south essex college

FURTHER & HIGHER EDUCATION

SOUTHEND CAMPUS

RESEARCH WITH PEOPLE

Research with People
Theory, Plans and Practicals

Nigel Holt
Bath Spa University

Ian Walker
University of Bath

palgrave
macmillan

First published 2009 by
PALGRAVE MACMILLAN

Palgrave Macmillan in the UK is an imprint of Macmillan Publishers Limited,
registered in England, company number 785998, of Houndmills, Basingstoke,
Hampshire RG21 6XS.

Palgrave Macmillan in the US is a division of St Martin's Press LLC,
175 Fifth Avenue, New York, NY 10010.

Palgrave Macmillan is the global academic imprint of the above companies
and has companies and representatives throughout the world.

Palgrave® and Macmillan® are registered trademarks in the United States,
the United Kingdom, Europe and other countries.

ISBN-13: 978–0–230–54555–7 paperback
ISBN-10: 0–230–54555–6 paperback

This book is printed on paper suitable for recycling and made from fully
managed and sustained forest sources. Logging, pulping and manufacturing
processes are expected to conform to the environmental regulations of the
country of origin.

A catalogue record for this book is available from the British Library.

A catalog record for this book is available from the Library of Congress.

10 9 8 7 6 5 4 3 2 1
18 17 16 15 14 13 12 11 10 09

Printed by CPI Antony Rowe, Chippenham, Wiltshire

For Sarah and Katie. We're sure it's just what they always wanted.

contents

Part 3   The really useful section

preface

There's an old saying that you may have heard: 'Give someone a fish and you feed them for a day; teach someone to fish and you feed them for a lifetime.' This nicely begins to illustrate what we would like to achieve with this book.

Over the years we have taught research skills to students from many different backgrounds, including sociology, political studies, education, psychology, economics, pharmacology, medicine and business management. The methods used to carry out research with people are basically the same regardless of the discipline you work in – a point we're keen to stress. Even though the projects here may not immediately appear entirely relevant to your subject, they are chosen to illustrate certain points and provide certain skills that you will then be able to transfer to your own discipline.

Different readers may come from different disciplines, but when doing research with people we are all interested in the same thing, behaviour. Why do people do things? How might we influence that behaviour? What happens to the behaviour in different situations? More specifically, how might people react to a new advertising campaign or what do they think when they look in a shop window, or showroom? The scientific study of behaviour is psychology. If, at times, this book ever feels like a psychology book, this is simply because you are studying humans and this always involves using some psychology, no matter what background you come from.

Often, the students we have taught have previously taken research design courses before coming to us. At first, we got very excited about this: we thought we could skip all the introductory material and focus on the more sexy advanced techniques (or perhaps just take three months off to go skiing). Instead, we found most students came to us so confused about what they had learnt, we had to go right back to basics with them. Far too many had attended their lessons and handed in their assignments, but never really understood what they were doing. They got bogged down in all the fine details of designs and tests and analyses and never grasped the reasons for using those things in the first place. They focused on their footsteps, but didn't know where they were walking.

In this book, then, we have tried throughout to help you understand the *why* of research just as much as the *how*. Rather than simply describe experimental procedures and calculations, we also show you the big picture: what are you trying to achieve with those procedures and calculations? This is, we feel, much more useful than a book which simply says 'Do this, then this, then this' and which leaves you not knowing why. This leads to superficial learning, which is soon forgotten.

Because we want you to understand what is happening when you conduct research, and what your ultimate goals are, we may at times simplify some complex points a little. We feel it is far better that you see the bigger picture and only 90% of the detail than it is for you to learn all of the detail, but miss the bigger picture entirely. This is an introductory book. You'll easily pick up later any details that we skim over, but if you don't grasp what you are trying to achieve at this stage it can take years to put that right.

Once you have learnt how to do research with people you will have the skills to answer any question you may ever want to ask. But you can only learn how to do research properly if your knowledge is given sound foundations. Our focus throughout is to build these foundations. We hope that you find our approach useful.

NIGEL HOLT,
Bath, England

IAN WALKER,
Salisbury, England

What's Covered Where*

	5	6	7	8	9	10	11	12	13	14
Research question		X	X							
Hypothesis testing	X	X	X		X			X		X
One-tailed vs two-tailed hypotheses	X	X								
Experimental method			X	X	X					X
Sampling	X		X	X	X	X	X	X	X	X
Pilot study	X					X				
Variables	X	X	X	X	X	X		X	X	X
Operationalizing variables		X				X				
Extraneous/confounding variables	X		X	X		X			X	
Design choices	X	X	X	X	X	X			X	
Order effects	X		X	X	X	X		X	X	
Control		X								
Blind Testing			X							
Placebo			X							
Standardized instructions			X	X		X			X	
Rating scales							X			
Experimenter effects			X					X		X
Linearity								X		X
Signal detection theory								X		
Data assumptions								X		X
Descriptive statistics		X	X			X	X		X	
Graphs	X	X	X	X		X	X	X	X	X
Comparing two means						X	X			
Comparing more than two means									X	
Correlational design/regression				X	X			X		X
Binomial test			X							
Chi-squared test			X		X					
Parametric vs non-parametric tests										X
Power						X				
Ethical issues		X						X		

* *Note*: many issues (e.g., ethics) run through all research. This table shows where issues are discussed in particular detail.

acknowledgements

Thanks go to Anna Van Boxel and Jamie Joseph at Palgrave for their gentle encouragement and spectacular patience whilst we were writing this book. Thanks also to Ryan North of qwantz.com for allowing us to use his cartoon in Section 1, and to the many students we have taught over the years who have helped us develop our approach to teaching research methods and who constantly show us that it really doesn't need to be difficult or boring.

part 1 thinking about research

You are already thinking about research

Right at this moment you are reading the first sentence of a book on how to do research with people. You can't be doing this by accident. We definitely remember asking our publishers to write something on the cover to say that this book is all about doing research. You chose to ignore this warning, so you must already be thinking about research – well done!

Okay, so we're being a bit silly here: it's the first book we've written together and we're a little giddy with the excitement. Bear with us, we'll have calmed down in a few paragraphs.

Actually, though, in amongst all this nonsense we are trying to make quite a serious point: you might well think that reading this book is the first step you have ever taken towards learning how to do research with people, but the truth is you have been thinking about how to study people all of your life. Pretty much from the moment you were born, you instinctively experimented with your caregivers to learn how they would react to various things you did – how else would you have learnt what is and is not acceptable in your culture? Today, every time you ask a question like 'I wonder why some people are more popular than others' or 'I wonder why people seem to get more aggressive when they drive a car,' you are setting up questions about people which could be addressed through systematic research. Indeed, if you put your mind to it, we are sure you would get at least part-way towards answering those questions right now.

And that is the point we wish to make: we are not about to teach you a completely new skill here. Instead, we are going to make you better at doing something you already know about, at least in part. Obviously we hope to teach you a lot of new information in this book. But we will also spend time taking rules and concepts that you already know in a fairly subconscious, intuitive sort of way, and making that knowledge more explicit. When you are properly aware of the ideas you already have about how research should be carried out, you can more easily use this knowledge when you conduct research yourself. You will also be better equipped to use other people's research: you will be able to spot mistakes in the data you come across, to know what questions you need to ask when you hear about research in the news, and to know which studies you can trust and which you cannot trust when making decisions about your own life.

Let us prove to you that you already know quite a lot about doing research with people, even if you have never thought about it before. As it happens we are both amateur pharmacologists and have worked away in our basements to produce a new drug called Holtodol. Holtodol not only makes you a great deal healthier and improves your memory, but also makes you more attractive to whichever gender it is you like to attract. Sounds good, doesn't it? So if we were to offer you some Holtodol, would you take it?

How about this: would you take the drug if we had tested it on two people, both 21-year-old men, for a week, and neither experienced any side-effects?

Would you take the drug if we had tested it on 10,000 people, with a mixture of men and women of various ages, for 10 years, and none of them experienced any side-effects?

We strongly suspect you would feel happier taking Holtodol in the second situation. The reason for this is that you already know, at some level, that although the finding is exactly the same – no side-effects – this is much more convincing when it comes from a large, mixed sample of people over a long period of time than when it comes from just two people over a few days.

Let us give you another example, which illustrates some of the issues that arise when we deal with people's feelings. There are two hospitals near where we live. Each claims its employees have the best working conditions in the area. Obviously they can't both be right, so we decide to put it to the test.

We take a member of staff from each hospital. Specifically, from Hospital A we take Professor Margaret Pritt, the 56-year-old Head of Ophthalmology, and from hospital B we take David Fish, a 19-year-old car park attendant. We ask each of them how happy they are at work. David Fish says he is 'really happy' whereas Margaret Pritt says she is 'fairly happy'. We therefore conclude that Hospital B treats its employees better, and suggest that Hospital A should change its working practices to be more like Hospital B.

Is this a fair conclusion? Should we really use this research to change policies throughout Hospital A? We suspect that right now you are violently shaking your head, and quite possibly wondering if you still have the receipt for this book so you can return it.

The thing is, we spoke to only one person in each hospital – there's every possibility we have chosen completely inappropriate people for our comparison. You can clearly see that the people we interviewed had very different jobs: one was the head of a clinical unit with decades of employment history and lots of responsibilities; her experience of work is likely to be totally different to that of a worker not long out of school. And it isn't just the differences in their jobs that might be a problem: David and Margaret are different genders, and are at completely different stages in their lives – middle-aged workers like Margaret could well be juggling their job with family responsibilities, which might affect their enjoyment of work. On the other hand, a younger worker like David might be affected by having less money and job security.

And all this is just the tip of the iceberg. There are a huge number of other problems with the study we have just described. For example, simply asking people 'how happy' they are is too vague and subjective: it would have been better to ask several questions, each using more objective terms, such as 'How often do you find you simply cannot face going to work?'. And is 'happiness' even the right thing to be measuring in a study of working conditions anyway?

So we are confident that when you read our description of the hospital study, you immediately felt there was something wrong with it, even if you could not put your finger on what exactly it was. This shows that, even when addressing a fairly complex question, you already have some knowledge of what is good and bad research. In the rest of this book we will be developing this knowledge and adding to it. What we will not be doing is teaching you something completely new.

What we are going to cover

The rest of Part 1 is going to lay some foundations before we get to the serious business of guiding you through how to plan and conduct research projects with people. We will start out by explaining the logic of how research works in Chapter 1, then Chapter 2 will look at the question of who will take part in your studies. Chapters 3 and 4 are an introduction to what you might do with the data you collect when carrying out research: Chapter 3 looks at how you can describe data and Chapter 4 introduces the tests that are used to see whether what you see with the people you test can be generalized to other people.

chapter 1

the problem with people: variation and hypothesis testing

From time to time, everybody who carries out research with people for a living wishes they worked with something a little simpler and more predictable. Sleep-deprived exploding panthers, for example. The problem is that, whilst people can be fascinating and amazing things, they are also maddeningly inconsistent. A physicist studying pieces of copper doesn't come in to work one day to find their blocks of metal are suddenly behaving wildly because it is windy outside (this happens all the time when studying small children). A biologist working with sheep doesn't have to worry about them having hangovers if they are tested early on Monday morning (as happens with some students). An engineer hanging weights on a model bridge to see how it flexes doesn't need to make allowances for the bridge getting better at its task with practice (as you would).

The point is that when we are dealing with people, with their memories and social lives and moods and beliefs, we have to be aware that every observation we make is the end product of a million different influences. Go and ask somebody what is their favourite colour. Done that? Okay, now think about the answer you received. Of course, the person you spoke to might simply have told you their favourite colour. But what if you then learnt they had the colour vision deficit known as protanopia, and so were not be able to tell red and green apart? This gives their answer a rather different complexion, doesn't it? And anyway, how can you be sure the answer you received is really that person's favourite colour, and not just a colour other people have told them they should like (as when five-year-old girls say 'pink')? Perhaps the person's favourite colour was orange but they told you 'black' because they wanted to appear moody and interesting. They might have said the colour of your shirt, because they thought your question was stupid and just wanted to get rid of you. If they know you, they might have said *your* favourite colour because they wanted to reinforce your friendship. They might have said 'mauve', simply because saying the word 'mauve' makes you smile (try it). Or they might have been tediously predictable and said 'blue'.

The point is, all you have from that person is the name of a colour. Is it their favourite colour, as you requested? It might be, but there are so many possible influences on their response that you just can't know that with any certainty. This means you can't reach safe conclusions.

Ian: I've just spoken to Anna and I now know her favourite colour is sea-green.
Nigel: Weird, because *I've* just spoken to Anna and I very much think you'll find her favourite colour is lilac.
Ian: Sea-green.
Nigel: Lilac!
Ian: SEA-GREEN!

And so on, until the fisticuffs begin. When this sort of thing happens, how can we ever find the correct answer?

One approach might be to anticipate all the various influences that could affect a person's behaviour and deal with them in advance. So you could try to discover somebody's real favourite colour by asking them a question like: 'Disregarding your recent experiences, and what you think I might be expecting you to say, and what your mother told you was her favourite colour, and what you feel Society thinks you ought to say, and any colour you might be looking at right now (unless it actually is your favourite colour, in which case don't disregard it), and the colour of your bedroom walls, and the colours of your toys when you were a child, and the magnificent mouthfeel of the word 'mauve'[1]... disregarding all that, what is your favourite colour?' You could try that, but you'd still fail to get a reliable answer

---

[1] The colour mauve has an amazing history, and is pretty much responsible for the modern world as we know it. Seriously. We really recommend reading Garfield, S. (2000). *Mauve: How One Man Invented a Colour that Changed the World.* Faber & Faber.

because you didn't realize that the person you are speaking to is a member of the Himba tribe from Namibia and so uses the same word to mean both 'dark red' and 'dark blue'.[2]

This is all by way of saying that tremendous amounts of variation and complexity are the norm when studying people. People differ from one another, and individuals differ over time, and so you cannot just measure things simply as you would with blocks of copper or model bridges. Nor can you hope to deal with this issue by anticipating all the factors which might affect people's responses, as we just attempted to, because, no matter how much you try to anticipate the influences on people's behaviour, people will always find a way to surprise you. Luckily, you do not need to do this, as procedures and techniques have evolved over the years to cope with people and their tricksy ways. These procedures and techniques are what this book is all about.

Most of the techniques we will cover involve testing groups of people rather than individuals. This helps you look past any individual quirks to reveal information about people in general (remember how you were happier with a drug tested on 10,000 people rather than two?). These techniques also tend to rely on using statistical analyses at the end of your data collection, to assess how well your choice of groups has worked. This last bit scares many people, but we promise we will make it very easy for you by making sure you understand what the statistics are for, rather than the intimate details of how they are calculated.

What we hope most of all is that by showing you the difficulties inherent in studying people, and how these can be overcome through good planning and design, human research can be a thing of beauty. And we mean that seriously. You will know when you have really grasped the issues involved in human testing by your emotional responses: reading about an ingeniously designed study which conclusively answers a difficult question will give you a rush of excitement, like hearing a great piece of music; seeing a badly designed study will make your nose wrinkle in disgust. The first time you find yourself squirming as you hear somebody describe a study in which they neglected to use a control group, take comfort from the fact you have at last developed the instincts of a great human researcher.

Good. Can I start doing research now?

Not just yet. Before you can do any research you need to make sure you know what question you are trying to answer, and this can take

---

[2] For more on the Himba and their descriptions of colour, see Adelson, R. (2005). Hues and Views. *APA Monitor on Psychology, 36*, 26.

more than one form. First, there is always a basic, straightforward question you are trying to answer, known as your **research question**. 'Do radar operators work better when they drink coffee?' and 'Do environmental issues affect people's decisions about how they travel?' are both examples of research questions.

It is very simple to decide what your research question is. Let's assume for a moment you come from a business management background and are interested in whether people who work for small companies feel more loyalty to their employers than people who work for large companies. In this case, your research question would simply be something like 'Do people who work for small companies feel more loyalty to their employers than people who work for large companies?' Alternatively, if you come from a medical background and are interested in whether people with gout feel better after taking Holtodol, your research question would be something like 'Do people with gout feel better after taking Holtodol?'

The research question is not a particularly difficult concept to grasp, we hope you will agree. It is simply a direct question you would like to have answered, and it often takes the form of a yes/no question (although it can also take other forms, such as 'What proportion of Holtodol users are aware they are treating their gout with a fictitious drug?').

It is a very good idea always to be clear about what your research question is, as this can really help keep your work organized. We have supervised quite a lot of students over the years who have come to us feeling overwhelmed by their research projects – a very common experience when people first have to design and conduct a substantial study on their own, especially in the Dark Ages before this book existed. In particular, we have heard many students say things like 'I've got so much material and I don't know what is relevant and what is not!' In almost every case, their problem was that, although they generally knew what they wanted to study, they did not have a clear research question. The solution was for them to take a step backwards (not literally – our offices aren't big enough for people to walk around in) and to write down, in a single sentence, the question they wanted to answer with their study. Once the research question was totally clear, and preferably written down somewhere prominent where it could be consulted regularly, problems of organization disappeared. Is the paragraph you've just written necessary for your report? Look at the research question – it'll probably tell you.

But, although a clear research question is terribly useful for organizing yourself, it is sadly not enough on its own for you to conduct research. For reasons we will explain in a moment, you cannot actually test your research question, no matter how hard you try. Instead, you must use the research question to generate something else, something which *will* let you do some testing: a **hypothesis**.

pedant point

The process of carrying out research can go by various names: you might refer to conducting a 'study', an 'analysis', an 'experiment', a 'project', an 'investigation' and so on. Most of these terms are interchangeable: there is no difference between saying 'I am carrying out an investigation of reindeer antlers' and 'I am carrying out a study on reindeer antlers.'

The one term that is reserved, and not synonymous with the rest, is 'experiment'. This is because an 'experiment' is a very specific type of study/investigation/project in which you make a change to some aspect of the world, whilst holding everything else constant, and look at the effects of that change.

It would be an experiment if you took a large number of people who had never ridden a unicycle, gave half of them unicycle lessons and half of them no unicycle lessons, and then looked at whether the group which had the lessons were better unicyclists. Subject to a few assumptions which we will explore later, this is a genuine experiment as the *only* thing that varied between the two groups of people is that one group had lessons and the other group did not – everything else was constant. If you found there was a difference

EXPERIMENTS, STUDIES AND INVESTIGATIONS

in unicycling ability between the two groups of people at the end of the procedure, you would be able to know with some certainty that it was caused by the lessons, as in every other sense the two groups were the same. This is an experiment, and it lets you make strong conclusions about cause and effect.

If, on the other hand, you asked some people how they felt about unicycling, this would be a *study* of unicycling, but it would not be an experiment. It would not be an experiment because you did not manipulate, or change, anything. It still would not be an experiment if you compared two groups of people – say a group of circus performers with a group of police officers – on their unicycling abilities. This is still not a true experiment because *you* have not caused the difference between the groups; it is simply a naturally occurring difference.[3]

It is quite common for people to mix up their terms and say 'experiment' when really they mean 'study', and to be frank we can't rule out the possibility that we'll do it before this book is finished. But we always try to reserve the word 'experiment' for situations where there is a true experimental manipulation and to use the word 'study' when we are talking in general terms. It is good practice to get used to doing this too.

Finding robust findings

Research with people generally takes one of two forms. First, research is sometimes purely exploratory. If you are the first person to investigate a new area, you generally just dive in and, using little more than educated guesses to guide you, start collecting data.

Imagine you were to discover tomorrow that trees can talk. This would be a totally new discovery. Your first action wouldn't be to go indoors and construct a careful research programme before doing anything else. No, the first thing you would do is ask a tree some questions! You would try to build some sort of understanding about

---

[3] To be pedantic about our pedantry, this sort of study can be called a *naturalistic experiment*.

your new discovery as quickly as possible in order that you could lay the foundations for later, more systematic research. This is exploratory research.

But most research is not like this. Instead, most research studies are in established areas. Some of this research tries to find answers to specific research questions like 'is poverty linked to crime?' and 'does eating saturated fat increase the risk of coronary disease?' Other research goes further to look at the mechanisms behind phenomena. For example, once you've found there is a relationship between poverty and crime, you might ask the question 'exactly *how* does poverty influence crime?' For now, we will focus on situations where you want to answer a particular research question rather than explore a brand new phenomenon.

When you carry out research to answer a specific research question, you really want to produce findings that are **robust**. This simply means that when you reach a conclusion at the end of your work, it is trustworthy. With a robust conclusion, nobody can come along afterwards and show that your conclusion is unreliable.

A lack of robustness was the problem we encountered when asking people about their favourite colours. After you asked someone their favourite colour, your conclusion was not robust because it was entirely possible for somebody to come along and contradict you, or to show that your method was faulty. If this happened, and somebody pointed out that your conclusion was unreliable, what response would you have other than insults and name-calling? That's the problem with conclusions that are not robust – they lead to undignified science.

Seeing into the future

So the conclusions you reach when you do research should be robust. But this alone is not enough, because you also want your conclusions to be *general statements about the world*. In other words, you want your conclusions to apply to new situations or people, not just the situation or the people you studied. For example, let's say you carry out a study to see whether a certain food additive affects children's behaviour. At the end of this study you will almost certainly want to be able to say something about how this food additive affects children in general, probably including children who have not yet been born. It would be pretty pointless if you could only make statements about the small specific group of kids that you studied.

What we are suggesting, then, is that *doing research is an attempt to predict the future*. We research things so that we can understand them, and when we understand something we can make statements about what is likely to happen in the future and why it is likely to happen. Consider this: what would happen if you set fire to this book right now?[4] This is something you have never done before, but you can almost certainly predict what would happen if you did it. The reason you can predict what would happen is that you have a good understanding of the various factors involved – fire, paper, the place you are reading, and so on. If you knew nothing about fire and how it behaves, you would not be able to make this prediction about something that has not yet happened.

This idea that research is an attempt to predict the future can be seen in all fields. If we are testing a new drug to see if it is safe, we are doing this because we want to know what will happen when people use it after our study is over – this is predicting the future. If we are looking at whether a new management technique improves workers' productivity, we want to know if it will work for people and in organizations we have not specifically tested it on – this is predicting the future.

Of course, humans have been trying to predict the future for thousands of years. In ancient Rome there was a type of priest known as an Augur, whose job it was to look at how birds were flying through the air and to use this information to decide whether the emperor's plans would be successful or not. (The 'birds' usually said the inbred sword-wielding psychopath was a genius and his plans couldn't possibly go wrong.)

Now you probably don't need us to tell you that if your attempts to predict the future are based around watching blackbirds, you will struggle to produce robust conclusions about what will happen tomorrow. But in a more subtle way, researchers had the same difficulty reaching reliable conclusions about people right up into the twentieth century. They would identify a research question and make observations to test it, only to find their conclusions were questioned later and there was nothing they could say to prove their findings were valid.

For example, a researcher might study a group of households and say 'I have seen evidence of greater intelligence in children who eat lots of fish.' But if another researcher came along afterwards and said 'I too looked at children who ate lots of fish and found no evidence of their being more intelligent,' the two researchers had no good way to establish who was correct. Each had a different idea about what would happen in the future to children who ate a lot of fish. As often as not the winner of the debate would be the one with the most forceful personality or, frequently, the biggest beard.

In the 1920s, the statistician Ronald Fisher, himself no stranger to facial hair, looked for a way to make research more robust, to deal with this problem. In doing so he gave us a new method to guide our

---

[4] Do not set fire to this book!

studies. His solution has come to be called **null hypothesis testing**, and it can be a slightly tricky concept to understand the first time you encounter it. However, the logic behind null hypothesis testing has transformed research, giving scientists a method for doing studies which produce robust findings unlikely to be questioned. As such, an understanding of how it works is important, so let us explain it by guiding you through a quick study. And, not lacking ambition, we are going to do our study on quite a big question: does gravity work?

Null hypothesis testing: gravity on trial

Pick up an object – nothing too fragile or valuable, please! – hold it up in the air and then let it go.

Did it fall down?

If not, kindly close this book and resume the demonstration when you have returned from orbit. If the object did fall down, it looks as though gravity is working. Excellent.

But the thing is, as researchers it is not enough for us to say 'it looks as though…' After all, from here it *looks as though* the sun rotates around the earth and it *looks as though* cows prevent fields from floating away by standing on them. Instead, we want to be *certain* about things.[5] So looking at the world and saying 'it looks as though…' is an easy way to make mistakes, and, in research, mistakes matter. Those of you reading this book towards a qualification will get bad grades if you carry out poor research; those of you who will do research for a living could damage your professional reputations. And those of you in biomedical fields could easily one day carry out research where a mistake would kill people. So let's get away from 'it looks as though…' and let's try to be more certain: pick up your object and drop it again.

Assuming it fell down once more, we now have two falls in a row and are getting a picture of how gravity works: objects that are not supported fall until they rest on something. But here is the key question: how many times would you have to drop your object and see it fall before you were *certain* this is how gravity works? Please decide on an answer to this question before reading further.

Unless you decided 'infinity' or something similar, you were wrong. Let us show you why.

---

[5] Or rather, as we will see later, we want to know *exactly how uncertain* we are about them.

If you pick any number – a billion, say – and drop the object that number of times, you will still not be *certain* about what gravity will do in the future. After dropping the object a billion times, you still cannot *know*, with 100% certainty, what will happen the next time. If we were to tell you that gravity makes objects fall down almost every time you drop them, but that just occasionally, instead of falling down, objects turn into winged badgers and fly away, well… you cannot *know* we are wrong.

You could, of course, test our suggestion by dropping the object once more, but the problem is still there: you have now shown the object falls the first billion-and-one times it is dropped, but you still cannot be *certain* what will happen the one-billion-and-second time it is dropped, because you have not yet seen it happen. Just as 'tomorrow' never arrives, 'the next time it is dropped' will never arrive for your object. Every time you test your object's behaviour again, a new, unseen 'next time' immediately comes into existence and you can do nothing to prove we are wrong if we continue to insist that at some point your object will turn into a badger. You do not have the ability to predict the future with certainty, as you would like.

Enough badgers – could we possibly have an example involving some pens in a box now, please?

But of course. We have a box with two pens inside – the two pens are identical in size, shape and weight, but one of them is blue and the other is red. We hope you can imagine somebody reaching into this box three times without looking and picking the red pen on each occasion (obviously they put the pen back after each attempt). Picking the red pen three times in a row wouldn't be a particularly unusual event – it would happen, typically, to one out of every eight people who reached into the box three times.

If you can imagine somebody reaching into the box three times and picking the red pen on each occasion, can you also imagine somebody reaching into the box four times and getting the red pen every time? If that is harder to picture, think of it this way: it is exactly the same event you imagined a moment ago, followed by the person reaching into the box one more time and getting the red pen again. Getting the red pen five times in a row is exactly the same as that, just with one more red pen at the end. And so on.

We realize we are now getting dangerously close to the sort of tedious statistical thought-experiment we didn't want in our lovely user-friendly book,[6] so let's get to the point: although we haven't met them all, we are reliably informed that there are now several billion people in the world. If a billion people each reached into our box 20 times, we would expect nearly 1,000 of them to select the red pen 20 times in a row. Selecting the red pen 20 times in a row, when there is also a blue pen inside the box, is something that *could* happen. That is what we are saying.

Now imagine we offered the box to you. We tell you, 'This box has a red pen and a blue pen inside.' How would you check our claim? You reach into the box and feel that there are indeed two pens inside. But, because you know we are nasty academics with a strange sense of humour, you immediately worry that we are tricking you and that both the pens are the same colour! You need some way of testing our claim that there are both a red pen and a blue pen in the box. You notice we have deviously designed the box so that you cannot see inside and so the only option open to you is to pull a pen out. You do so: it is, unsurprisingly, red.

Having seen a red pen come out of the box, you replace it and carry on testing our claim, pulling a pen out of the box over and over, until you have done it 20 times. The pen is red on every occasion. Now, we claimed there were a red pen and a blue pen in the box. What could you say *for certain* about our claim at the end of your experiment? You would agree with the first part of our claim: there is definitely a red pen in there – you have a frankly tedious amount of evidence for this. But what about the second part of our claim, that there is also a blue pen? Can you say it is true? No, because you haven't seen it. Can you say it is false? Again no, because it might be in there and you have just been unlucky in not picking it on any of your attempts – you might happen to be one of those 1,000 people out of every billion who get the red pen 20 times in a row. The fact is, you can say *nothing* definite about whether or not the blue pen exists at this stage. Sure, you can say you *believe* there is no blue pen in the box, but you have no way of knowing *for certain* that it will not appear the next time you reach into the box.

This principle is really important when we do research with people. Let's return to the idea of testing a new drug to decide if it is safe. In fact, let's say you are testing the specific research question 'Does Holtodol cause side-effects in users?' You find a willing volunteer, give them a big dose of Holtodol and find they are fine afterwards. Do you therefore conclude 'No, Holtodol does not cause side-effects'?

We suspect that after testing just one person you would not be happy coming to this conclusion and would want to see more data. Good for you!

---

[6] Consider yourself lucky we're not yet talking about tossing coins.

So let's say you give the drug to 1,000 people – or even 10,000 – and still find no side-effects. Can you put your hand on your heart and say the answer is 'No, there are no side effects, Holtodol is 100% safe, it never produces side-effects and I would be happy for my mother to take it right now'?

We hope by now you would not be able to say this without some feelings of doubt, even if they are only small ones. We hope you see that, no matter how many people you test, there is always a possibility, however slight, that Holtodol is dangerous to some people and that you have, through a quirk of chance, met only people who are unaffected by it. The next person might be different. And just as tomorrow never arrives, nor does the 'next person'.

But this isn't satisfactory at all: it looks as though we can test an idea over and over and over but still never know anything for certain! And this is just what Fisher realized: as long as we go on testing the idea that we will see something happen, but not seeing it, there is always a 'next time' or a 'next person' which could change everything.

Null hypothesis testing

Fisher's ingenious solution to this dilemma was subtly to change the questions we ask when we do research. Realizing that we can test ideas over and over without ever reaching a definite conclusion, he suggested we test the opposite idea instead.

Original idea: on earth, gravity makes unsupported objects fall
New idea: on earth, gravity *does not* make unsupported objects fall

So instead of predicting that something happens, we predict that something *does not* happen. This probably sounds fairly trivial, but it is really a big difference. Ask yourself this: how many times would you have to drop your object to test this new idea that gravity *does not* make things fall? Again, decide on an answer before reading further.

The answer is almost certainly 'one'. Go on, try it: drop the object again. If it fell down then you have conclusively, absolutely, indubitably and forever demolished the idea that objects do not fall when you let them go, and you have done this with only a single test. When we test the idea that an event will *not* happen, research becomes much easier. If you give an event a fair opportunity to happen and it does not, then your claim that it doesn't happen is probably true; if the event does happen, even once, you know for certain that your claim is false. Either way it's good.

And this is the basis of all research. We start with an idea we are interested in, which as we have seen is called the research question.

Step 1. Research question: Do dogs eat bananas?

Based on this, we derive an **experimental hypothesis**, which is a specific prediction that something will happen.

Step 2. Experimental hypothesis: We will see a dog eat a banana.

But this is not entirely suitable for research. If we see a dog eat a banana than we have an answer to our research question. But if we go our whole lives watching dogs and never see one eat a banana, we learn nothing for certain. For all we know, dogs eat bananas a lot, but only when nobody is watching. Or perhaps they eat bananas only in the dark, or perhaps it is only dogs in Chad who eat them. Or perhaps they do eat bananas, but only a different variety of banana than those we are using in our study. We therefore don't bother with this idea and come up with something else to test, as Fisher suggested. We test the opposite of the experimental hypothesis, the idea that nothing is happening…

Step 3. Null hypothesis: We will not see a dog eat a banana.

You only need to see one dog eat a banana to know for sure that this null hypothesis is false. This then gives you an answer to your research question (yes, dogs eat bananas). If, on the other hand, despite your giving dogs ample opportunity to eat a banana in front of you, this does not happen, your null hypothesis is probably correct and you again have an answer to your research question (no, dogs seem not to eat bananas).

pedant point

EXPERIMENTAL HYPOTHESES

During our last bit of pedantry we said the word 'experiment' had a very specific meaning and could only be used to describe studies in which we manipulate one aspect of the world and look at the effects of doing so, as a way of establishing cause and effect.

It is therefore a little confusing that we use the term 'experimental hypothesis' to describe any specific prediction, even if the study we are conducting isn't a true experiment. This is a fair point, and in our defence we have to say that these are not our terms. If it helps, you might want to use the more technical terms, which are 'H_1' for the experimental hypothesis and 'H_0' for the null hypothesis. Or you might favour the term 'alternative hypothesis', which you will find used in some sources. The problem with the term 'alternative hypothesis' is that, although it makes a lot of sense if you are approaching hypothesis testing from a statistician's perspective, it doesn't make much sense if you are learning about hypothesis testing from the applied approach we are using here: as we have shown, this hypothesis is always developed *before* the null hypothesis, so it seems odd to call it the alternative.

Oh, and whilst we're here being pedantic, can we point out that it is 'one hypothesis' and 'two hypotheses'? You already knew that? Excellent.

Null hypothesis testing made as non-threatening as possible through the use of pasta sauces

(If you feel you have already understood null hypothesis testing, feel free to snort derisively right now and jump straight to the final section below, entitled 'A last point'.)

At this stage you would be forgiven for thinking this has all been really quite complicated – and it's only chapter 1! Don't worry: null hypotheses are the most difficult thing in this whole book and we definitely do not expect you to have grasped every aspect of this in a single reading – we are expecting that you will come back and read the material above a few more times as you work through the rest of the book. And it is only when you start to design studies of your own that it will start to become second nature to you.

Having said this, before we move on we would like to try and cement the concept in your mind just a little bit more. To do this, we will talk you through the sorts of thought processes we would use when we select the hypothesis for a study. This should illustrate what goes on with research questions and hypothesis testing when planning research for real.

Nigel: I'm cooking pasta tonight.

Ian: Nice.

Nigel: Yes, so I'm off into town to get some tomatoes for the sauce.

Ian: Why would you do that? Tomatoes are vile!

Nigel: You philistine! Tomatoes rock. Tomatoes rock the hardest.

Ian: Please tell me you're joking.

Nigel: You're just weird about vegetables.

Ian: Fruits.

Nigel: You know what I mean.

Ian: There's no way you should be making a tomato sauce for your pasta when you could make a cheese sauce instead. Cheese sauce is far better. Why else is cheese sauce so much more popular? That is a fact, my friend: a cold, hard fact.

Nigel: I don't –

Ian: Faaaaaaact.

Nigel: That is so *not* a fact! You just made it up. If anything, there's no difference. It just happens I'm having tomato sauce tonight, but they're both equally good sauces and they're both equally popular.[7]

Ian: Oh yes? Well let's settle this – with science!

Nigel: Right. So what's our research question? I suppose it's going to be something like 'Is one sauce more popular than the other?'

Ian: Yes, which means the hypothesis we'll test will be something like 'One sauce will be chosen more often than the other'.

Nigel: Right, let's get to work.

Ian: No, hold on: we're not there yet. We can't test that hypothesis. Think about it: suppose we speak to forty people and the majority prefer tomato sauce, that doesn't answer our research question. For all we know, if we tested forty more people the majority of those would prefer cheese and cancel out our original finding.

Nigel: Fine, so we won't test forty people – we'll test a hundred if it makes you happy. That way we've got both lots of people you've just described and a few more as well.

Ian: No, that's still no good. Even if we test one hundred people, that still won't tell us whether the sauces are equally popular or not. For all we know the next hundred might be totally different to that hundred, and we've no way of knowing that without testing them as well.

Nigel: So we do that. In fact, let's test a million people!

Ian: Still no good. Even if we ignore the fact it's practically impossible to test that many people, it still doesn't let us make a decision about our hypothesis. If we test a million people, we still can't be *sure* one sauce is more popular than the other. The next million could be different. The only way we could ever know for sure would be to test every person on the planet all at the same time. This is getting us nowhere.

Nigel: So what do we do?

Ian: We need to stop trying to test that experimental hypothesis. What we need to do is use it to create a null hypothesis. Instead of testing the idea 'One

---

[7] You're probably thinking this is all invented for the sake of your education, but tragically we have this conversation about once a month.

sauce will be chosen more often than the other' we need to test the idea that there's nothing happening: we test the idea there is no preference. We use a null hypothesis like 'There will be no difference in how often cheese sauce and tomato sauce are chosen'.

Nigel: Yes, that'll work. We test a reasonable number of people, which will give any preference a chance to show itself. If we still don't see a preference then we'll accept our null hypothesis that there isn't one. But if we do see a preference we'll reject our null hypothesis and accept our other hypothesis, which was 'One sauce will be chosen more than the other'.

Ian: Either way, we can settle on one of the hypotheses as a conclusion.

Nigel: Hoorah!

You might remember that at the top of this section we told people who were already happy with the concept of null hypothesis testing to skip on to the next section. So whilst those insufferable know-it-alls aren't looking, we would like to share a snippet of information with you more assiduous readers, which is this: because the null hypothesis is always simply suggesting *you will not find an effect*, it is very common for people not to bother even stating it when they write about their research. So if you see somebody say 'We tested the hypothesis that soldiers run faster than civilians,' what they mean is they tested the null hypothesis that there was no difference in running speed between soldiers and civilians. If you see somebody say 'My hypothesis was that the longer people spent studying, the better their exam score would be,' what they are telling you is that they tested the null hypothesis that there was no relationship between study time and exam score. Even if somebody doesn't mention it, they *did* test a null hypothesis. It's just that sometimes you have to work out what it was for yourself.

A last point

Null hypothesis testing is a really important aspect of how we carry out research. It provides a method which most researchers agree allows us to obtain robust findings. We've guided you through some examples to show where this procedure came from and how it is used, but, as often happens in life, this is a concept which you can grasp in more than one way, and different people prefer different explanations. So to finish we would like briefly to sum up null hypothesis testing in a slightly different manner. If our explanation so far hasn't worked for you, perhaps this will make it clear.

Let's consider a question for which you have no evidence one way or the other. We are working together in a room right now, and we would like to ask you this: 'Is there a cat in this room with us?' What would you say, given that you cannot see us? There are two possibilities here: either there is a cat or there is not. Without any evidence one way or the other, which would you choose?

Many people in this situation, having to choose one situation over the other with no evidence at all, would choose the simplest option. Keeping things simple is generally a really good idea – something we'll say a lot more about soon. In this case, it is much simpler to assume there is no cat. A room, when it is built, does not have a cat in it. It is not the natural state of a room to contain a cat and extra effort has to be made to get a cat into a room, so it is clearly simpler to assume there is no cat. (You may have heard this described as 'Occam's Razor'. This is the idea that, when you have to choose between options and have no reason to favour any one option, you should always choose the simplest option. The principle gets its name from a mediaeval English monk called William of Occam who first described it.)

In research, the null hypothesis always states that nothing is going on – there is *no relationship* between two measures; giving people a new drug *won't* affect them; there is *no cat* in the room. The null hypothesis, then, always represents the simplest explanation. We need a good reason to abandon it in favour of a more complex explanation.

As we will see in later chapters, when we study a research question we collect evidence. It is only when that evidence clearly points towards a more complex explanation that we abandon our nice simple null hypothesis. It is for this reason that we focus on the null hypothesis, and describe research as testing it – deciding whether to keep it or reject it. See Box 1.1 for a little more on the types of hypotheses you might choose.

(There was no cat in the room, by the way.)

Box 1.1 One- and two-tailed hypotheses

You will almost certainly encounter the terms 'one-tailed hypothesis' and 'two-tailed hypothesis'. These are slightly odd names, and refer to the shape of certain graphs which we won't go into here. However, their meaning is very simple.

A two-tailed hypothesis predicts that there will be an effect in your data

A one-tailed hypothesis predicts that there will be an effect in your data, and *says what that effect will be*

So, for example, consider these two hypotheses:

1. Women will drive better than men
2. There will be a difference in how men and women drive

The first hypothesis is more specific: it predicts an effect and says specifically what that effect will be; the second hypothesis simply predicts an effect. We call the first a one-tailed hypothesis and we call the second a two-tailed hypothesis. It is called 'two-tailed' because the effect can go either way – women could be better drivers than men or men could be better drivers than women.

Test yourself

Here are some experimental hypotheses. For each, decide if it is one- or two-tailed. Remember: a two-tailed hypothesis predicts there will be an effect and a one-tailed hypothesis predicts exactly what the effect will be. The answers are just below.

1. People from Chile will be less patriotic than people from Argentina.
2. Eating sugar will lead to changes in people's moods.
3. People who swim regularly will have more supple limbs than people who run regularly.
4. Boys and girls attending school have different numbers of friends.

Now here are some research questions. For each, what would be the experimental hypothesis and what would be the null hypothesis if you were carrying out a study? Also, for each experimental hypothesis you produce, is it one- or two-tailed?

1. Do left-handed people write at a different speed from right-handed people?
2. Does eating cheese in the evening give people nightmares?
3. Does learning to ride a motorcycle make people more alert to road dangers?

Answers

1. One-tailed: we predicted a difference and said exactly what it would be.
2. Two-tailed: we predicted a difference but didn't say which direction it would go in – sugar could improve or impair mood.
3. One-tailed.
4. Two-tailed.

Research questions

For each of these, your wording might be slightly different to ours, but make sure you have said the same general thing we have. In particular, it is quite possible that you have generated one-tailed hypotheses where we used two-tailed, and vice-versa.

1. Experimental hypothesis: There will be a difference in how fast left- and right-handed people write. Null hypothesis, which will be tested: There will be no difference in how fast left-and right-handed people write. Here we've produced a two-tailed experimental hypothesis – we've predicted a difference but not said which way round it will be.
2. Experimental hypothesis: People who eat cheese in the evening will experience more nightmares than people who do not eat cheese in the evening. Null hypothesis, which will be tested: There will be no difference in how many nightmares will be experienced by people who eat cheese in the evening and people who do not eat cheese in the evening. Here we've produced a one-tailed hypothesis – we've not only predicted a difference but we've also predicted exactly which group will experience more nightmares.
3. There are actually two approaches to this one, depending on whether you design a study comparing motorcyclists with non-motorcyclists, or whether you design a study which teaches people to ride a motorcycle. The fact you can study the same question in more than one way is a theme we'll say a lot more about.
    a. Experimental hypothesis: Motorcyclists will perform better in a road danger test than equivalent non-motorcyclists. Null hypothesis: There will be no difference between motorcyclists and non-motorcyclists in the road danger test. Here we've used a one-tailed hypothesis.
    b. Experimental hypothesis: Learning to ride a motorcycle will increase people's scores on a road danger test. Null hypothesis: There will be no change in people's scores on a road danger test when they learn to ride a motorcycle. Here we've used a one-tailed hypothesis – the two-tailed version would predict a change in test scores instead of an increase.

chapter 2

who will you study? samples and populations

Back in Chapter 1, we said 'doing research is an attempt to predict the future'. In an ideal world we would just leave that statement to stand as a pithy and profound insight which people might like to consider for our gravestones. But unfortunately, much as we would like to be remembered as the people who said 'doing research is an attempt to predict the future!' we are now going to have to explain why this is only true most of the time.

The point we were making in Chapter 1 is that when you study people, you are usually doing this to find some sort of general lesson or conclusion which you can use to judge other people – people you didn't actually study. When he was a student intern, Ian worked on a project which tested a group of children with developmental dyslexia.[1] The researchers didn't do this because they were interested in that particular set of children, nice as they all were. Rather, they studied those children to try and learn something about dyslexia in general. This information now allows us to predict what we might see in other children with dyslexia, including children who are not yet even born. When we carry out research, this sort of future-prediction is generally what we are aiming for. But there are exceptions.

---

[1] Goulandris, N.K., Snowling, M.J., & Walker, I. (2000). Is dyslexia a form of specific language impairment? A comparison of dyslexic and language-impaired children as adolescents. *Annals of Dyslexia*, vol. 50, pages 103–120.

Let's say we go into a workplace and carry out a survey of the people who work there. We might ask them whether or not they are happy at work, for example. There is more than one reason we might do this. First, and most straightforward, *we might just want to know whether those people are happy at work*. Simple, eh?

In this sort of situation we are not trying to do anything clever. We aren't attempting to discover general principles about people and we aren't trying to learn anything which will let us predict the future. Instead, we are just working to learn a particular piece of information about a particular group. This is essentially what happens when governments carry out a census. A census is just a really big exercise in finding out how things stand on a given day. What proportion of the people in this country, today, is male? What proportion of people in this country, today, live in rented accommodation? If a census is carried out this year, it is primarily to discover how the country looks right now, not to make predictions about what will happen in the future.

One of the nice things about this sort of research – which we might as well call **summative research**, as the aim is to 'sum up' how things stand at a certain point in time – is that it is always easy to decide who you will study: you want to study *all of the people you are interested in*. In a census, the government tries to get information from every household in the country. At the time we are writing this, Ian's university has just carried out a survey of how satisfied its employees are: the survey went to everybody who works at the university. So when carrying out summative research there is no question of who you will study: you will study everybody you are interested in.

You can probably tell immediately that summative research projects can involve an awful lot of participants, and so a lot of data. Ian's university employs several thousand people – this was a lot of information for the surveyors to compile and manage. A government carrying out a census has millions of households to keep track of.

However, there are plenty of situations where you might want to do summative research with smaller groups. We both teach courses to groups of students numbering from somewhere around 12 to somewhere around 200. At the end of each course we survey the students to see how they found the lessons and if they think there are ways we could do things better.[2] In this case, we are doing summative research: we simply want to sum up the experience of a specific group (the students who just took our course) at a specific time (the semester just finished). The participant numbers are small and

---

[2] Of course, if the results come back with any negative comments we just shout *'Ungrateful wretches – damn their eyes!'* and storm around in a sulk for a couple of days. (In our heads, it's always the nineteenth century.)

manageable and so summing up their experiences isn't difficult. You may very easily come across small groups like this that you wish to summarize somehow, and many of the methods in this book will be useful to you if you do, especially the methods for describing data we cover in Chapter 3.

Going beyond your participants: inferential research

So much for summative research. The other, usually more interesting, type of research is **inferential research**. This is where you *are* interested in predicting the future: this is where you want to learn something general, where you want to reach a conclusion that applies not just to the people you studied, but to other people as well. The dyslexia project we mentioned above was inferential research: a group of children was studied not as a way of summarizing that group's abilities, but as a way of learning something about children with dyslexia in general.

When carrying out inferential research you study a group of people, find out something about them, and then use this information to estimate, or *infer*, what you would have seen if you had tested a larger group of people. The group you test is known as the **sample**, and the larger group that you generalize the findings to is known as the **population**. So the process goes like this:

1. You identify a population that interests you (more on this in a moment).
2. You select a group of people from this population – a subset of the population – to be your sample.
3. You study this sample of people and discover something about them.
4. You use the information you have gathered to infer (estimate) what you would have seen if you if you had tested the whole population.

But if there is a certain body of people you are interested in, why not test them all? Why only test a subset of them? The answer is that in many circumstances it just isn't practical. But that depends on what your population is.

What is my population?

You may remember back in Chapter 1, we said it was really helpful when carrying out research always to be sure you know what your research question is. Well, we were right: this is important. But it is perhaps *even more important* always to be certain what your population is. And it can be different in every study.

The difficulty, and the reason we will labour the point a bit here, is that the word 'population' means something different when doing research than it does in everyday life. Usually when we use the word 'population', we are describing the people who live in a certain place. So we refer to 'the population of India' or 'the population of Rome', meaning the people who live in a particular country or city.

In a research study, the population is *the group of people you want to reach a conclusion about.* If you carry out a study to learn whether or not chiropractors are mostly extroverts, the population you are interested in is 'all the chiropractors'. If you carry out a study to look at how often drivers in New Zealand are involved in collisions, the population you are interested in is 'all the drivers in New Zealand'. At the end of the dyslexia study we wanted to be able to make statements about every child with dyslexia. Therefore the population we were studying was 'every child with dyslexia'. This included children not yet born. Notice how different this is from the usual use of the word 'population'. Notice how, although the word *can* be linked to geography (as with our New Zealand example), it usually has nothing to do with where people live and can easily involve people scattered all over the world, as with the chiropractors.

So you have probably now realized why, a lot of the time, we do not study whole populations: they are just too damn big. There are almost certainly too many chiropractors in the world for you to study them all. There are *definitely* too many children with dyslexia for you to study them all – to say nothing of the fact that dyslexia is a complex condition, such that identifying everybody who has it is difficult.

The issue of populations being too big to study becomes particularly pressing when you want to reach conclusions about *human beings in general.* This is something human researchers need to do all the time. When a psychologist, for example, looks at how short-term memory works, they want to reach a conclusion about how *everybody's* short-term memory works, including everybody alive right now, everybody who will be alive in the future and everybody who was alive in the past. *Everybody ever* is the population. Clearly testing the whole of this population presents certain logistical difficulties.

The same principle often applies in medicine, biology and related disciplines: when somebody carries out research on how blood vessels dilate in response to hormone changes, they want to know how this happens for everybody, including you, us, Isaac Newton, everybody in Papua New Guinea and Elvis Presley. Clearly testing all these people just isn't possible.

Of course, on some occasions you *can* test the whole population you are interested in. Let's say you are interested in what the people who live in your street think about the level of road traffic that passes by: in this case the population is 'the people on my street' and you could probably survey the whole population quite easily. As such, when your population is small enough your work becomes summative and there is no need to do any sampling or inference (this also means you don't need to use any statistical analysis). But in general, most research questions require you to study a sample of a bigger population. This is where it gets interesting.

What makes a good sample?

You study a sample – a subset of a population – when for one reason or another it is not practical or possible to study the whole population. You want to learn something about the sample and for this to be true also of the population. When this happens you have learnt something about a lot of people by studying just a few – which is great, as there are no medals for doing more work than necessary. What you do not want to do is to learn something about the sample and presume it is also true of the population when in reality the sample and the population are not the same.

So the key principle we want to communicate here is this: ideally, your sample will be *exactly the same as your population, but smaller.* Your sample should be the population in miniature; it should be completely *representative* of your population, but be a manageable size. We should warn you, we are about to use the word 'representative' a lot.

You might remember back in Chapter 1 we talked about inventing a new medicine called Holtodol. Like all medicines, Holtodol needs to be tested before it can be used widely, to ensure it is safe. If we test it on a sample of people and see no problems, we will infer that it is safe for the whole population and start selling it. So, if there is going to be a problem in the population, we want to see that problem in the sample first. In other words, we want the sample to behave just like the population, to *represent* the population.

So what can you do to try and make sure your sample is as representative as possible of its population? This is not simple, as you usually have no way of knowing what your population looks like in advance. To show you what we mean by this, imagine you discover tomorrow that some people sweat beer. Woo-hoo! You immediately set out to discover what proportion of people have this amazing ability. Clearly testing everybody in the world isn't an option so you have to test a sample. You apply yourself to this project with uncharacteristic assiduity and find that 5% of the people you tested have sweat made of beer. What proportion of people in the world sweat beer? The answer is you don't know, as you haven't tested them all, but your best guess will be 5%. Is this estimate correct? Critically – and this is the point we are making – you've got no way of knowing: the only source of information you have is what you saw in your sample. This means your sample had better be good. (As well as anything else, what you learn from this sample will likely affect how you distribute party invitations in the future.)

If a good sample is so important, how do you go about ensuring you get one when doing research? There are two main things you need to consider. The first is that you must choose a sample of the right size, and the second is that you must choose the right people to be in your sample. Let's take these issues in turn.

How big should my sample be?

When we first mentioned our new drug in Chapter 1, we asked whether you would be willing to take it. We asked whether you would take the drug if we had tested it on two people and neither experienced any side-effects. We then asked if you would take the drug if we had tested it on 10,000 people and none of them experienced any side-effects. We were confident you would be happier with the larger sample.

But why were you happier with the larger sample, even though you had not yet read this section of the book on sample sizes? The answer is that you already intuitively knew something about samples and populations: other things being equal, *the larger the sample, the more likely it is to be representative of its population.* If you have had any training in statistics then this principle might make sense to you immediately, but if not, here is a non-mathematical illustration to make things clearer.

We need a population for this illustration, so we might as well use the 180 students who are taking Nigel's Hearing, Speech and Language class this year. Now, obviously if we wanted to know something about a population of only 180 people we should probably test everybody, but let's pretend for the moment that we can't do this and so need to test a sample. This particular group has 100 women and 80 men in it, meaning the women make up approximately 56% of the population and the men approximately 44%.

Normally, of course, as a researcher you don't have this sort of information about the population – you have to guess what the population looks like from the sample you end up with. So let's forget for a moment we know what the population really looks like and see what we would estimate about the population if all we had to guide us was a sample of it.

For the purposes of this demonstration we gave all 180 people in Nigel's class a unique number and then used a random number

Table 2.1   Samples drawn from a population which is 56% women and 44% men

Sample size	First attempt	Second attempt	Third attempt	Average
5	2 women (40%) 3 men (60%)	4 women (80%) 1 man (20%)	5 women (100%) 0 men (0%)	**73% women** **27% men**
15	9 women (60%) 6 men (40%)	11 women (73%) 4 men (27%)	7 women (47%) 8 men (53%)	**60% women** **40% men**
30	17 women (57%) 13 men (43%)	19 women (63%) 11 men (37%)	16 women (53%) 14 men (47%)	**58% women** **42% men**

generator to select samples of them. We took three samples of five people, three samples of 15 people and three samples of 30 people, and the way these samples broke down between men and women is shown in Table 2.1.

Tempting as it was for us to fudge these data[3] to make sure they supported our point perfectly (as if we would ever do such a thing!), we genuinely created the data in Table 2.1 at random. Recall that, in the population, there were 56% women and 44% men. Which of the samples in Table 2.1 looks most like this? It is pretty clear that the larger the sample, the more it tends to look like – or *represent* – the population. In particular, our smallest samples are very misleading – just look at our third attempt to pick a sample of five people: there were no men in it at all; the sample was totally unrepresentative of its population.

So you can see that if we knew nothing about the population and were having to estimate, or *infer*, what it looked like from a sample of people, the smaller our sample is, the less accurate our judgements about the population will tend to be.

So the more, the merrier?

Yes, there is a real sense in which, when you are sampling populations, the more people you can get the better. You would not go far wrong if you aimed always to study as many people as you can possibly manage to test. But, in practice, when you are deciding how many people to study in your sample you need to strike a balance between various

---

[3] Did you notice we wrote '*these* data'? That's because 'data' is a plural word – in fact, it's the plural of 'datum', which is Latin for 'a given thing'. We're all in favour of viewing language as a democracy in which word uses change and evolve according to the will of the majority, but on this one we have to take a stand: when we abandons grammars and use plural without following rule we's in troubles.

If you're ever not sure, substitute the word 'numbers' and you'll see when a sentence is wrong. When people write things like 'We took the data and put it in an analysis...', this is just like writing 'We took the numbers and put it in an analysis...'. You know that little feeling of discomfort you just felt reading the second version? That's what we experience *every day* reading the work of people who don't know that 'data' is plural. It's plural. It really is. Plural. Data: plural. More than one.

factors: studying more people helps ensure more representative samples, as we have seen; but the more people you study, the more time and money it takes. The number of people you test in any given study will be a compromise between wanting the largest possible sample and practical constraints.

There can also be a problem of diminishing returns: eventually you reach a point where testing more and more people gets you less and less benefit. To show you how diminishing returns work, we will extend the data in Table 2.1 by taking some bigger samples, as shown in Table 2.2. What you can see here is that, although our samples got more representative as they moved from five to 15 to 30 people, after this point making the sample bigger didn't really do a great deal to give us a more representative sample of the population. This is essentially because the samples were already pretty representative with 30 people in them; there just wasn't much scope for them to get a lot more representative as we tested more people.

Diminishing returns notwithstanding, there are still plenty of good reasons why it is always better to have a larger sample than a smaller sample – in particular, the larger the sample the less your results are affected by odd people who give extreme scores, known as outliers (we'll say more about outliers in Chapter 3). And the larger the sample, the lower the likelihood of getting a freakish sample which looks nothing like the population (more on this shortly). But, despite all this, when doing research in the real world there comes a point where testing more people doesn't really give you any clear benefit. Interestingly, in Table 2.2 this point seems to have come somewhere around a sample of 30 people.

The reason we say this is interesting is that, for statistical reasons that are too complex for us to go into here, 30 is a bit of a magic

Table 2.2   Samples drawn from a population which is 56% women and 44% men

Sample size	First attempt	Second attempt	Third attempt	Average
5	2 women (40%) 3 men (60%)	4 women (80%) 1 man (20%)	5 women (100%) 0 men (0%)	**73% women** **27% men**
15	9 women (60%) 6 men (40%)	11 women (73%) 4 men (27%)	7 women (47%) 8 men (53%)	**60% women** **40% men**
30	17 women (57%) 13 men (43%)	19 women (63%) 11 men (37%)	16 women (53%) 14 men (47%)	**58% women** **42% men**
60	36 women (60%) 24 men (40%)	29 women (48%) 31 men (52%)	34 women (57%) 26 men (43%)	**55% women** **45% men**
100	56 women (56%) 44 men (44%)	63 women (63%) 37 men (37%)	59 women (59%) 41 men (41%)	**59% women** **41% men**
140	79 women (56%) 61 men (44%)	86 women (61%) 54 men (39%)	76 women (54%) 64 men (46%)	**57% women** **43% men**

number in sampling.[4] This means you can often use 30 people as a rule of thumb when deciding how many people to test. *Like all rules of thumb, this will very often be wrong*, but just tuck it away in the back of your mind somewhere: it is always good to test as many people as possible, but if you have at least 30 people in each group you study you will probably be okay (unless you are looking for race events live adverse reactions to a drug, obviously).

Please do not get obsessed with this number 30. It is only a *very* loose guideline. It only applies to study designs where you compare groups of people, and you should always aim for more people per group in most circumstances. Indeed, in principle there are always advantages to collecting as many data as possible – every extra person you study makes your sample closer to the population. The closer the sample is to the population, the less you are having to infer what the population looks like. And the larger your sample, the less likely you are to overlook a discovery.

Finally, if you want to get much more scientific about this then we'll just alert you to the existence of a technique called **power analysis**. This is a way of calculating in advance how large your sample needs to be for a given study. Power analysis is rather beyond the scope of this book, and all we want to do here is make you aware that it exists for if you ever need it.

Sample size: a final word

Our discussion of sample size is a little different from what you will find elsewhere. Some people get terribly serious about there being a 'right' number for any given study and might be somewhat surprised at how we have treated the subject here. So, even though we will probably get hate mail for it, we prefer to tell you how it is in the real world. In everyday research, people more often choose their sample sizes based on how much time and money they have available, and how easy it will be to find participants, than on careful power analyses. It is far more common to hear people say 'I'm teaching a class of 94 people tomorrow – if I get them all to do my test that should be enough people' than it is to hear people say 'My power calculation said I need two groups of 47 people. Where might I find them…?'

(The reason we can be a bit cavalier about this is that in research there is a safety net. Every study you conduct involves statistical analysis, which assesses the sample you used and can let you know whether your sample was too large or too small. Many analyses, especially when you use a technique called regression, also test the people who went into your sample. So we're definitely not suggesting that you work blind.)

---

[4] If you want to know more, look up the relationship between the normal distribution and the *t* distribution. The issue of effect sizes is also relevant.

Who goes into my sample?

We have looked at why, within reason, you want your sample to be relatively large. But knowing the number of people you will test is no good on its own. If somebody tells you to test 300 people, your first response will probably be to say 'Okay, but who?' Let's now turn to this question of who the people in your sample will be.

As we have seen, the single most important aim when sampling people for a study is to get a sample that is *representative* of the population. At the time we are writing this chapter, we are also working with an aerodynamicist on a project looking at whether some motorcyclists suffer hearing loss (with high-speed winds buffeting motorcycle helmets, it can get pretty noisy inside). If we were to take a sample of motorcyclists and find that some proportion – 20%, say – showed signs of hearing loss, our best guess would have to be that this same proportion of all motorcyclists show signs of hearing loss.

But what if our sample was somehow unrepresentative of the population? In this case, our judgement about the population would be faulty. At one point, when planning the study, we discussed doing all the testing on a set of police motorcycle riders, because we knew we could get access to this group quite easily. But then we realized this group was almost certainly not representative of motorcyclists in general: not only do they spend far more time riding their bikes than is typical, meaning they have more exposure to noise than most riders, but they also use radio equipment which plays directly into their ears, possibly affecting their hearing in a way most bikers do not experience. There was every reason to suspect, then, that police riders would show more evidence of hearing damage than normal. Fortunately we spotted the potential problem with this group in advance, but if we had not we would almost certainly have ended up with a sample which did not really represent the population properly and we would probably have overestimated the amount of hearing loss amongst bikers in general.

In this case, we came close to getting a potentially biased and misleading sample because we were choosing the sample using a method called **opportunity sampling**. This is just one method for choosing the people who will make up a sample, and we will look at it, and the other methods that exist, now. Each has advantages and disadvantages. In particular, some sampling methods allow you to be more confident than others that you are getting a representative sample. Why don't we therefore use these high-confidence methods all the time? As you will see below, it is largely a question of logistics.

Random sampling

Imagine you need participants for a study on what people think about cheese. Now it just happens that both of us have strong feelings about cheese, and would really like to get into your sample to make sure our opinions on cheese are represented. If we learnt about your study we would email you and ask if you needed volunteers, because we'd love to come over and help. Really, it's no trouble. What time suits you?

You can probably see that if you selected your participants for this study based on the people who volunteered, you could very easily end up with a sample which over-represents people who really care about cheese, one way or the other. If 98% of the population have no interest in cheese at all and only 2% are passionate about it, when you announce you are looking for volunteers for a survey your eventual sample will likely have these percentages reversed.[5]

Bias in samples can also arise in other ways. You might go out and conduct your cheese survey by speaking to people in the street. In this case, you could inadvertently bias your sample by where you stand – you could be just around the corner from a cheese seller without realizing it, meaning you again end up with a sample far more interested in cheese than the general population.

These sorts of bias cannot happen if you use random sampling. This method is very simple in principle: you give every member of the population an exactly equal chance of being included in your sample. As such, there is no way people's strong opinions can affect the likelihood of their being in your sample and there is no way an accident in your planning, like standing in the wrong place, can cause any bias either. People get into your sample if their number comes up and are left out of your sample if it does not, and that's the beginning and the end of it. The result: no bias, and, as long as it is sufficiently large, you can be very confident that a random sample will represent the population from which it was drawn. Random sampling allows such confidence, and has been proven with statistical techniques in such a convincing way, that many bodies, especially in medicine, practically oblige researchers to use the technique.

Admittedly, it does remain possible that even using careful random sampling you will be really unlucky: you might, just through pure chance, end up with a higher proportion of hard-core cheese-lovers in your sample than there is in the population. But the critical point is that the probability of your sample being biased like this goes down in a mathematically predictable way as your sample gets larger. Indeed, you can look back at Table 2.1 to see a small demonstration of this.

---

[5] Read these last two paragraphs again, changing the word 'cheese' to 'religion', 'abortion', 'immigration' or 'legalizing drugs', and you'll understand the power of self-selection when it comes to distorting samples.

So the fact random sampling rules out any possibility of systematic bias makes it a really good sampling technique, giving you every likelihood of getting a nice representative sample of your population. Indeed, random sampling is often seen as the 'gold standard' sampling method, to which researchers should always aspire. But if it is so good, why don't we use it in every study? Why does this book even bother to discuss other sampling techniques?

The answer is that random sampling can be difficult to achieve: making sure everybody in the population has an equal chance to be included is complicated at best, and often downright impossible. For example, when doing research where we want to reach conclusions about human beings in general, we might view the study's population of interest as 'everybody'. How on Earth could we give every human being an equal chance of being included in a sample? There's just no way. We don't even know who they all are. And most of them are dead, or not born yet.[6]

But even with smaller, more constrained populations, difficulties still arise. Imagine we decide to take a random sample of the students at one of our universities. In principle this will be easy: every student has a unique number which is used to keep their records organized – it would be a simple matter to choose numbers at random and select a sample this way. Doing so should give us a nice unbiased sample, shouldn't it?

But imagine you are one of our students and you get an email one day saying 'You have been randomly selected to take part in a study. Come to room 8.22 on Wednesday morning'. You would quite probably just delete the email. It would be not only rude but also unethical of us simply to expect people to participate in our study. And the fact that we cannot oblige people to take part means that even when we sample randomly we will almost always end up with a sample which is biased to some extent. Specifically, even if we wanted our sample to be the people whose numbers we selected, in practice it would be the people whose numbers we selected *and* who did not mind coming out to help. This sample could easily show some systematic biases. For example, it might consist of people who were more generous – or perhaps more meek – than average. This might make them unsuitable for a study that could be affected by personality. A group of unusually meek people wouldn't be suitable if we were conducting a study on how people work together in groups, say. People having the right to refuse to take part in a study is an issue to a greater or

---

[6] This last point means that when looking at people in general there is no such thing as a true random sample, and anything that looks like a random sample is actually a cluster sample, using the single cluster of 'people who happen to be alive right now'. Just as the cluster sample we discuss later in this chapter saves you travelling around the country, using the cluster of 'people who happen to be alive right now' saves you a lot of tedious travelling through time.

lesser extent in all 'randomly sampled' studies, and is something to look out for in other people's research reports – what proportion of people refused to take part? Was there any evidence of one type of person refusing more than another?

Another practical difficulty with random samples is that producing genuinely random numbers is surprisingly difficult. A fact not enough researchers know is that computers cannot produce random numbers. Instead they produce what are called *pseudo-random* numbers. This means the numbers are sufficiently muddled to look random to us, but frankly this isn't difficult as we are terrible judges of such things. In fact the numbers computers produce are not genuinely random, and are sometimes surprisingly predictable. (Computers, at least right now, just can't do random things; they are machines, like car engines, where one event follows another in a strictly predictable pattern.)

In many cases where you want a random sample, you would do as well using the old-fashioned approach of picking names or numbers from pieces of paper in a hat (as long as you have jumbled them sufficiently – and you have made sure the pieces of paper are all the same size and texture, haven't you?) or using something like a lottery machine. Just be aware that there are two ways of doing this: *with replacement* and *without replacement*. 'With replacement' means that after picking each name, it is replaced before the next is drawn. This in principle keeps the probability of choosing each person the same. (Imagine there are five names in the hat. If sampled *without* replacement, the first person has a 1 in 5 chance of being picked, the second person has a 1 in 4 chance, and so on.)

Finally, we should just clear up the difference between a random sample and a **randomized control trial**. A randomized control trial (RCT) is where the participants are randomly allocated to the various conditions in a study. As an example, let's say we are testing a new drug and need to give some of the participants the drug and some a placebo. How do you decide who gets the drug? A very poor way of doing this would be to meet all the participants and give the real drug to ones whose faces you liked and the placebo to the people you didn't like. This would be a terribly biased study.

A way of doing this allocation without bias would be to use a random process for each person – for example, you could toss a coin for each person and if it lands on Heads they get the drug and if it lands on Tails they get the placebo. (Note that what we have described here, with the coin tossing, is a true randomized control trial, and it is possible the two groups would end up with different numbers of people in them. It is common to see pseudo-RCTs, where the researchers ensure the two groups end up the same size. This process is not quite as good.)

The point is that the 'random' in 'randomized control trial' refers to how people are allocated to the various conditions – it does not mean the sampling is random, and it is perfectly common to do randomized control trials on non-random samples, like opportunity samples. So just be careful you don't confuse the two terms.

Systematic sampling (or *n*th name sampling)

This has a lot of the advantages of random sampling with the further advantage of being really simple. You put the names of your population in a list. When you know how large your population is and how large your sample has to be, you can easily divide one number by the other to work out an interval. For example, if you need a sample of 25 people out of a population of 1000, you select every (1000/25 = 40) 40th person on the list as your sample. As long as there is no systematic bias in how the names are ordered, this should give you something a lot like a random sample.

In practice it can be difficult to produce a list of names without any systematic bias in their order. Alphabetical order is definitely out, and the order in which people volunteered to be considered is also going to be biased. In reality, getting a completely unbiased list order is essentially the same problem as true random sampling. And there is still the issue we saw with random sampling, that your final sample can easily be biased by refusals to participate.

Cluster sampling

Here we use naturally occurring groups to make sampling more convenient than with random samples. Let's say you are interested in how schools are dealing with the issue of bullying, and let's also say you decide you need to visit a sample of 300 schools to conduct interviews. With a random sample, the 300 schools might – indeed, *should* – be scattered all over the country, making your task really difficult, expensive and time-consuming.

A way of dealing with this is to find some way that schools are already clustered together in groups. For example, you might use cities or counties. Then, instead of choosing schools at random, you choose *cities* or *counties* at random and visit all the schools in each of these selected. This technique should still take you to various parts of the country, but involve rather less travelling overall as many of the schools will be close together.

Opportunity sampling (or convenience sampling, or grab sampling)

This is where you simply do your research on a convenient group of people. When academics like us do studies on groups of students, this is opportunity sampling – we have the *opportunity* to test the students so we do. Another example of an opportunity sample is when somebody tests their colleagues, or neighbours.

Spotting opportunity samples can also be slightly more difficult. If you advertise for participants – if you put a notice on the Web, for example, asking people to take part in your study – this is also an opportunity sample as your volunteers are a convenient sample you have the opportunity to study: the people who happened to see your advert and volunteer.

Opportunity sampling – especially on students – forms a really large part of the published literature in psychology, sociology, economics, and various other fields. The fact so much research takes place using student samples is often used as a criticism of how science progresses: students tend to come from a fairly narrow range of ages, and to an extent a fairly narrow range of social classes. Therefore, the argument goes, what we learn from them can't be generalized to people in general.

We would argue that there are plenty of situations where student opportunity samples are perfectly acceptable – experimenters just need to use their judgement. When we are looking at basic abilities, students can provide a perfectly good sample of the human population. For example, if a psychophysicist wants to study how the perception of a sound varies with its intensity, there is no reason at all to think students' hearing systems will be different to everybody else's. If, on the other hand, a political scientist is interested in people's views on property ownership, a student sample is probably less suitable.

real-world view: opportunity samples

Barbara Tabachnik and Linda Fidell,[7] in their magnificent advanced statistics book, make a really interesting claim about the relationship between samples and populations. They say that whilst, in theory, samples are chosen to represent populations, in the real world populations are usually determined by samples.

What they are suggesting is that most samples in the real world can probably be thought of as opportunity samples. As such, if you want to know the population a study refers to, you need to scale up the sample. Let's say we carry out a study to see what is the quietest sound people can hear, on average, and so we grab a sample of students from Nigel's university and test their hearing. What is the population in this study? We would like it to be 'human beings in general', but strictly speaking the population is really 'people, like the students at Nigel's university'. So the sample defines the population rather than the other way round. The practical implication of this is that most studies' findings are arguably not as generalizable as they appear to be.

[7] Tabachnik, B. and Fidell, L. (2001). *Using Multivariate Statistics* (4th Edition). Boston: Allyn & Bacon.

Stratified sampling and quota sampling

These are techniques often employed in public opinion surveys and political polls. The aim of stratified sampling and quota sampling is really interesting, as they are all about representativeness: the techniques very deliberately seek to ensure, through careful control, that the sample used in a study looks just like a smaller version of its population, which is of course what we want.

When using **stratified sampling**, the researcher looks at the population and how it can be broken down into different groups, or *strata* (the plural of *stratum*, which is Latin for 'layer'). They then carefully ensure their sample breaks down in exactly the same way. For example, if the population is half male and half female, the sample will be chosen to be half male and half female. If the population's ethnicity breaks down as 60% Caucasian, 10% Asian, and so on, then the sample will be chosen to break down in the same way.

Stratified sampling has two main benefits. First, it helps ensure minority groups are not overlooked in a sample – something that is clearly important when working in areas like political opinions. Second, it can in theory allow the use of smaller samples than some other sampling methods. Let's say only 1% of your population consists of women, from a certain ethnic group, aged between 55 and 64 and coming from a middle-income bracket. If you wanted to ensure this group was represented in your sample and you were using random sampling, you would need to use a really large sample to give such a small group a good chance of being represented. With stratified sampling, however, you do not need to worry. If 1% of the population falls in this group, you know 1% of your sample will.

But this strength of stratified sampling can also be a cause for concern. Let's say you want a sample of the people in your country so you can ask them about their political views. Political views tend to vary with age, gender, ethnic group, income bracket and so on. Each of these divisions gives you smaller and smaller strata, and every extra division multiplies your sampling difficulties. Let's put some numbers to this to show you what we mean. Imagine you are working towards a sample of 500 people. That will be 250 male and 250 female participants.[8] Let's focus on the men for a moment: to reflect the population's varying levels of wealth you might need to break the 250 men down into 75 from low-income families, 125 from middle-income families and 50 from high-income families (this is in

---

[8] In reality the ratio of women to men is not so simple, and varies by age. There tend to be slightly more male children than female children, but by the time we reach older age brackets (over 65, say), men's lower life-expectancies mean there are more women than men.

itself a clear oversimplification of how wealth is distributed in society). Then, amongst the 125 middle-income men you need to break them down by age, ethnicity, and the region they live in... With all this subdivision, you can see how easy it would be to end up with a single 33-year-old middle-income Asian man from the North-East of the country representing every middle-income Asian man aged between 25 and 34 in the country's whole North-Eastern region! That one man has some real power, as you will take whatever he says to represent the view of thousands of people. What if he is an outlier? What if he happens to have extreme views? What mechanism do you have to spot it if he does?

We would like to suggest that stratified samples also have the potential to be misleading for another, slightly more abstract, reason. When working with people, stratified samples are nearly always stratified by demography (the study of groups within society). The final sample will be carefully stratified so there is exactly the right ratio of men to women, low-income households to high-income households, and so on. The sample is demographically a perfect microcosm of society.

Our suggestion is that the care with which the sample is balanced demographically can encourage people to assume the research findings will also be nicely balanced and representative. But there is no reason to believe that demographic balance in the participants will ensure any sort of balance in the research results. If there are only one or two men representing all the 25- to 34-year-old middle-income North-Eastern Asian men, as in our illustration above, how were those men chosen? Strictly speaking, in stratified sampling they should be randomly selected from all the 25- to 34-year-old middle-income North-Eastern Asian men. In real opinion polling the chances are they fell into one of two groups. First, they might have volunteered to be on a panel of people whose opinions could be surveyed from time to time. Volunteering for such things is not something most people do, so immediately you have to worry about how representative these people are. Second, they might have answered the telephone when a surveyor called their home (no doubt during their evening meal) and stayed around to deal with some questions. Answering a telephone surveyor's questions is also not something the majority of people do. Again this raises questions of representativeness.

(Interestingly, what we have just described above is actually **quota sampling**. Quota sampling is exactly the same as stratified sampling with one exception: whereas in stratified sampling the strata are filled through random sampling, with quota sampling the strata are filled through opportunity sampling. We would argue that practically all stratified sampling in the real world is actually quota sampling.)

Another practical consideration with stratified sampling is that a researcher using this technique has to make some difficult decisions about the strata that matter. Let's stick with the example of political opinion polling: it is very likely that age, gender, income group and ethnicity will be important strata that affect people's political opinions. But what about voting history? What about education level? It is not difficult to think of plenty more potentially important strata: every extra one you add at least doubles the number of participants you need. Do you add another stratum, and make your task twice as difficult? Or do you leave it out and risk introducing a bias into your sample?

We have slightly exaggerated the difficulties of stratified sampling here: in practice there may be as many as three or four people in a sample representing all the 25- to 34-year-old middle-income Asian men in the North-East of the country. What we want to communicate to you is that you cannot simply assume that, just because a sample is demographically representative of a population, the way it behaves will also be representative of that population. The issues of how you select the specific people to test, and the biases that can be introduced at this stage, still exist, and all the concerns we discussed above in relation to random and opportunity sampling can still come into play.

In particular, stratified and quota sampling only make sense if people's opinions or behaviours are genuinely related to their demographics. For example, there is no real systematic relationship (that we know of) between a person's gender and their musical tastes. As such, stratifying our sample by gender does nothing to help us achieve representativeness if we want to learn about this subject, except perhaps fooling us into thinking we have managed to achieve representativeness in our sample when we have not. So stratified samples and quota samples have a lot to offer, but just be careful: that's what we are saying.

Judgement sampling

We have devised a new technique for catching criminals. It works by coating every object of any value with strong glue. Whenever a thief steals an object it will become permanently stuck to their hands, making it easy for the police to catch them – they just need to drive around looking for people with computers and telephones hanging awkwardly from their fingers.

Imagine we approach the police with this idea and, somehow overlooking the fairly glaring flaws in our plan, they decide to test it to see if it works. What the police would probably do in this case is pick a single city and try it there. If it works in the test city, they will make the idea national, in which case we become rich.

But which city would be used for the test? Obviously, the city would need to be 'typical' or 'representative' of the whole country. If they made the selection by looking at some data and saying 'This city looks like it should be representative – it's an average size and has the same sort of demographic breakdown as the whole country,' this would be judgement sampling: they would be using their judgement to select a naturally occurring group of people to act as a sample.

Judgement sampling can perhaps be seen as a form of cluster sampling where the clusters are chosen by people rather than randomly.

Matched-pairs sampling

This is where you take a group of people for testing and compare them with another group of people who are the same in some way. Most usually, the first group is a naturally occurring sample of people and the second group is chosen to fit them.

As an example, let's say you have a group of athletes that you have access to for some reason – an opportunity sample, essentially. You might be interested in whether they are different from non-athletes. For example, you might want to see whether they have, on average, fewer friends than non-athletes, perhaps thanks to all the time they spend training, or because their compulsion to run really fast makes them abstemious and dull. You therefore need a group of non-athletes for the comparison. And what you ideally want is a group of people that is exactly the same as your group of athletes, but made up of non-athletes.

A random sample of non-athletes probably would not be the best choice in this situation. Athletes tend to be quite young: a random sample would include lots of people who are much older, and who probably have different patterns of friendships. Another approach would be to take a second opportunity sample – a group of students, for example – where everybody is about the same age as the athletes, but this still doesn't guarantee that the two groups are essentially the same except for the athletics.

Perhaps the best option here would be to go through your athletes one-by-one and select participants who are a close match. If your first athlete is a 23-year-old North African woman from a middle-class background, you make sure the first person in the non-athlete group is a 23-year-old North African woman from a middle-class background. And so on for the rest of your athletes. If you do the matching carefully enough, you should end up with two groups which are essentially the same, except for the factor you are interested in, which in this case is the athletics. You can then be reasonably confident that if you find the athletes do indeed have fewer friends than the non-athletes, it is the athletics background that is responsible for this difference.

This approach can be particularly useful when your first group is relatively small and you need to do everything you can to ensure the second group is well-matched.

Probably the best known examples of research using matched-pairs are twin studies. There are various forms of twin study, but the most powerful are studies which seek out identical twins who were separated at birth and raised in different environments. These are a matched-pairs design because, for each person in the first group, there is a person in the second group who is *genetically identical* but raised in a different home. Careful research can use this matching to determine the extent of genetic influences and upbringing on personality, intelligence, and so on.

Snowball sampling

This technique will almost certainly give you a biased, and possibly a totally unrepresentative, sample. You use it when no other method is practical because you are interested in secretive or otherwise hard-to-reach groups. It is used when studying criminals, drug-users and people whose activities, whilst not illegal, are still secretive – people with eating disorders, for example.

The idea of snowball sampling is that each participant finds you one or two more participants. You start with just one person and, after testing them, you ask them to pass on your details to other people they know who are in the same group. So, if you have found one burglar, you ask them to pass on your details to other burglars they know. (Note that you don't ask them to give *you* the details of other burglars. On the one hand, they'll probably just refuse; and on the other hand, it would be unethical to request individuals' contact details without their consent.) When a second person gets in touch and you have tested them, you again ask them to pass on your contact details to any other burglars they know. If each person you test passes your details on to one or two more people, you can eventually get a suitably sized sample of hard-to-find participants even though you found just one person yourself.

The problems with snowball sampling all centre on being unable to know whether your sample is representative or not. This is partly because you cannot know what the population looks like. It is also because all your participants will know one another to some extent: they probably all come from the same area, or frequent the same websites, and the fact that they know one another makes it likely that they have been exposed to the same influences, and might also discuss your research with one another. Ultimately you just cannot know whether a snowball sample is representative or not, but, when hard-to-reach participants might tell you something interesting, it can be your only option. You just have to use caution when interpreting your findings, and need to place less weight on them than you would with more reliable sampling methods.

Checking your sample

One of the things we have tried to show you, in describing the various sampling methods above, is that, even if you are using the most promising methods, like random sampling, there are very plausible ways you might end up with some sort of bias in your sample. For this reason it is always a good idea to check your sample at the end of your study to see if you can spot any signs of this. Have a look at your participants' characteristics: are there more women than men? Is the average age of your sample surprisingly low or high, or is there very little variation in age? (This sort of information is usually reported in people's study reports, so it is also a good idea to get into the habit of looking for any biases in other people's samples when you read about their research.)

As well as looking at your sample's gender, age and so on at the end of the study, look at the results you obtained from them and be open to the idea that they might be biased. If you carry out a survey to discover how much people like cheese and find that 88% of people say they like it, you will probably be excited that you have learnt an exciting fact about the nation's level of cheese-adoration. But you always need to be open to the idea that this is not what you would have found if you had tested the whole population and that your finding is actually spurious. Every result we obtain is suspect to some extent. This is why, when we carry out inferential research, we use inferential statistics to check our findings. And that's what Chapter 4 is all about. But before we get to that, tradition dictates we get Chapter 3 out of the way first...

chapter 3

how will you describe your findings?

In the previous two chapters we covered a few things – particularly hypothesis testing and sampling – which you simply must know before you ever test a single person. Now, we don't want to suggest that having read those two chapters you are ready to go out and test people straight away – there is plenty more we want to teach you about how to plan and conduct research first, and we will do this with the practicals that make up the next part of this book.

First, however, we would like to jump ahead in time a little, to the point where you have collected some data and have to decide what to do with them. That way you will be prepared for when you start to carry out research on people and find yourself accumulating information. This chapter will look at how you can summarize and describe your findings; the next chapter will introduce you to the statistical analyses that are used after you have carried out inferential research.

It can be very useful to think of research as having two stages. In the first stage you collect data and in the second stage you analyse them to see what they tell you. If you think about research in this way, you should see that the second phase – the data analysis – has nothing to work with except the data you collected in the design and testing phase: if the numbers you eventually process are faulty, your conclusions will be faulty, so you really need to focus on making sure those numbers are good. Computer scientists have a term that describes this well: GIGO, which stands for 'garbage in, garbage out'. If you put meaningless information into a computer, you can't expect to get anything useful out again. In research, if you put bad data into your analyses – if you forget to use a control group or don't counter-balance your design properly – it doesn't matter what the analyses say, your conclusions are unreliable.

So our main focus in this book is on giving you the skills to design and conduct your studies well. And because of this, the information in this chapter and the next is not intended to teach you everything there is to know about the statistics you will eventually use on the data you collect. We deliberately chose to describe what you need to learn about statistics, rather than teach you the subject in detail ourselves, because many universities and colleges teach statistics separately from research design. And those of you who *are* learning statistics at the same time as research methods will always be better off choosing a statistics textbook that matches your level of mathematical skill – one size doesn't fit all when it comes to statistics, we find, and those of you who are less confident about mathematics will want a different textbook than people who are prodigies.

Instead, what we have tried to do with this chapter and the next is provide *the introduction to statistics most human scientists should read first, before they ever touch a statistics book*. Our introduction will provide a solid foundation if you go on to learn what you need to know about statistics, and will be enough for you to understand all the most important concepts even if you never learn any more. We have written this material based on years of experience teaching statistics to human researchers and have taken a lot of care to explain as clearly as possible concepts we know people often find difficult; in places where we think it is important we have even gone into more detail than most statistics books.

These two chapters should, in particular, be a good introduction for people who are nervous about the subject of data analysis, as we know many people are. We have particularly tried to focus on data analysis from a practical perspective. We do not get bogged down in theoretical debates, interesting as these can be, but rather tell you what you need to know, explain why things are done the way they are, and alert you to some of the common mistakes people make, to help prevent you falling into those traps.

So whether this is the beginning of a long and happy relationship with statistical analysis, or whether you just want to learn a few techniques to get research done and answer questions without burdening yourself with too much theory, we hope we will set you off down the right path.

First things first: categories and continuous measurements

Carrying out research with people – which, if you've read this far, we assume you want to be able to do – is all about measuring people.[1] When it comes to measurement, the first thing you need to know is that all data fall into two broad types: **categorical data** and **continuous data**.

Categorical data are things like gender and race and nationality, where there are a limited number of categories, or groups, to which people can belong – a small set of pigeonholes they can be put into, if you like. Continuous data, on the other hand, are measures like a person's height, the length of time it takes them to peel a potato, or how much money they have – things that can take a vast range of different values, perhaps even an infinite number of different values.

Usually it is easy to tell whether something is a categorical measure or a continuous measure. The temperature in a room is continuous, as it can take almost any value and can undergo tiny changes. A person's nationality is categorical: there is a limited set of different nations you can belong to and there is no such thing as a tiny change in nationality.

Some measures can be a little more subtle, however. What about shoe sizes – are these a continuous measure or a categorical measure? Actually these are categorical, as shoe sizes change in steps (ha ha ha) rather than changing continuously (there is no size 14.227, for example). But this is not really an obvious idea, especially as shoe sizes are described with numbers rather than with names, like genders and nationalities. And even experienced researchers would probably argue about whether 'the number of windows in a building' should be treated as continuous or categorical.[2]

---

[1] This is a big fat lie: there are at least two substantial categories of human research which are not about measuring people. The first is the case study, where a researcher writes in detail about an individual or an organization – usually one that is remarkable in some way – in order that lessons might be learnt from it.

The second major type of research with people which does not involve any real measurement is work from a social constructivist viewpoint. Researchers who follow this postmodern approach try to understand people by using techniques like 'discourse analysis' and 'interpretative phenomenological analysis'. These methods ~~subjectively cherry-pick people's words to ensure the researcher finds exactly what they wanted to find and never has their prejudices challenged~~ objectively reveal important truths and are completely unaffected by the personality or preconceptions of the researcher.

[2] It's the fact you can't have half a window that makes this question so difficult.

Finally, when a categorical measure only has two different categories, as gender does, it can also be called a **dichotomous measure** ('dichotomy' comes from the Greek word for 'apart', and means a sharp division). So gender is a dichotomous variable because you are either male or female; life status is also dichotomous: a person is either alive or dead. Dichotomous variables can become important in more advanced statistics as they allow us to use a process called 'dummy coding', which is a way of getting categorical variables to work in powerful statistical tests where they cannot normally be used.

The distinction between categorical and continuous measurements really becomes important when we start to consider levels of measurement. Oh, here we go now...

Levels of measurement: a number is not always a number

Is '14' a number? You might be surprised to learn that the answer is 'sometimes'.

The idea that a number is not always a number – an idea we can probably trace back to Stanley Stevens (1946)[3] – surprises most people when they first learn it. We grow up assuming the number 14 is always the number 14. When there are more than 13 objects but fewer than 15, then we have 14 objects. It should be simple.

However, the number 14 can actually perform different roles, and when you are reporting or analysing the results of your research it is really important to know what role is being performed by the numbers you see. Being sure about this can stop you making some embarrassing mistakes, as we will show you in a moment.

The various roles that numbers can play are called 'levels of measurement', because the same number – like '14' – can be doing different *amounts* of measurement, ranging from measuring nothing at all to measuring quite a lot. There are four levels of measurement you need to know about, and we will take them in order from the lowest amount of measurement to the highest.

The nominal level of measurement

This is where numbers are acting as names ('nominal' comes from the Latin word for 'name'). Somewhere you can see nominal numbers every day is in sports, where the numbers on the players' shirts

---

[3] Stevens, S.S. (1946). On the theory of scales of measurement. *Science, 103,* 677–680.

usually represent not some quantity or measurement, but rather individual players, or certain positions. Number 6 is not necessarily a better player than number 3, and they are definitely not *twice as good* at their sport as number 3. These numbers – 3, 6, 14, and so on – are just names for the players (or, as in rugby, for the positions they play in). They happen also to be numbers, but they are being used here as names. This is an important point.

There is no special reason that numbers get used as names this way: in many areas, like sports shirts, people could just as easily use letters, squiggles or Ancient Egyptian hieroglyphics. The numbers are used simply because a set of unique symbols is needed to identify individuals and this is a set of unique symbols we all know well.

Other places where you might come across nominal numbers in everyday life include public transport routes (bus number 7 is not necessarily worse, or slower, than bus number 10; 7 and 10 are just unique names for routes and are not really numbers at all). You also see nominal numbers in postal codes. Ian's first job was in Germany where, like in the United States, the postal codes are five-digit numbers representing zones within the country. Ian's apartment was in the part of Germany known to the postal service as 04103; the next zone along is called 04315, but despite it having a higher number it isn't in any way better, further away from the capital city or anything like that; the two numbers are just names for places.[4]

You can perhaps see that nominal numbers are going to be useful when you need a quick and simple way of describing categorical data. Let's say you are collecting data on dietary habits from a group of people. It is very common to represent categories like this using numbers, so you might use 1 to represent 'eats anything', 2 to represent 'vegetarian', 3 to represent 'fruitarian' and so on. The numbers are just short, convenient names for the various dietary categories you have considered.

Now here's the important thing: because these numbers are just acting as names, it would be a *really big mistake* to use them in any sort of analysis. It would, for example, mean nothing if you took an average of these numbers. *People make this mistake all the time. It is very easy to do.*

When category names happen to look like numbers, averaging them together isn't the only mistake people make: they sometimes put them through full-blown data analysis. Let's say that, as well as dietary preference, you also have a measure of how many times each

---

[4] Before we get lots of emails from Germans, we have to admit that these numbers aren't strictly nominal: the zero at the start of the codes tells us that both places are in the southern part of eastern Germany and, more specifically, 04 tells us they are both somewhere in Leipzig or thereabouts. But the rest of the number is essentially arbitrary. *Alles in Ordnung?*

person in your sample visited a doctor in the past 12 months. It would be very easy to look at these two columns of numbers in a spreadsheet and think 'Hmm … I could correlate those two measures to see if there is a relationship between dietary preference and health …'

This would not work! Your dietary preference numbers are not real numbers. They might look like numbers, and as far as your computer is concerned they can be processed just like numbers, but they are *not* numbers – they are just names and you should not do any calculations with them whatsoever.

These mistakes happen particularly because a lot of statistical software forces you to use numbers to describe your categories. So always make sure you know which numbers are nominal and never try to calculate anything with them. Even experienced researchers fall into this trap from time to time.

The ordinal level of measurement

Ian: Have you made the arrangements for the conference yet?

Nigel: I was just doing it. Look, we've got a choice of three hotels. There's a 3-star hotel which costs 80 a night, a 4-star hotel which costs 120 a night and a 5-star hotel which costs 300 a night. And it's all on expenses! So … five star luxury?

Ian: Hold on, that doesn't make any sense. If we move from the 3-star hotel to the 4-star hotel, the cost goes up by 40. But if we move from the 4-star hotel to the 5-star hotel, the cost goes up by 180. That's crazy! Surely the cost should go up by the same amount every time there's an extra star?

Nigel: Ah, but it doesn't work like that. Going from 3-star to 4-star *isn't* the same change as going from 4-star to 5-star. You're forgetting that hotel ratings are ordinal numbers, which is an ironic mistake from a statistics teacher. So, do I put us down for the five-star hotel? Free slippers … ?

A 5-star hotel has better facilities than a 4-star hotel, which in turn has better facilities than a 3-star hotel. As the name suggests, you can put ordinal numbers into order. The higher an ordinal number is, the better something is, or the more of it there is.

But the key thing is that, although you can put ordinal numbers into order, you cannot learn anything from how far apart the numbers are. This is often easiest to explain by looking first at numbers that are not ordinal, like the number of books somebody has. If Nigel has five books, you have four books and Ian has three books, the difference between you and Ian is *exactly the same* as the difference between you and Nigel: one book. A difference of one book is the same difference whatever number you start with.

Ordinal numbers, such as hotel star ratings, do not work like this. The difference between a 5-star hotel and a 4-star hotel is not exactly the same as the difference between a 4-star hotel and a 3-star hotel.

Any numbers like these, which can be put into a meaningful order but where the distances between numbers do not mean anything, are working at the ordinal level of measurement.

Perhaps the most common example of an ordinal measure that you will encounter is the rating scale. When you see questions such as ...

'How was the service you received today? 1: Excellent – 2: Good – 3: Poor – 4: Terrible'

... this is ordinal: everybody would agree that 'excellent' is better than 'good', which is better than 'poor', which is better than 'terrible', but there would be no clear agreement on whether the difference between 'excellent' and 'good' was exactly the same as the difference between 'terrible' and 'poor'.

The interval and ratio levels of measurement

These are the levels of measurement where the numbers contain the most information. Most numbers in the real world are found here; indeed, most numbers in the real world are ratio measures.

Interval and ratio numbers can be put into order like ordinal numbers but they also have another property: the distances between them are meaningful in a way that the distances between ordinal numbers are not. The number of books somebody owns has this property: the difference, or *interval*, between three books and four books is the same as the difference between four books and five books: one book. If Ian travels 700 kilometres, you travel 800 kilometres and Nigel travels 900 kilometres, the difference between your journey and Ian's is exactly the same as the difference between your journey and Nigel's: 100 kilometres.

So both interval and ratio scales allow us to learn things from how far apart the numbers are. Where the two levels of measurement differ from each other is here: a number is a ratio measure if it has a true zero point and it is an interval measure if it does not. A 'true' zero point is when zero means there is absolutely nothing of whatever you are measuring. Money has a true zero point, and therefore is a ratio measure, because when you have zero money you have *no* money. Time is like this also: when you spend zero seconds on a task, you spend *no* time. When you have zero books, you have *no* books; and when you travel zero kilometres, you have travelled *no* distance. We could give examples of ratio measures all day, as there are so many of them.

So if a ratio measurement scale is defined by its true zero point, what is the 'false' zero point that gives us an interval scale? Perhaps the most obvious example you will encounter in the real world is temperature when measured in Celsius or Fahrenheit. With both these temperature scales, zero does not mean there is *no* heat – you can tell this by the fact there are plenty of temperatures below zero, like −14 degrees. (Temperature in Kelvin, on the other hand, sets zero as the coldest temperature that can possibly exist in the universe, and so *is* a ratio measure.)

The only other example of an interval measure you are likely to encounter is calendar year. In all mainstream dating systems, the year zero is not seen as the beginning of all time. As such, calendar years – 1439, 1881 and so on – are interval numbers, like temperatures in Celsius and Fahrenheit. Other forms of interval measure are relatively rare (see the box on Likert scales).

You can do almost any sort of data analysis with interval and ratio numbers and for most purposes you can treat the two levels of measurement as the same. The key advantage of ratio numbers' zero point is that, as the name suggests, it allows you make statements about ratios, or proportions. If we spend 1 hour reading and you spend 2 hours reading, you can say you have spent *twice as long* reading as us. If you own 200 books and we own 400, you can say we own *twice as many* as you, or equally that you own *half as many* as us. Ian has three pets and Nigel has two: Ian has one-third more pets than Nigel.

You cannot use this sort of language with interval scales, where there is not a true zero point. If the temperature in room A is 10 degrees and the temperature in room B is 20 degrees, you cannot say it is twice as warm in room B. If this doesn't make sense to you,

real-world view: likert scales

Likert scales (which we both pronounce 'lie-curt', although admittedly it should probably be 'lick-er') are a very common type of question used in surveys. You have almost certainly seen these; they are questions which look like this:

How much do you like cheese? (circle a number)

Not at all   1 2 3 4 5 6 7   A great deal

The numbers from Likert scales are usually analysed as interval data. This is the elephant in the room[5] of research statistics as there is *no way* Likert scales are really interval measures. If you give a rating of 6 for the question above and somebody else gives a rating of 5, can we guarantee you like eating cheese more than them? Can we rule out the idea you might be using different criteria to make your judgements? And we are sure you can imagine a situation where two people answer a question with the same number – 6, say – but do not feel exactly the same emotion. As such, we have no way of knowing that the numbers we get from Likert scales can even be put into order, let alone be treated as interval data, and yet people regularly average them and do full-blown parametric statistics on them as if they were real numbers. This includes us. It's weird, frankly.

---

[5] If you are not familiar with this lovely phrase, it refers to something incredibly obvious – as an elephant standing in the room would be – that nobody is mentioning for some reason, usually out of embarrassment or because nobody else is mentioning it.

consider temperatures that include zero. If you feel you ought to be able to say 20 degrees is twice as warm as 10 degrees, what temperature would be twice as warm as zero degrees? What temperature would be half as warm? This language of ratios just doesn't work without a genuine zero point.[6]

Life was simpler a thousand years ago when zero hadn't been invented.

Levels of measurement: a summary

	Nominal	Ordinal	Interval	Ratio
	Smallest amount of information	←	→	Largest amount of information
Examples	Sports players' shirt numbers, public transport routes, gender	Hotel star ratings	Temperature in Celsius or Fahrenheit, calendar dates	Temperature in Kelvin. Most real-world measures: money, years of experience, people in a room, etc.
What can you do with the data?	Count how often they appear	Everything you can do with nominal data, plus you can say if one is higher or lower than the other and take the median	Everything you can do with ordinal data, plus you can average them, take measures of dispersion, add them to or subtract them from one another	Everything you can do with interval scores, plus you can multiply and divide them with one another and describe them in ratio terms ('twice as much money')

As a final point, note that you can often choose to measure the same thing at different levels. For example, you could measure how much money somebody earns by asking them 'How much money do you earn?', which would give you a ratio measure. Or, you could ask the same question in an ordinal form, like this...

How much money do you earn?

1. Less than 15,000 per year
2. 15,000 to 24,999
3. 25,000 to 39,999
4. 40,000 or above.

The other interesting thing that has happened here is that you have moved from a continuous measurement to a categorical measurement.

Describing your data to other people

When you have collected measurements from a sample of people, one of the first decisions you will need to make is how you will

---

[6] We have seen wine experts make this mistake when writing about storage temperatures!

Table 3.1   Raw data from 11 of the participants who provided data for research investigating how quickly 4 tasks would be completed under two different management styles

Participant number	Management level 1				Management level 2			
	resp1	resp2	resp3	resp4	resp1	resp2	resp3	resp4
1	5.2	4.3	4.6	5.3	6.3	4.5	5.5	4.2
2	4.3	5.5	5.6	2.3	4.7	3.3	4.5	3.3
3	5.5	4.5	6.7	3.2	5.5	5.8	6.1	4.5
4	6.5	4.5	6.6	4.3	6.6	4.2	5.3	5.2
5	3.4	3.2	4.4	3.3	5.2	6.6	4.4	4.5
6	3.3	4.5	3.5	5.2	6.5	7.3	3.3	7.2
7	3	3.4	4.4	5.3	6.3	5.5	5.5	6.4
8	4.3	4.4	4.1	6.5	5.5	5.6	7.6	4.4
9	3.4	4.5	5.2	4.3	6.6	5.5	6.5	7.4
10	4.6	5.4	4.3	5.4	6.6	4.3	3.2	6.6
11	4.5	6.5	4.6	5.1	6.5	5.8	4.9	6

communicate what you have found to other people. The simplest way is just to give them your raw data. If you have tested a group of 60 people and taken five measurements from each, you have 300 measurements in total. You could simply present people with a large table containing all 300 measurements.

When you do this, you will find you are rewarded by people turning to you and saying, 'And just what am I supposed to do with this?'

The point is, a large table of raw scores has one really big advantage: it is complete. Nothing is hidden, nothing is distorted by any calculation. The problem is, a large table of raw scores also has one really big disadvantage: it is complete. As such, it will almost always be overwhelming, leaving people unable to spot any patterns at all. Table 3.1 shows some of the data from one of our projects. Look at Table 3.1 and decide what we found. No idea? That's because raw data, although often the only way of communicating results to other people without losing any information, does not make for clear communication.[7]

In most circumstances, what you need for describing your data to other people clearly are two things. The first is a measure of how, overall, the people you looked at tended to perform. This is known as a measure of **central tendency**. You also need a measure of how much people varied from one another in your study, known as a measure of **dispersion**. Let's look at these two things in turn.

---

[7] There are some ways of communicating small amounts of raw data whilst also showing an overall pattern. We will see this when we go on to look at scatterplots.

Measures of central tendency (averages)

Have a think about any group with which you are involved. Colleagues in a seminar group or class perhaps, or people you work with. It is possible you may find yourself wondering whether you are older or younger than many in your group, or taller, or shorter. To do this you would find it useful to have an idea of the average age (or height) of those in your group. This average age is a *summary statistic*. It is a single number that tells us something rather useful. It is a number that describes the centre of a set of numbers.

In fact, the word 'average' is not quite accurate enough. You'll not be terribly surprised to hear that there are a number of different 'averages'. The most common are the **mean**, **mode** and **median**. Collectively they are known as measures of **central tendency**. Each of these measures has good and bad points that make them useful for some things and not others; we'll cover each in turn.

The mean

This is what most people are talking about when they say 'average'. It is more accurately called the **mean** or, even more accurately, the *arithmetic mean*.[8] To work out the mean, all you do is add up the numbers you have and divide by however many of them there were. For instance, if you took a set of people from an office and measured how many hours each worked on a given day, you might get these data:

6.5   8.0   8.25   9.0   6.5   8.6   8.25   9.5

The mean number of hours worked is calculated by adding up the numbers (which gives you 64.6) and dividing by 8 (the number of values in your data set, also known as N, for 'number'). If you could be bothered to do this you'd find that the average number of hours worked in this particular office was 8.08.

The main issue with the mean is that it can be powerfully affected by any extreme values, known as **outliers**. Let's imagine your office workers are joined by an insomniac, who works 22 hours in a day. This changes your data set to:

6.5   8.0   8.25   9.0   6.5   8.6   8.25   9.5   22

The mean of this set of numbers is 9.62 – the value has been pulled up considerably by this one person and no longer really represents all

---

[8] This is because there are other types of mean, such as the *geometric mean*, but you have to be doing some pretty advanced work before you need to know about these.

the other people in the office: it is higher than everybody's working hours, except for the one outlier, and so clearly doesn't really sum up this set of numbers very well.

The pros and cons of the mean can be summarized as follows:

Advantages of the mean	Disadvantages of the mean
It uses all the data in the set in its calculation, and shows changes in the data set when they occur.	It is a very sensitive measure of central tendency, so sensitive in fact that it is very severely influenced by values in the data set that might be described as 'outliers' or 'rogue values'. The resulting mean may not be very representative of the data set.
Its calculation is simple to do and widely understood – it is a useful summary statistic as most people understand what it is and how you arrived at it.	If you have two outliers (one high and one low) their effect on the mean is cancelled out. The mean does not reflect these outliers.
It is part of many more complicated statistical procedures.	A mean value for discreet values such as 'the average number of cars in a family' may well be misleading as the value often comes out with a fraction, for example 1.4 cars, or the infamous 2.4 children!

The median

The major disadvantage of the mean is that it is easily distorted by extremely large or small scores in the data set. The **median** does not suffer from this disadvantage, and is actually very insensitive to extreme values.

The median is simply the central value in the data set. Not the arithmetic central value, but the number that is literally in the middle once you have arranged your data in order from the smallest to the largest. Consider the following data set. We have seven numbers here, each referring to, let's say, the number of hours of television watched by seven different people:

$$5 \quad 7 \quad 3 \quad 9 \quad 12 \quad 4 \quad 8$$

First, take the data set and arrange them in numerical order. This gives us:

$$3 \quad 4 \quad 5 \quad 7 \quad 8 \quad 9 \quad 12$$

With a small data set like this it is very simple to find the central number: it's the value in the middle of the row. Really, it's that simple. Here the value in the middle is 7 – it is in the middle because there are three numbers below it and three numbers above it. So the median of this data set is 7.

When the data set is relatively large, you can use spreadsheet software to order the data for you. It's simple enough to do. And it is also simple to work out what the central number is: all you need to know is how many numbers there are in your data set. For instance, if your data set has 213 numbers, the position of the median number is given by:

$$(213 + 1) / 2$$

that is to say: 214/2, which is 107.

So the median value in a data set with 213 values in it is at position 107 when the data are ordered in numerical value. Find the 107th number once you have ordered your data and there's your median.

One place the median is used a lot is in medical research where survival rates are calculated. Let's say there is a disease – statisticitis, say – which kills people eventually, but everybody survives a different amount of time. What you will find is that some people will die quite soon, some will live for a while and a few will go on living for a really long time before succumbing to the disease. These few people with very long survival times, although lucky individuals, would distort the mean survival time. By working as outliers, they would make the mean look larger than it should, like the hard-working office worker we described above. The median isn't really affected by outliers, though, and so would be used instead of the mean to describe the 'average' survival time.[9]

The advantages and disadvantages of the median are summarized below.

Advantages of the median	Disadvantages of the median
Outliers and rogue values do not affect it. If you have a data set with more large numbers than small, or more small numbers than large (a skewed distribution), then the median is a good measure to use for this reason.	When there are very few values in the data set, and the values differ a lot, the median is not very representative. For instance, if your data set is 1, 4, 5, 5, 160, 190, 13000 the median is 5, which doesn't really summarize those data well.
As long as you're not worried about tied values and the data set is relatively small, it's very simple to calculate.	The exact values of the numbers in the data set are not taken into consideration in its calculation.

Issues with the median: an even number of values in the data set

In the example we used (number of hours of television watched), we cunningly chose a data set of seven people. This is because we knew that eight people – or indeed *any* even number – would cause a small problem. Let's add one more value to the data set to show you why. When ordered, our eight-value data set becomes:

1   3   4   5   7   8   9   12

---

[9] If you want an example of a study which does this, here's one we've chosen more or less at random: Ugurel, S. et al. (2008). Impact of the CCR5 gene polymorphism on the survival of metastatic melanoma patients receiving immunotherapy. *Cancer Immunology Immunotherapy*, 57, 685–691.

You can see there is no 'central' number any more. An even number of data points means the median now lies somewhere between the fourth number (5) and the fifth number (7). To work out the value between 5 and 7 is simple enough though: you simply take their mean (see why we covered the mean first?). In other words, add them up and divide by 2. Like this:

$$(5+7) / 2 = 6$$

If you have a large data set with an even number of values in it, you calculate the position of the median value in exactly the same way as we did above. What you'll find, though, is that you'll get a fraction as a result. For instance, if you have a data set with 108 values in it, then the position of the median value will come out as 54.5.[10] What this means is that the median value lies between position 54 and position 55. To find the median in this case, add up the values at positions 54 and 55 and divide by 2. Not really a major problem after all.

Issues with the median: tied values in the data set

Tied values are not always a problem when calculating a median. If the tied values happen to be at the midpoints of an even-numbered data set, then the tie is a positive blessing as it means that you don't have to worry about calculating the average of the two central numbers, since they are both the same. However, tied values elsewhere in the data set can sometimes mean the median value is not very representative of the overall data set. If this is the case, statisticians often recommend a more complicated calculation which takes into consideration how often the different numbers appear. We'll not go into details here, but, just to explain the logic behind this, consider the following data set, which refers to the number of doughnuts eaten by members of the police force in a small provincial police station in a month. To save you the trouble, we'll tell you that there are 22 values in this data set, and we've put them in numerical order for you. Since there are 22 values, the median value is between positions 11 and 12. We've printed these in bold for you.

1	1	1	2	2	2	2	3	3	3	**3**	**5**
5	5	5	5	9	9	9	9	11	11		

This means that the median number of doughnuts consumed is 4 (the mean of 3 and 5). Not a bad median value actually, and one which is reasonably representative of the data set.

---

[10] $(108+1) / 2 = 54.5$.

However, we would get a better median value if we could in some way consider the number of times each value appeared in the data set. You can do this if you feel the need. The number you would arrive at would not be 4 as it is in our earlier calculation; the median you would calculate if you were to consider the frequencies of each of the values in the data set would give you a more accurate position between the 11th and 12th values. It could be nearer the 12th value or nearer the 11th value (that is, not right in the middle) depending on the values in the top half and bottom half of the data set. However, as we said, we're not going to spend time on that here. It is, frankly, dull, and of interest to relatively few people. If you would like to know more, or are in need of a very accurate median for your data set, you'll find details of how to do this elsewhere.[11]

The mode

The **mode** or *modal value* of a data set is simply the most common value in that set of numbers. Imagine you were collecting data on how often different people in your community used a public transport service in a given week. Once you've completed your data collection you may well end up with something like the numbers below. Each value refers to a single person and shows how often they used public transport in the previous week.

$$3 \quad 3 \quad 3 \quad 5 \quad 5 \quad 5 \quad 5 \quad 6 \quad 6 \quad 7 \quad 7 \quad 7$$
$$8 \quad 9 \quad 9$$

The most common number of times people used public transport is 5. This means that the modal value for this data set is 5.

In some cases two numbers appear equally frequently as the most common values. For instance:

$$1 \quad 1 \quad 2 \quad 2 \quad 2 \quad 6 \quad 6 \quad 7 \quad 8 \quad 8 \quad 8 \quad 9$$
$$12$$

In these cases we say that the distribution is **bimodal**. It has two modes, with the values 2 and 8 each occurring three times. In these cases you should report both modal values.

Advantages of the mode	Disadvantages of the mode
Can be used with categorical data. Extreme values do not affect the mode. It is often interesting or useful to know the most frequent number in a data set, and the mode provides this information.	Sometimes in small data sets lots of numbers appear with equal frequency. In cases like this the mode is of no use at all. The exact value of each item is not included in its calculation.

[11] For example, Greer, B. and Mulhern, G. (2002). *Making Sense of Data and Statistics in Psychology*. Palgrave.

What's the point of having more than one measure of central tendency?

The answer is that each is useful in different situations. You choose a measure of central tendency based on what you want to say about your data. Also, some levels of measurement only allow certain measures of central tendency to be used. The table below summarizes where each of our three measures of central tendency is appropriate.

Level of measurement	Measure of central tendency to use
Interval or ratio	The mean is most appropriate here, but you might also use the mode and the median in some circumstances.
Ordinal	If the data can be 'ranked' then you can use the median but not the mean.
Nominal	If the data are placed in categories then the mode is appropriate.

Measures of dispersion

Take a look at these data. These are the ages of two groups of people:

	GROUP A	GROUP B
	0	18
	10	21
	20	22
	30	20
	40	19
Mean:	20	20

The two groups have exactly the same mean age. But, even though the groups are the same age on average, you can see that group A and group B are far from being identical: in group A there is much more variation than in group B, where the participants are all roughly the same age. These different amounts of variation could easily matter. For example, what if you expected the people in each group to study together? It is pretty obvious that the five people in group B, where everybody is similar in age, could probably be educated together whereas the five people in group A could not. But if we had just given you the two groups' mean ages you would not have seen this big difference between the groups.

So when summarizing a set of data it is not enough to provide a measure of central tendency alone, as this can disguise real differences between groups. A measure of central tendency should always be presented along with a measure of how much the scores vary from one another, known as a measure of *dispersion*. There are four main measures of dispersion that you need to know about.

The range

This is the simplest measure of dispersion and is simply the difference between the highest score and the lowest score. Look again at the table of ages above. If we were to summarize these and include the ranges, we would say group A had a mean age of 20 with a range of 40 and group B had a mean age of 20 with a range of 4.

We got the range 40 by subtracting the smallest score in group A (0) from the highest (40), and the range 4 by subtracting the smallest score in group B (18) from the highest (22). You can see how when the means are given with ranges this is a lot more informative than the means were on their own.

The range has a really powerful advantage over the other measures of dispersion described here, which is that you do not need any training in statistics to understand it. As such, it is probably the best measure of dispersion for when you are describing your research findings to laypeople.

The disadvantage of the range is that it can be strongly affected by any outliers – extreme values – in your data. Here is a quick demonstration of how outliers can be a problem with the range measure.

We have a set of people whose mean age is 20 with a range of 40. This sounds like quite a mixed group of people, doesn't it? In fact, it sounds just like group A in the table above.

The thing is, it would also be possible for a group to have a mean age of 20 with a range of 40 if their ages were 0, 40, 20, 20, 20, 20, 20, 20, 20, 20, 20, 20, 20, 20, 20, 20, 20, 20, 20, 20, 20, 20, 20, 20, 20, 20, 20, 20, 20, 20, 20, 20, 20, 20, 20, 20, 20, 20, 20, 20, 20, 20, 20, 20, 20, 20, 20, 20, 20, 20, 20, 20, 20, 20, 20, 20, 20, 20, 20, 20, 20, 20, 20, 20, 20, 20, 20, 20, 20, 20, 20, 20, 20, 20, 20, 20, 20, 20, 20, 20, 20, 20, 20, 20, 20, and 20. This doesn't look quite so mixed, does it?

So the range, whilst better than no measure of dispersion, and whilst good for communicating with people who do not know about statistics, can hide some important information about a group thanks to its sensitivity to outliers.

Oh, and as a final point, some people prefer to write the range as a single value, like this...

Mean = 20, range = 4.

...whereas others prefer to write it by giving the lowest and highest value, like this...

Mean = 20, range = 18–22.

There is no real difference between these and you should feel free to use whichever form you prefer the look of. The second version is perhaps slightly easier to read, as long as it is clear you have used a dash rather than a minus sign!

The interquartile range and interpercentile range

The interquartile range is a version of the range which should not be affected by extreme scores, and it is really quite a simple idea. If you line up all your scores from the lowest to the highest, the interquartile range is the middle 50% of the scores. Look at this set of 12 scores, which we have arranged from the lowest to the highest:

2	4	5	7	8	10	13	14	15	17	19	96

Bottom 25%   Middle 50%   Top 25%

The mean of these 12 scores is 18.25 and the interquartile range – calculated from the central six scores – is 7 to 15. So, if we were describing this set of numbers to somebody, we might say something like 'Our data had a mean score of 18.25 with an interquartile range of 7–15.'

You can see how the interquartile range deals with extreme scores – outliers – by the magnificently simple method of totally ignoring them: if only we could deal with all life's difficulties this way!

Remember the big set of ages in the previous section, which had a mean of 20 with a range of 40, even though almost everybody in the group was aged 20? If we were to use the interquartile range, we would describe these data as having a mean of 20 with an interquartile range of 0 (20 minus 20). We're sure you'll agree this value of zero, indicating no variation, can give a more accurate picture of what the group looks like.

The main difficulty with the interquartile range is that somebody without any statistics training will run away if you use the word 'interquartile' at them.

The interquartile range is making use of **percentiles**. If you take a set of scores and arrange them from the lowest to the highest, you can find a score which a certain percentage of the scores fall below. That sounds a bit abstract, so here are some examples:

- The 50th percentile is the score where half the participants scored that value or less.
- The 76th percentile is the score where 76% of the participants scored that value or less.

In the row of numbers shown just above, all the participants scored 96 or less, so 96 is the 100th percentile (100% of people got this score or lower). The 25th percentile is 5, as 25% of the participants got this score or less. 15 is the 75th percentile, as 75% of the participants got this score or less.

Percentiles quickly communicate how a person's score stands in relation to other people's scores. If you take a test and score at the 93rd percentile, this means only 7% of the population are better than you on this test. Well done!

Percentiles are often used in education, where it is common to want to know how well a child is performing relative to their peers. You will find that quite a lot of the public understand the concept, and so you can sometimes get away with using it to communicate with people who have not had statistics training. (But sometimes you cannot – judge your audience carefully and, if you're not sure, use a different measure.)

Hmm. We seem to have just spent four paragraphs explaining percentiles, so let's get back to the point we wanted to make, which was this: the interquartile range uses the 25th and 75th percentile points to discard the top and bottom quarter of the scores when calculating the range, but working with quarters is not the only option. It is also fine to use other percentiles to remove the top and bottom scores when working out the range. For example, you might use the 10th and 90th percentiles to remove the most extreme 10% of scores from the top and the most extreme 10% of scores from the bottom to look at the central 80% that remain.[12] This will remove fewer scores from the range calculation than the interquartile range, dropping only the most extreme 20% instead of the most extreme 50%, which is quite a lot of scores to remove from your data.

The standard deviation

The second measure of dispersion you need to know about is the **standard deviation**. The word 'standard' here really means 'average'. So the 'standard' deviation is essentially the 'average' deviation – the typical amount by which the numbers in a set of scores differ from the mean. The standard deviation and another measure of dispersion known as **variance** (which we'll discuss next) are closely related – in fact, one is simply the square root of the other.

Before we go on, we should just say a little more about how a set of scores will vary. Because the mean of a set of scores is always right in the middle of those scores, there is always just as much variation above the mean as there is below the mean. As such, all the variation

---

[12] If you want to see a study that uses the 10th–90th interpercentile range, have a look at Graw, P., Kräuchi, K., Knoblauch, V., Wirz-Justice, A. and Cajochen, C. (2004). Circadian and wake-dependent modulation of fastest and slowest reaction times during the psychomotor vigilance task. *Physiology & Behavior, 80,* 695–701.

around the mean score always cancels out to zero. For example, the scores 4, 5, 7 and 8 have a mean of 6. If you look at how each score varies around this you see that ...

4 is two points below the mean (−2)
5 is one point below the mean (−1)
7 is one point above the mean (+1)
8 is two points above the mean (+2)

The problem is that −2, −1, +1 and +2 add up to zero. This would suggest there is *no* variation in the scores! Clearly you need to get rid of the negative values somehow, and you can do this by 'squaring' each value (multiplying it by itself), because any negative number multiplied by another negative number produces a positive number. So, for example, you would get rid of the minus sign on the number −2 by squaring it: $-2 \times -2 = 4$.[13]

Using the numbers above, squaring all the differences would change them to 4, 1, 1 and 4. The difference between each data point and the mean is now positive, which is a good start. You then take the average of these numbers, which gets you $(4 + 1 + 1 + 4) / 4 = 2.5$.

However, this is still quite a large number – it was made using squared deviations, and so exaggerates how much our scores varied around the mean. To finish things off, then, you take the square root of this number finally to get a really useful estimate of how the data were dispersed. This number – which in our example is 1.58 (the square root of 2.5) – is the *standard deviation*. This gives us a useful feel for how much, on average, each score in the data set differed from the mean.

Lost? Don't panic. A swift summary of how to do the calculation should make it clear.

Step 1: Subtract each score from the mean to get its deviation, then square each of these deviations
Step 2: Add up all these squared values
Step 3: Divide by the number of scores you had (take the mean squared deviation)
Step 4: Take the square root of this number and you have your standard deviation

The thing about the standard deviation is that not only does it give you a good idea of how the scores you have vary around the mean,

---

[13] You might ask – quite rightly – why we don't deal with negative numbers simply by ignoring the minus signs. This is a perfectly valid approach, as far as we are concerned, but doing this makes proper statisticians shriek in agony and, in extreme cases, send nasty emails. They prefer to get rid of a minus sign by squaring a number then taking the square root.

but it is a terribly useful number in more complicated statistics that you might use later.

Variance

The final measure of dispersion we should talk about here is the **variance**. Once you've figured out how to work out a standard deviation it couldn't really be simpler. All you need to do is take your standard deviation and square it (multiply it by itself). That's really all there is to it.

The word 'variance' sounds a lot like 'variation', and this is useful thing to bear in mind. That is, the variance is a measure of how much, in total, the values in your sample vary around the mean. Lots of statistical tests make use of this concept – most strikingly the technique called 'analysis of variance', which is all about analysing the variance in your data to see where it came from.

Illustrating your data

Numbers are great. No, they are, really. We know that many people just hate them, but more often than not people are actually very comfortable with the concept of 100 being larger than 75. It really is, often, that straightforward, for all that we tried to upset your preconceptions when we talked about levels of measurement.

The problem with numbers, though, is rather like the problem with rodents. On their own, or with one or two of their friends, they are just fine: easy to keep track of and actually rather nice. However, when they get together with lots of their friends, the effect is rather different. Keeping track of one of them in amongst the often rather uncomfortable result is not easy, and identifying patterns is close to impossible.

What we always tell our students, and each other when we occasionally forget ourselves, is that as researchers we are in the business of telling other people what we have done, as clearly, and as carefully, as possible. We want people to know what our results are with the minimum effort. You don't want to have to wade through hundreds of pages of textbook to find the snippet of information you want. You go straight to the index, and turn to the correct page. Think of the poor people who will be reading your reports, or listening to your presentations. If you ever have the misfortune to present findings at a symposium or conference where the delegates have already sat through a good number of presentations in an overly warm room immediately after lunch when everybody is sleepy, you'll see how important it is to present things as clearly as possible. Presenting your data in an easy-to-see and easy-to-read way, with the minimum of thought and interaction, is absolutely necessary.

You also have to remember that those reading your reports are not always as clued in as you are to the details of your study. They may well have a completely different background and be reading your work for a particular reason. Journalists are a great example of this. If copy for a publication or newspaper is due in at the end of the day, they may not have time to read everything as carefully as people might like them to. They read for specific information, quickly looking for material they can use in their copy. Give it to them! And the best way to do this is with graphics and tables.

Graphs

A good graph really is worth a thousand words. A bad one is worthless – worse than worthless: it may well be horribly misleading. There are a whole load of different ways to display your data graphically and, as with many tasks in research methods, there is often more than one way to crack the nut properly. But sometimes there is a right and a wrong way, and in most cases one way of representing your data on a graph is more desirable than the others. Knowing how to choose the right graph, and how to make it show exactly what you want, is an important research skill. It's such a shame to design and carry out an elegant and careful project, only to fall at one of the final jumps.

Oh, and one last thing before we go any further: we've lost count of how many times we've been told by people we have worked for, and people who have completed coursework for us, that 'graphs are really simple' and 'everyone knows how to draw and read a graph'. Don't underestimate the power a clear and well-designed graph can have. Everyone does not know how to choose and draw graphs, as evidenced by some coursework we have marked and, indeed, some academic papers and textbooks we have read and conferences we have attended! So now we'll go through the types of graphs you might like to consider when you express your data.

The Pictograph

Pictographs are funny things. You don't really see many of them in academic papers, but you may well find them in professional reports, or news items where those dealing with the data are interested not so much in exacting detail, but rather in getting a message across to readers and viewers in an interesting, fun and engaging way, as quickly as possible.

The pictograph uses 'icons' that refer to a portion of the data. It does this to reduce the physical size of the graph and to decrease the amount of information that the reader of the graph has to take in. Here's an example:

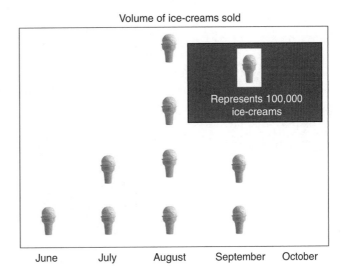

In this example the data have been compressed and reduced so that every 100,000 ice creams are represented by a single image. The pros and cons of this sort of representation are rather easy to see. On the positive side, they are simple to read and look friendly and non-threatening. On the down side, they can oversimplify the data. Accuracy is lost in a trade-off with simplicity. In our example, depicting 38,000 litres of ice cream would involve slightly less than half an ice cream icon, which would not be terribly easy for people to read as a value.

People don't need specialist training to read a pictograph, which is one of their major strong points. They are easily accessible. Remember your audience when you are drawing a graph.

Histogram

This is a common sort of graph. You'll be very used to seeing them, no doubt. The horizontal line across the bottom – which we call the x axis if we're being technical – is a continuous variable split up into categories, or intervals. The vertical line – the y axis – indicates how many times that particular category was seen in a set of data. So, in the histogram given here, you can see that age runs along the x axis, with younger people at the left and older people at the right. You can see from the y axis that there were more people aged 41–50 in our sample than any other age, and can see how the ages of the people we studied varied.

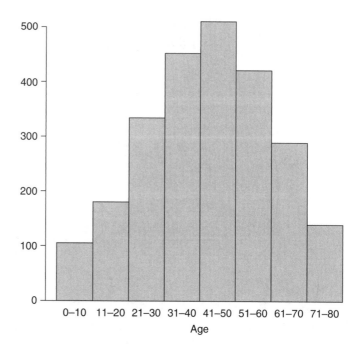

Notice that there are no gaps between the bars in a histogram. This is because the x axis scale is continuous from one end to the other, even though it is split into categories. This is what distinguishes a histogram from a bar-chart.

You would use a histogram if you wanted to depict how a group of people varies by, for example:

- Distance (time to reach work from different distances away)
- IQ (scores on tests given particular Intelligence Quotient scores)
- Age (number of overseas trips taken by different age-groups)

Bar-chart

A bar-chart is rather like a histogram in that it is constructed from bars, and often records frequency (how often something is seen) on the y axis. The difference between the two is that here the x axis is not continuous. Instead, it contains discrete categories or groups.

Below we have a graph indicating different categories of wildlife and how often each was seen on a safari trip. This is the kind of thing you need to know if you are a wildlife fan and are faced with a choice of three sites for your safari. Plotting the data like this makes it extremely easy for people to find the information they need quickly.

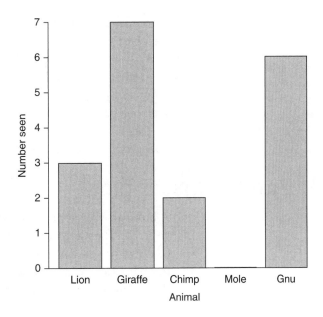

The kind of things you would use a bar-chart for might include:

- The types of vehicles driven along a road over a period of time (cars, trucks, motorcycles, etc.)
- Numbers of items in different categories in a typical shopping basket
- Number of different types of domestic birds present in a garden or park
- Number of different diseases or injuries presenting at a clinic
- Number of male and female employees in a business.

However, you would not use a bar-chart in a situation where you only had one category. This is wasteful and pointless. Simply presenting the count of instances as a number in your text (e.g., 'We saw six lions'), is much better than plotting a graph when there is no comparison to be made with another category.

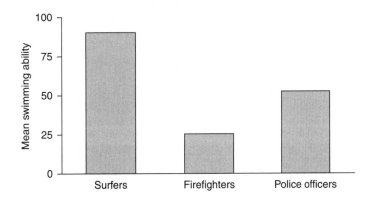

You would also not use a bar-chart if you wanted to represent a proportion. Remember. The bar-chart is about frequency, or number of times something occurs, not the proportion of times it occurs.

If you are representing proportions you will probably want to use a pie-chart (see below).

As well as showing the frequency with which things were seen, a bar-chart can also be used to present average scores for different groups of people, as with the surfers police and firefighters on the previous page.

This is very common and is a simple and effective way to show how groups differ on a measure.

Box-and-Whisker plot

A box-and-whisker plot is one of those things you don't really draw yourself. They are the sort of things you ask your computer nicely to draw for you, usually when it is busy helping you do some sort of mathematical wizardry. The box-and-whisker is a rather complex thing, but it very usefully, and at a glance, identifies the median, ranges, percentiles, maximum and minimum in your data. This is quite a lot, really, for one graph that takes up very little room! In our example we have used data showing the change in quality of life ratings for a group of patients taking the experimental drug Holtodol.

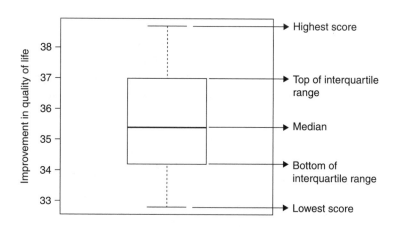

Box-and-whisker plots are useful for all sorts of things. If you have data and need to depict some of the 'harder to see' aspects of it, such as the median and the range, then you should really consider these. The downside, of course, is that they are quite difficult to understand for people who are not used to looking at data, so make sure you remember your audience!

Line graph

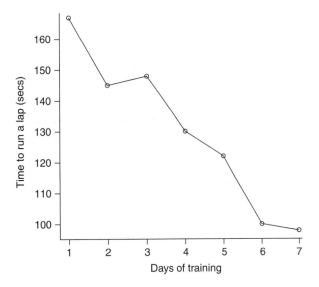

The line graph is another common way to represent data. They are quick and simple and a very visual way of getting your point across. In these data we have 'days of training' on the x axis and 'time to run a lap' on the y-axis. As you can see, the data indicate that the more this person trained, the faster their running speed became, at least over the number of days we have measured here. These data might therefore lead us to conclude that training is a good thing for athletes to do.

pedant point

JOINING THE DOTS IN LINE GRAPHS

In the line graph we have presented here, the dots which represent the measurements are joined together. This is because the data represent change over time – each data point is part of a sequence. As such, it is right to join them with a line. When the data points do not form part of a sequence it is proper not to use a line to join the points – indeed, you should consider using a bar-chart instead. If you really want to use a line graph and your data do not come from a sequence, you need to make it clear in your text that this is the case.

In the next section of this book we will identify the things that you measure as *dependent variables* and the things that we vary (or that vary naturally) as *independent variables.* For example, on a study looking at the effect of practice on violin-playing ability, the amount of practice is the *independent variable* and the ability (measured presumably as ability to pass tests, or ratings given by experts) is the *dependent variable.* Look back to this section once you are an expert on all that and you'll see that with line graphs the independent variable is always on the *x* axis and the dependent variable always on the *y* axis.

Pie-chart

The pie-chart is superb for depicting percentages, or proportions in categories. They are very visual indeed. In our example we have used a pie-chart to show the distribution of music preferences in a group of high-school students.

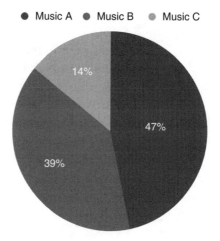

You can use pie-charts for anything that involves a proportion or a percentage. The key thing to remember is that they always show how a single thing (a population, or an amount of money, say) is broken down into parts. Examples might include:

- The proportion of people in a community who celebrate Christmas and the proportion who do not
- How 'film-genre' preference breaks down in a group of film-goers
- How government income is spent on different things, like defence, health, education etc.

Scatterplot

The scatterplot is a special kind of graph that plots a person's score on one thing along the *x* axis against their score on another thing on the *y* axis. Unlike line graphs, bar-charts and so on, where only one measurement is being recorded, the scatterplot records two measurements at once. Let's say you want to see if people who enjoy hunting also watch violent films. If this is the case, you would take a group of hunters, and ask then to tell you how many hunting trips they had taken in the last year, and how many violent films from a list they had seen.

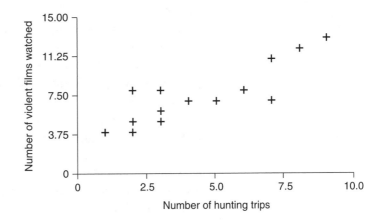

Notice how each person is represented by a single point on the graph, and how each point captures two scores. Our scatterplot seems to suggest that the more hunting trips a person takes, the more violent films they like to watch. So a scatterplot identifies how one thing varies with another, and can be extremely useful for illustrating the relationship between two measurements. You might draw a scatterplot if you were interested in:

- The relationship between drinking and smoking behaviour
- The relationship between money earned and money spent
- The relationship between the number of trees planted in a local town and the residents' happiness
- The relationship between how many pets people own and their anxiety

How measurements vary among lots of people: the normal distribution

So far we've talked about measures of central tendency and how values in a data set might vary around the mean – measures of dispersion.

When you collect data on a relatively small scale, which is what most of us will ever do in our research with people, this is usually all that is needed. A mean and a measure of central tendency will express all you and others need to know about your data.

When you have a large number of data, however, from lots of people, the way they are distributed can often reveal patterns. Allow us to illustrate. If you were to ask 10 people to estimate how many hours they watch television each week you will get 10 numbers. It's easy to calculate a mean from these numbers and also a measure of dispersion around this mean, such as the standard deviation.

But if you were then to ask more and more people about their television viewing habits, you would start to find a particular pattern appearing when you look at how often each value appears in your data set. Specifically, what you would find is that the distribution of scores would begin to look a little like a 'bell-shape'. Very few people would watch no television at all, and very few would watch 24 hours a day. Most people would watch an amount somewhere in the middle of the two extremes. The more people you have in the sample, the more your frequency distribution will look like this bell-shaped curve. What's happening here is that your data are beginning to approximate what is known as the **normal distribution curve**, or more simply the **normal distribution**. In actual fact the curve is called a 'Gaussian' distribution, named after the German mathematician Karl Gauss who first described it, and identified a rather spectacular mathematical formula for producing it.

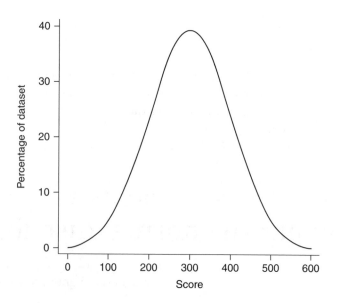

The normal distribution crops up almost everywhere in research with people. If you collect a lot of measurements of, say, people's heights, shoe sizes, the amount of weight they can lift up, the amount of money they spend at supermarkets in a year, the distances they would be prepared to walk to work, the hours they spend bicycling, or the days they would be prepared to wait to see a medical specialist, your data will almost always begin to resemble a normal distribution like this, with lots of people scoring somewhere close to the mean and fewer and fewer people appearing as you move away from the mean. In fact, if you ever collect a large amount of data from human beings and these do not begin to approximate a normal distribution, this might be evidence to suggest that something quite peculiar is going on. This should also set alarm bells ringing for your statistical analyses: most statistical tests assume your data take this normally distributed form. Therefore any conclusions you might draw from them could be in doubt if your data do not.

Thankfully, many many measurements we take from people do follow the normal distribution, with most people being around the mean and fewer and fewer people appearing the further from the mean we look. Knowing this is very useful, because the normal distribution has certain important characteristics which arise almost magically from its shape:

1. The normal distribution is symmetrical about the midpoint.
2. The mean, mode and median all fall at the midpoint.
3. The tails of the distribution never quite reach the horizontal axis.[14]
4. In a normally distributed data set, just over two-thirds of people (actually 68.26%) fall within one standard deviation of the mean. So if the mean of a set of scores is 100 and the standard deviation is 20, 68.26% of people will have a score between 80 and 120.

That last property of the normal distribution is very useful indeed. If you know that your data will eventually approximate a normal distribution, you can use this assumption to tell you all sorts of things about individuals.

As an example, let's say someone has already collected data from 10,000 people on a measure of 'entrepreneurial potential' and let's say these data look a lot like a normal distribution (most people have a level of potential that is around average, and not many people have

---

[14] This is only really true for theoretical distributions. When we do research with people there are usually very real endpoints. Take people's heights, for instance. You'll never get someone 400 cm tall, or someone of 2 cm in height. In this case there are very real endpoints, and so your data will only ever 'approximate' the normal distribution, where the Gaussian curve's tails never reach the horizontal axis.

really high or really low levels). You would know, from your careful reading of this paragraph, that 34.13% of the population must have an entrepreneurial potential score between the mean and one standard deviation above the mean. You also know that 47.72% of the population have a score between the mean and two standard deviations above the mean, and that 49.87% of the population have a score between the mean and three standard deviations over the mean. As such, if you administer the test to one of your employees and find that their score is higher than the mean plus three standard deviations, you instantly know that they are in the top 0.13% of the population in entrepreneurial skill. So paying them a little more money to keep them working with you might be a very good idea indeed! Similarly, if the person got a score less than three standard deviations below the mean, you would know they are in the bottom 0.13% of the population, so promoting them to head of entrepreneurial activities might not be such a great move.

How about one more example to illustrate the point? Let's consider professional sport: playing games to earn vast amounts of money. How hard can that possibly be? We reckon it's not in the slightest bit like a real job. Take that Tiger Woods man, for example: we think he's basically a show-off. All he does is turn up and hit a few golf balls into some holes, and his trick is that he takes fewer shots to do it than the others. We reckon we could do that. No, we reckon *anyone* could. So we head off to the driving range.

Let's say we decide to measure, or **operationalize**, 'golfing skill' as 'how close to the flag somebody can get with one shot'[15] and so we set up a red flag as a target. We get people to hit the ball from the same spot each time, using the same club and identical balls, so that the only thing to change from shot to shot is the person doing the hitting. Each of our participants hits a single ball to the flag and the balls are left where they lie. Every evening the distance between each ball and the flag is measured and recorded. After 3 days we have a few hundred or so people who have helped us in our quest for sporting brilliance, and in our proof that golf is much easier than it looks.

Data after 1 day

Number of balls at different distances from the flag

61–70 cm	51–60 cm	41–50 cm	31–40 cm	21–30 cm	11–20 cm	0–10 cm
1	23	0	39	0	2	1

---

[15] Yes, we know golf is much more than that – we're using this as an illustration.

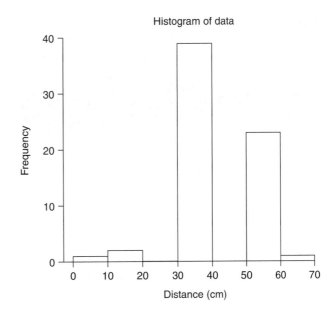

Data after 2 days

Number of balls at different distances from the flag

61–70 cm	51–60 cm	41–50 cm	31–40 cm	21–30 cm	11–20 cm	0–10 cm
3	23	16	55	10	13	1

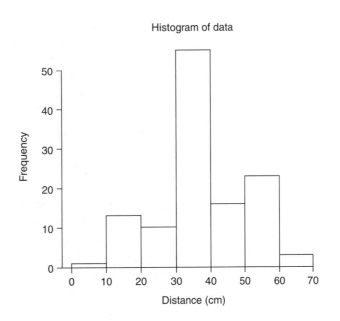

Data after 3 days

Number of balls at different distances from the flag

61–70 cm	51–60 cm	41–50 cm	31–40 cm	21–30 cm	11–20 cm	0–10 cm
5	26	37	57	30	17	2

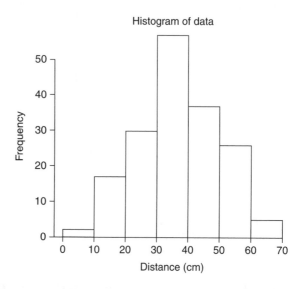

Well, that's a surprise. We felt certain that golf would be easier than that. Instead it seems some people are rather good, getting very close to the flag, and some are pretty bad, missing by quite a long way. Most people, however, are neither really good nor really bad: they are 'reasonable' and fit between the two extremes. So Tiger Woods is rather extraordinary in his ability after all, and making millions at golf isn't as simple as we thought (although there is more research to be done we reckon: we clearly need funding to spend a few weeks in Florida and Spain carrying out further studies).

This procedure also illustrates another interesting point about normal distributions. You can see how the graph begins to look more and more like a normal distribution as we included measurements from more and more people. This is something you will often see: for many of the things you might measure in people, the more people you have, the more the measurements of their behaviour will begin to resemble a normal distribution. And, critically, the opposite of this is also true. If you are measuring something that is normally distributed in large numbers of people, it often will not be normally distributed in small numbers of people. This is an important point which researchers too often forget. It matters because, as we said earlier, most of the statistical tests used in research assume the data are normally distributed.

When working with small numbers of people, they very rarely are. An awful lot of research – even from professionals – is actually slightly suspect for this reason. Let's now look a little further at this issue of analysing data when the distributions are not normal.

What to do when your data just don't look nice: skewed distributions

It is just lovely when you collect a load of data and they look like a normal distribution when you plot them. It's like magic when that happens. You actually begin to believe what you are told in books like this.[16] Life, unfortunately, is often not that straightforward. People have a habit of behaving in a way that is not entirely predictable. We think it is this unpredictability that makes people so fabulously interesting. However, what it also means is that often, when you examine frequency data, you'll end up with something that looks like a normal distribution curve that has been pushed to one side or the other, rather than the nice symmetrical curve you would like.

A recent job of ours gives a good example of this. We did some work for a museum that was interested in how often people came to visit. The museum had a policy of making each ticket to the museum valid for 1 month. This meant that once people had bought a ticket they were allowed to return to the museum as often as they liked for the following 30 days. We asked staff to note how often people returned, adding a 'revisit' mark to their visitor book each time the person came back for another look at the collection. We stopped collecting data after about 2 months, and drew them up into a table to help our organization and to tell us what values to plot in our graph.[17] We'll not reveal the name of the museum if you don't mind, but the data are real enough.

Here's our *frequency table*. In the left-hand column we have 'number of visits' and in the middle column we have 'frequency', so we can see that 90 people visited once, 112 people visited twice and so on. We have also included a third column here headed as 'cumulative frequency'. This is simply a running total of the number of visits as we follow the table down (so 283 in the third row is the number of people who visited either one, two or three times).

---

[16] The only possible reason we would ever lie to you would be in an attempt to makes things clearer, for your own good. Really. Everything in this book is almost entirely true. Honest...

[17] Remember, you don't need really need to draw up a table as well as plotting a graph. That's often considered as 'over-egging the pudding'. One or the other (a table *or* a graph) is usually sufficient, but you should always follow the accepted data-displaying etiquette of the area or publication in which you are writing.

Number of visits	Frequency	Cumulative frequency
1	90	90
2	112	202
3	81	283
4	80	363
5	50	413
6	12	425
7	16	441
8	5	446
9	4	450
10	2	452

It is easy to see that 90 people only visited the museum once, but quite a few came back more often. The frequencies from this table can be plotted to reveal their distribution:

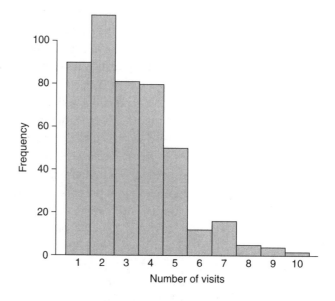

This shows us that the frequencies are not normally distributed. Instead, most visits to the museum are bunched up on the left-hand side of the figure. When data are bunched up to one side like this instead of being distributed symmetrically, like in a normal distribution, we say the data are **skewed**. A consequence of this is that if you were to calculate the mean of these data you would find that it does not fall beautifully at the point of highest frequency (the mode), as it would in a normally distributed data set. Rather, the mean would fall more towards the right. (If you are interested, the mean number of visits in these data is 3.11, which is not the same as the modal value of 2.) In this case, then, the data are **positively skewed**, meaning the mean value is *higher* than the mode value. More than half of the values in this particular data set occur at a higher level than the modal value.

You might also imagine a data set that is skewed in the opposite direction. How about 'number of hours of video games played each week by those who own a games console'? You might find that many people use their console a reasonable amount, with some using it a great deal. Some may not use it too much, but hardly any would not use it at all, or very little. The distribution might look something like this if you plotted it:

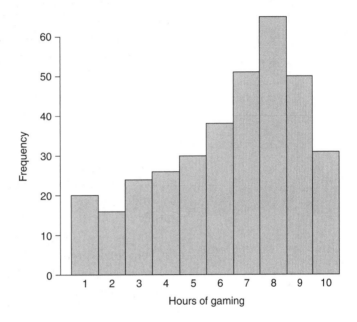

In his case the mean number of hours spent gaming is actually less than the modal value, meaning that more than half of the scores in your data set fall below the most common number of hours played. These data, then, are **negatively skewed** – they are asymmetrical with a tendency to bunch up on the right-hand side of the chart.

The problem with skewed distributions, as we have suggested, is that you cannot make the same assumptions as when you have normally distributed data. You saw earlier, when we talked about entrepreneurial ability, just how useful these assumptions can be. And we also mentioned how all the clever mathematical procedures you may wish to run on your data also work on the assumption that they are normally distributed. If the data do not meet this assumption, the results of your analyses cannot be relied upon. All is not lost however! We can do something to help.[18]

---

[18] We are at this point in danger of turning our user-friendly book into a nightmare for some people by talking about things that generally don't interest or bother them. If you are one of those people, then feel free to skip this and move on to the Doing

Transformations for skew

The first thing to say here is that, even if you have some skew in your data, it is not the end of the world. Some of the statistical tests you might use in analysing the data, even though they assume that you have a normal distribution, are actually rather flexible. Statisticians would say that these tests are 'robust'. The t-test is a very common statistical procedure which you will almost certainly use at some stage, and it is rather robust. The same goes for the common test known as 'analysis of variance'.

However, having said this, it is always nicer to have data that look like a normal distribution, and a skewed data set – a set of data where the distribution isn't symmetrical – can be 'transformed' to resemble a more normal distribution in a few different ways.

The very first thing to do is to plot the data graphically. It will be pretty obvious from looking at the graph whether you have a problem with skew. What you are aiming to do with a transformation is make the skewed distribution *look* symmetrical, as it would look if you had a normal distribution. The thing to remember here is that whatever you do to your data to make the distribution look symmetrical, you have to do it to *all* the data. You can't go about adding a bit here, multiplying a bit there, and plotting one bit or the other on a different scale. But as long as you do the same calculation to all the scores in a set, you can do pretty much anything to your data in an attempt to make them look like a normal distribution.

The simplest way to change the shape of the distribution is to change the scale on the x axis. Most graphs have a **linear** scale. This means that the scale stays completely regular as you move along it: every time you move from one point to the next on the axis, the score goes up by the same amount.

But this does not have to be the case. It is possible to change the axis so that some parts of it are more 'squashed up' than other parts. A common way of doing this is with a **logarithmic** transformation. If you turn the x axis from a linear axis (where each point on the scale is one more than the previous point) to a logarithmic axis (where each point on the scale has a value several times larger than the previous point) your data will be a significantly different shape. This kind of transformation is only really appropriate if you have heavily skewed data because its influence is rather powerful.

Research section. Doing research is much more fun. You may like to come back to this bit once you feel more confident, or if you collect some data and the distribution begins to bother you. Keep it in mind, that's all we are saying. Put a 'read this later' note in the book or something.

A non-symmetrical (skewed) distribution, where there are more people scoring below the mean than above. On the left is the original distribution and on the right is the distribution after taking the logarithm of all the scores.

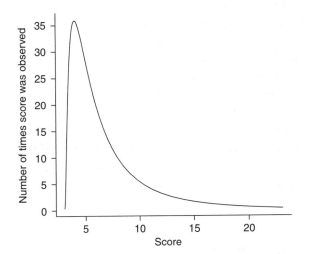

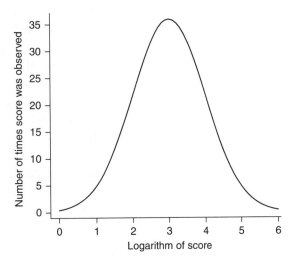

You might also consider a **power** transformation. That is, you take your original set of scores and raise each to the power of 2 (square it) or 3 (cube it). Perhaps the most useful data transformation of all, which is also a power transformation, is to take the square root or cube root of all your data. Taking the square root of your data usually changes the x axis to get rid of positive skew in a data set really nicely, and this is a good thing to know as positively skewed distributions are something you will see a lot. But do note that you can't use a square root transformation if you have any negative values in your data, because it just makes everything positive. If you do have any negative values then you will have to consider a cube root transformation.

A non-symmetrical (skewed) distribution, where there are more people scoring below the mean than above. On the left is the original distribution and on the right is the distribution after taking the square root of all the scores.

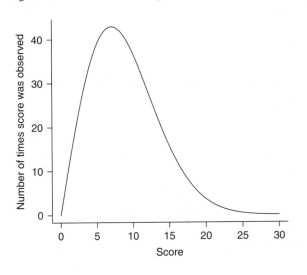

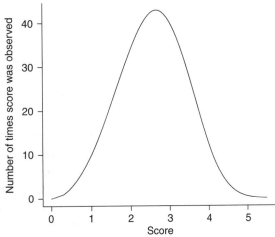

This is a good time for us to show you exactly how these data transformations are working to correct skewed data, as the square-root transformation makes it quite easy to see what is going on. As we've just said, taking the square root of all your measurements is a neat way of making your distributions look symmetrical when they are positively skewed. If you look for a moment at the diagram showing a positively skewed distribution, you should be able to see that it is the scores over on the right-hand side – the ones with higher values on the x axis – which need to be changed more than the scores on the left-hand side if we are to make the distribution symmetrical.

The clever thing with the square-root transformation is that the influence of square rooting a number is larger the bigger the number was originally, which is exactly what's needed if you're to alter the right-hand side of the x axis more than the left-hand side. Look at this:

Original Number	Square root	Difference
4	2	2
9	3	6
16	4	12
25	5	20

You can see that the difference between a number and its square root is bigger the larger the number is. Small numbers only change a bit when you take the square root but large numbers change a lot. This should show you how the square-root transformation works to alter the high end of the x axis more than the low end. All the other transformations work in similar ways, although we've illustrated it with square roots as they are the easiest to visualize.

A final neat trick for sorting out distributions is the **reciprocal** transformation, where you replace each score in your data with 1 divided by the score. If you are measuring something like 'accidents per kilometre driven' you will definitely have skewed data, because the numbers involved are really small (most people have far less than one accident per kilometre!). You might tidy these data up by flipping things round, to measure 'kilometres travelled per accident' instead, which will give you much bigger numbers to work with. For example, let's say somebody drove a car for 200,000 kilometres and crashed three times. You can see that the data are much more manageable expressed as kilometres per accident (200,000/3 = 66,667) than as accidents per kilometre (3/200,000 = 0.00015).

Reversing, or rearranging, your data like this is absolutely fine. You have not altered some of the data and not others. Rather, you have manipulated all of the data in exactly the same way. (You may still have a problem with outliers, though, so be careful to note their presence and account for them if you can.)

Once you have performed any transformation on your data, plot them again and see if you are happier with the distribution. There are a few rules of thumb that you might consider here, variously described as the '15/40' rule, or the '40/15' rule, or sometimes the '15 limit'. What this means is that, if you have 15 participants or fewer, your data may well look normally distributed but you must be careful. You have to be *really* sure with small data sets like these that you have no skew or outliers. If you do, then the skew, or extreme values of the outliers, will heavily influence your calculations, so watch out.

If the number of participants in your data set is somewhere between 15 and 40 you are on the right track, but you still have to be careful. If you can, try your analysis with the outliers in, and then again with the outliers removed, to see if it makes a big difference. If it makes a huge difference then you might consider a transformation and trying the analysis again. So, with between 15 and 40 people, proceed carefully and keep an eye on skew and outliers.

The best thing to do is to collect at least 40 data points. If you have more than 40 then you are really doing well and can generally (but definitely not always!) not worry too much about the influence of skew or outliers. Still, we've had experiences where the data look very odd and a transformation has really helped bash them into shape – even with quite large numbers of participants. If you go on to learn more about statistics – or use a statistician to do your analyses – then you can deal with this issue in more depth by using something called *residual analysis*.

Data distributions, skew and transformations – summing it all up

If you've just got to this point and had never heard of data transformations before, you might well be thinking 'What the ... ?' We sympathize: it's not a completely easy subject to grasp, and it often only becomes completely clear when you get involved with statistical analyses yourself. But just to end this chapter nicely, let's try to sum up skew and transformations as simply as possible.

When you measure something in a lot of people, those measurements are usually normally distributed. Take height: most people are around average height (these measurements would be seen in your data often), and as you move away to more extreme heights – very tall or very short people – you will see fewer people in your group.

Because normal distributions are so common, a lot of statistical tests assume the data being tested are normally distributed. If your data are not, you might be confusing your test, and the results it gives you might be misleading as a consequence.

Therefore, when your data distribution is skewed – not symmetrical – it is a good idea to change all the scores so that it becomes symmetrical.

If you do some sort of calculation, such as taking the square root, with *all* your measurements, this will often make the distribution look symmetrical, and will avoid confusing your statistical test.

We know that a lot of people, when they first learn about data transformation, get the feeling that it must be sordid cheating for a researcher to fiddle with their measurements to make them look the way they should. It's not. It's a completely acceptable and normal thing to do. Just make sure you are honest about it and describe your transformation when you write up the report of your study.

chapter 4

south essex college
FURTHER & HIGHER EDUCATION
SOUTHEND CAMPUS

what have you found? inferential statistics

Chapter 3 was all about describing your findings, both to yourself and to others. It may seem slightly odd to talk about describing your findings to yourself, when they are your own findings, but this is actually an important step in research. Describing your results to yourself helps make sure you are completely certain about exactly what it is you found. We once carried out a study on an aspect of decision-making and it was only later, when we were describing the results to somebody else, that they said 'Oh, so you've shown...' and then pointed out a second result we hadn't even noticed we had discovered! So describing your data is not just for telling other people what you have found, it is also for your own benefit.

Once you have collected your data and described them, the next step is to decide what is the answer to your research question. This is the straightforward question you are hoping to answer: 'is crime related to poverty?' or 'does learning to juggle make people more co-ordinated?' Remember how in Chapter 1 we explained why you can't test the research question directly and so test a *null hypothesis*, the idea that you will find no effect? And remember in Chapter 2 we discussed how you test a sample of people because it is not practical to test the whole population?

It is now, after you have designed a study and collected the data, that these ideas all come together. Because the final stage of your research is to say to yourself: *okay, I've seen something in my sample – would I see the same if I tested the whole population? Can I generalize these findings?* And the way you answer these questions is by looking at whether the null hypothesis is correct or not. See how everything fits together?

Scaling up your sample

If you were able to test the whole population you are interested in – if you carried out *summative research* – then your task essentially ended when you described the data. If you have tested a whole population, and you didn't make any mistakes with your design or data collection, then *whatever you find is the truth about your population.* If you are interested only in the people who live in your street and you test them all, you have found out what you needed to know about the people in your street. It's that simple.

In most research, however, you are not able to test the whole population that you are interested in. In this case, you test a sample which you hope is *representative* of the population. So the normal situation at the end of a study is that you have tested a sample of people, found out something about them, and must then answer the key question: *would I have found the same thing if I had tested the whole population*? How do you answer this question, without actually going out and testing the whole population? The answer is, you do it with **inferential statistics**. Back in Chapter 2 we described the process of testing a sample of people as *inferential research*, because you use the sample to work out, or *infer*, what the population looks like. Inferential statistics are what you use to do this.

p, the magic number

If you go on to learn more about statistics – and we hope you will – you might well find the subject slightly overwhelming at first. We know we did. We happen to have a statistics book with us right now which we were using earlier for a research project we are working on. Flicking to the back we see that it is – yikes! – nearly 1,000 pages long. That is a *lot* of information and if you saw this book you would have every right to be a bit nervous about having to learn it all.

So we're going to let you into a secret, which should make understanding inferential statistics a lot easier. *All statistical tests do exactly the same thing: they calculate a number called* p. That's it. If you remember this, you have already learnt most of what you need to know about statistical analysis. We're being serious.

The letter *p* stands for 'probability'. The probability of what? Well, we'll tell you that in a moment, but first we want to make sure everybody is happy with the idea of probability in general. You might know all about probability, in which case feel free to skip the next section, but if you're at all shaky on the concept then here's a refresher...

Probability: a short refresher course involving coffee cups

Probability is one of those words people use every day, often without completely understanding what they are saying. For our purposes, probability is a number. It is a number with a value somewhere between zero and one, and it tells you how likely it is that something will happen.

When there is a probability of zero, this means something *will not happen*. There is a zero probability that you will fly by flapping your ears. There is a probability of zero that you will turn into an octopus one day. These things will not happen.

A probability of one means something *will happen*. There is a probability of one that we will die some day. Much as we don't like to think about it, this *will* happen.

But most of the things that go on in the world have probabilities somewhere between zero and one. Most things have in-between probabilities like .25 or .76. And interpreting these is really very easy.

If something happens with a probability of .50, it happens half the time. If you toss a coin and catch it, it will land on Heads half the time. So we say Heads has a probability of .50. If you were to toss a coin over and over and over, it should come up on Heads 50% of the time thanks to Heads having a probability of .50. This shows you that probabilities and percentages are really the same thing. If you feel happier with percentages, you should feel free to multiply any probabilities by 100. So a probability of .50 becomes 50%, for example (.50 x 100 = 50).

We have each drunk two cups of coffee whilst writing this morning, and, as we couldn't be bothered to wash the cups before refilling them, the table we are working at has four coffee cups on it. These four cups are each a different colour: one is red, one is green, one is orange and one is blue.[1] If Nigel closes his eyes and Ian mixes the four cups up, there is a one in four chance that Nigel will choose the red cup. A one in four chance can be written as ¼, which can also be written as .25 (1 divided by 4 = .25). So there is a probability of one in four, or .25, that Nigel will choose the red cup – if we did it over and over, he would almost certainly choose the red cup 25% of the time.

---

[1] Once again, we're not just making this up for your education: it's all true. Brightly coloured cups are very fashionable at the time we are writing this.

Okay, so what does p tell us when we do research?

There are two answers to this: there is the 'proper' answer and the easy answer. We'll give you both and you can choose to use whichever makes the most sense to you. Just remember the 'proper' answer is the one to use when you are writing up your research for other people to read!

Let's say we carry out an experiment to see whether men and women, on average, differ in their driving ability. It clearly isn't possible to test *all* the men and women in the world, so we test a sample of them. We take a group of people and put them in a driving simulator. We find the men make six errors each on average and the women make four errors each on average. It looks as though the men are worse drivers. So should we go out right now and tell the world that men can't drive as well as women?

The answer is no (sorry girls). And the reason we can't just go right out and tell the world what we found is that the sample we used might have been odd in some way. It is possible that, just through bad luck, we got some particularly bad men in our sample (or some particularly good women). Or it may be that, just through pure bad luck, our men just performed a little bit worse than they normally would on the day we tested them. But how likely is it that this happened? That's exactly what p tells us when we run our statistical test.

The actual test we use doesn't matter for now[2]; what matters is that after carrying out our driving test, and after all the calculations are done, we get something like this:

$$p = .16$$

And what does this tell us? As promised, here are the two answers.

The 'proper' answer: p is the probability of seeing scores at least as extreme as yours if the null hypothesis is correct. That is, it is the probability of seeing scores like this just by chance.

The easier answer: p is the probability you are wrong if you say you have found something interesting.

Let's look at this in a bit more detail.

As you saw in Chapter 1, all research involves testing a null hypothesis, and this always predicts that *nothing interesting is happening* – that whatever you thought might happen will not happen. Now, in our sample the men made six driving errors on average whilst the women made four, and our calculations gave this finding a p value of .16. Taking the 'proper' approach, this p value of .16 means there is a .16 – or 16%, if you prefer – chance of seeing scores this different or more if the null hypothesis is

---

[2] In this example, it would probably be a *t*-test, if you must know.

true. If men and women do not really differ in their driving ability, there is a 16% chance of seeing the men make six errors and the women make four just as a fluke – just by being unlucky with the particular people you happen to test, for example.

So our statistical test's '$p = .16$' tells us there is a 16% chance of seeing this difference between men and women if the null hypothesis is true. Or, if we use our easier explanation of p, *there is a 16% chance we will be wrong if we conclude men and women drive differently.*

But what does this *mean*?

When we compared men and women's driving we saw a difference in the number of mistakes the two groups made – the men made more errors than the women. But our analysis then told us there is a .16 probability of seeing an effect like this if the null hypothesis is true, and men and women do not really differ in driving ability. In other words, if men and women are really the same, there is a 16% chance of seeing this difference in our sample just by accident. However, this isn't really what we want. We've got a probability measure when what we wanted was a straightforward answer to our research question. So what do we conclude about men's and women's driving? Are men and women different or not? How we do use this .16 number to answer that?

On the face of it, it looks as though we should conclude men and women *are* different at driving. If there is a .16 chance we are wrong saying this, that means there must be a .84 – 84% – chance we are correct if we say men and women are different, no?

Well, yes. There is actually. Probabilities always add up to 1, and so if there is a .16 probability of us being wrong, there must be a $(1 - .16 = .84)$ .84 probability of us being right. But let us ask you this: is an 84% chance of being correct high enough?

Imagine that, instead of looking at people's driving, you are testing a new drug. You find there are no side-effects in your sample and after running the statistics you are 84% certain that there will be no side-effects in the general population. Would you release your new drug on the world if there was a 16% chance you would be wrong about it being safe?

We're really hoping you thought 'no' just then. But even if you thought 'Yes: yes, I *would* release it!' you wouldn't be allowed to, as there are plenty of regulatory bodies who expect much better evidence about medicines' safety before they allow them to be sold.

And even if we leave aside questions of life and death for a moment, your reputation as a researcher will always hang on any statements you make. If you conclude you have found something and you are wrong, this could be disastrous for your career.

The problem you face as a researcher is that there is only one way of having zero doubt about the population you are interested in: test everybody. If there is even a single person in the population whom you have not tested, you cannot know for certain how they will behave. So you will never be in a position of having zero doubt unless you test the whole population – which is usually impossible, as we saw in Chapter 2.

So if you can't expect ever to have zero doubt about how the population will behave, how much doubt is okay? We suggested that when p is .16, this is too much doubt – a 16% chance of being wrong with your conclusion is too great a risk to take with your reputation as a researcher. So if zero doubt is impossible and .16 is too high, the answer to how much risk you will accept must be somewhere between 0 and .16!

In fact, it depends what you are testing. If you are exploring something where being wrong doesn't matter too much – people's attitudes to teddy bears, say – you might accept a greater risk of making a mistake than if you are clearing a new medicine for human use. In this latter case, you *really* don't want to get it wrong. And if you are exploring a brand new field you might accept more risk of being wrong than if you are working in a well-established field.

The level of risk you will accept has a name: **alpha**, usually written with the Greek letter alpha, which is α. So, for example, you might decide to set α to .10. This means you are prepared to accept up to a 10% chance of being wrong when you reach your conclusions. Or, more strictly, this means you are prepared to accept up to a 10% chance of rejecting your null hypothesis when in fact it is true.

So alpha is .10?

Sometimes. In fact, over the years a standard alpha level has become established in human research, at .05. This means that, in most studies, the researchers are accepting up to a 5% chance of their conclusions being wrong. They accept the idea that there is up to a 5% chance the results they obtained emerged just by chance, rather than because of anything interesting.

If your research conclusions really matter – if you are testing a medicine, say – then you will probably set α to something lower, such as .001. If you are exploring a new area and are happy to risk making mistakes for the chance of new discoveries then you'll probably set it high, to say .10. Nobody ever sets α higher than this, and .05 is the norm in the great majority of projects. You will see the number .05 everywhere when you carry out and read about research.

Speaking of things you will read about, you will almost certainly come across the word 'significant' a lot when you read other people's research. This is a very misleading word that means different things to different people. You will see sentences in research reports like this:

'When we looked at how much they like teddy bears, we found a significant difference between Canadians and Americans.'

When you read something like this, all the researcher is saying is: 'my p value was lower than .05, and so I have rejected my null hypothesis. I have decided I discovered something about the population in my study (residents of North America, in this case).'

This is *statistical significance*: a result is 'statistically significant' whenever its p value is lower than α (usually .05). So when something is statistically significant, this means that what was seen in the sample probably reflects something real about the population.

The problem is that almost everybody in the real world uses the word 'significant' to mean something else. When most normal people say 'this is a significant result', they mean 'this is an *important* result'. When a researcher says 'this is a significant result', they are saying nothing about how important the result is: they are talking only about their p value.

So a research project can have results which are significant, but not significant. We told you it was misleading, didn't we?

Summing it up

This has been a lot of new information. So we're going to attempt the impossible: we're now going to sum up the whole field of inferential statistics in one short paragraph. If we pull this off it'll make all other textbook authors look like losers. Okay, here goes…

When doing research, you test a sample of people and calculate the probability that what you saw in your sample will not generalize to the population. If the probability of your findings not generalizing – if the probability of your findings being wrong – is higher than alpha (which is usually .05), you conclude you haven't found anything. If the probability of your findings not generalizing is lower than alpha, you conclude that the population would probably show the same findings as your sample.

Ha-ha! One short paragraph, as promised. Now let's make it more concrete by using a couple of examples.

An example of significance testing involving music

We decide to carry out an experiment to see whether people can learn new information better when they are reading in silence or when they are listening to music. (You probably have your own opinion on how you best learn. We think silence is the best way to learn, but you might be ~~wrong~~ different.)

We take two substantial groups of people and get everybody to read three pages of information before answering a set of 10 questions about what they read. One of the groups reads the information in silence and the other group reads it with music playing in the room. We find this:

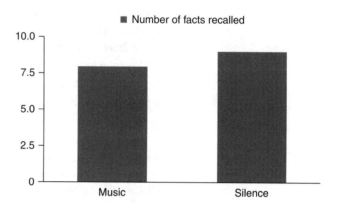

So it looks at though people remembered more after reading in silence. But before we can state this as our conclusion we have to do a statistical test. We do this because the difference between the Music group and the Silence group was fairly small, so there are two possible explanations for the difference. It could be that it really is better to learn in silence. Or it could be that learning in music and learning in silence are really the same but we just happened, by accident, to get slightly better learners in our Silence group. If this is the case, the difference we have seen wouldn't generalize to the larger population.

So we do a statistical test and get the result $p = .22$. What this tells us is there is a .22 – 22%–probability of seeing a difference this size if the null hypothesis is correct. In other words, there is a .22 probability the difference we saw was just accidental, and we would not see the same if we tested the whole population.

Recall that the usual value of α, our decision-making criterion, is .05. Our value of p is much larger than this. We therefore accept the null hypothesis – music makes no difference to studying. We conclude that music and silence are the same, and that the small difference we saw in our graph must just have been a fluke, caused by the particular people we tested being, by accident, slightly unrepresentative of the whole population.

An example of significance testing involving gearboxes

So we have discovered that it makes no difference whether people study in silence or when listening to music.[3] Flushed with the success of this discovery, we decide to expand our work to see whether the same thing is true of physical tasks. We therefore visit a large factory and find two groups of workers manufacturing gearboxes.[4] For a month we get one of the groups to work in silence and the other group to work with music playing, and we find this:

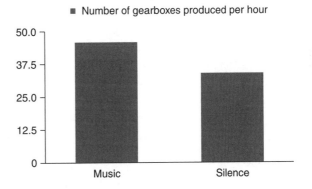

■ Number of gearboxes produced per hour

So it looks as though listening to music made the workers more efficient. But is this a real difference? Would we see the same thing if we tested the whole population? Or is the difference on our graph just a fluke, caused by our particular set of workers being unrepresentative in some way? Would this difference disappear if we tested a lot more people? A statistical test will help us know.

We carry out a suitable test and it gives the result $p = .02$. This means there is only a .02 probability – a 2% chance – of seeing a difference this large or bigger if the null hypothesis is correct, and if there is no real difference in the population. In other words, there is only a 2% chance we would be wrong if we said music helps people work. This p value is nice and low – less than the usual α level of .05. We would therefore accept the small risk of

---

[3] We should emphasize that we made these data up. Don't blame us because you struggled to revise after listening to music all the time. But do feel free to use what we teach you about research skills to do this experiment for real. We'd be interested to hear what you find.

[4] Ian once spent a summer doing this when he was a student. Much of his work involved removing a metal cog from each gearbox and replacing it with a plastic one so the gearbox would wear out sooner. Capitalism, eh?

being wrong and conclude that yes, listening to music really does make people work faster.

It's fairly simple, really. And we aren't kidding when we say that if you understand this example, you have understood the main principles of all statistical testing.

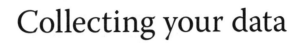

2 part

doing research

Collecting your data

Right, you've got the idea. You've cleared a little space in your diary and now all you need to do is get the information from the general public. What you have so far is an idea, a *hypothesis*. But hold on ... you can't just go out and collect data. The first thing to do is to consider all the design options open to you.

Design

We know we do it for a living, and may be biased, but when you are dealing with people a well-designed project is a thing of beauty. There is a certain elegance and artistry involved in making sure you have designed your project as carefully as possible. The trick is to think of how your project can go wrong at this stage, and design it so that nothing under your control can possibly ruin what would otherwise be a Nobel prize-winning procedure. The first rule, though, is that you should never try to solve all the problems and questions you can think of in one single project session. The more complications you introduce, the more there is to go wrong. So a *very* important rule we will return to time and time again is this:

Keep It Simple!
(KIS for short)

You may even see this rule elsewhere as 'Keep It Simple, Stupid' (KISS). Keeping things simple means you are more likely to see things happen with your procedure. You are less likely to hide effects or discoveries of interest in an overcomplicated design. Also, unless you keep things simple, you'll not be sure what is causing the change or behaviour that you are observing.

What do I need to know?

The first thing is to identify the various factors you need to consider in the design process. One of these is the *hypothesis* and we've already discussed that. A well-thought-out hypothesis makes everything else pretty simple. But before you start writing things down in your notebooks, and sending your data to newspapers and academic journals for publication, we should really cover a few more things that will be of use to you.

In this section we'll describe how you actually go about doing research with people. In the previous section we introduced the theory which gives us the rules, sets sensible guidelines. This is extremely important. It helps us to avoid making mistakes before we start, mistakes that can be more than a waste of time – they can be a waste of money and resources too. It's worth highlighting one of the rules we laid out in the previous section again. Before you dive in head first, ask yourself this.

Are you sure you know what you are doing and why you are doing it?

If your answer to this question is 'no' then take a deep breath, get yourself another blank sheet of paper and take a little more time to think it through.

We have decided on three examples of the kind of research you may find yourself doing with people, and we'll go through these together in some detail, highlighting the kind of typical errors people often make when they embark upon research with people. Once we've done this you'll be ready to get stuck into a series of practical workshops.

How do I use this section of the book?

The examples we have decided to use may or may not appear entirely relevant to your field of research. The principles used in the design and execution of the examples are, however, transferable to a whole range of projects, and the examples have been chosen to best illustrate these, so stick with us.

The best way to use this section is to read through it carefully, noting down areas that you feel might be important in any investigations that may relate to your area of interest, and taking in the approaches described in all the examples. Then, when carrying out your own projects, or working on one of the practical workshops later in the book, you should flick back to this section to refresh your memory of how to do things and what to look out for with different types of research with people. You'll also notice words and phrases in this chapter that are detailed in the glossary. The definitions are very useful, but there is no substitute for a practical example when learning to apply the sometimes abstract and peculiar terms which form the 'jargon' of research methods. For this reason, we think one of the best things about this section of the book is that it will clarify terms you may feel the need to look up in the glossary, where you'll find not only a definition, but also, in the index, page references to where the terms are used elsewhere in the book.

Can I just get on with it now?

Right, you've read Part 1 and have got the idea. You've cleared a little space in your diary and now all you need to do is get the information from the general public. What you have so far is an idea, a *hypothesis*. But hold on... you can't just go out and collect data. The first thing to do is to consider all the design options open to you.

chapter 5

designing a study: running for the bus

Ian:	QUICK! It's the bus. I can see it coming. RUN!!
Nigel:	You've got to be joking, I'll never make it, not with these bags.
Ian:	Well give me some then. Now run! The next one won't be for another hour and it's freezing out here.
Nigel:	Take another bag then.
Ian:	If I take another bag I'll not be able to run fast enough.
Nigel:	You sure?
Ian:	No, I'm not sure. OK … give me another bag and I'll give it a try.
Nigel:	I think … I think we should probably do this properly …

Running for the bus is a regular event for those of us for whom 'time-keeping' is not terribly strong. If you've ever tried running for a bus with shopping bags or sports kit, you'll know how difficult it can be with heavy bags flapping about around you, doing their best to trip you up. In our example, we suggest the *number* of bags you are carrying can influence the likelihood of your making it to the bus stop before the bus pulls away.

This is a perfect example of our KIS rule. Aha! you may say, it's not just the number of bags that influences your bus-catching ability is it? It's also got something to do with the weight of the bags, and also the shape of the bags, which influence how awkward they are to carry. Yes, of course you're right. But here we are getting into complicated ground. The KIS rule is clear, and we must keep it simple. Once we know the answer about the number of bags, *then* we can design different procedures to see about the influence of weight and shape.

Ok, I want to know about running with bags. What do I do first?

The first thing to do is get it completely straight in your own mind what it is you are trying to find out. This is one of the great things about thinking logically about research. It makes you think clearly, and it makes you focus on what's important in your research. So first, as we discussed in Part 1, you need to formulate a hypothesis.

In this case you have the idea that carrying bags makes you run slower, so you can afford to choose a 'directional' or 'one-tailed' hypothesis. In other words you don't need to ask whether 'carrying bags *alters* the speed at which you can run'; you can cut straight to the more specific 'carrying bags makes you run *slower*'. In fact, we could probably do a bit better than that. We could say something like:

'the more bags you carry, the slower you run'

We have our hypothesis. Now all that's left to do is test it.

What statistical tests am I going to do?

Oh dear, false start. You see, you're doing that thing that millions of researchers learning their trade do. You're making the terrible mistake of thinking that doing research is all about mathematics. We'll remind you of this as we go on, but it is terribly important for us to explain that research is mostly about careful design and thinking. Mathematics and statistics are really only a tool that researchers use to help them make a decision once all the data have been collected. So banish this question from your mind for a minute, and take solace in the knowledge that we are going to spend most of our time thinking and doing – the fun parts of research.

How many bags will I use?

Good question. This is what you have control over. As project designer you cannot control how fast the person runs, you'll leave that up to them, but you can hopefully influence this by loading up your runner. This is really what got you interested in the problem in the first place. Do a little fieldwork, and try and control this as carefully as possible. See how easy it is to run with bags yourself, and try to get a feeling for whether carrying, let's say, three bags is enough to make a noticeable difference from running with only one bag. This is a little like a **pilot study**, where you try out something to see if a decision is sensible before you dive in to the research itself.

Next you'll need to try and control things carefully. It would be extremely annoying if you gave your runner one bag to carry, then gave them a second to see if it made a difference only to discover later that the second bag was five times heavier than the first. Each bag will need to be a standard weight. Decide on this and stick to it. Two large packets of sugar in each bag might be a good compromise.

So you now have three bags, each weighing the same amount. You have just constructed your **independent variable (IV).** In our case the IV can be described as:

'*the number of bags of standard weight being carried*'.

And in this particular case, our IV has **three levels:**, one, two or three bags.

How will we do our measuring?

You'll have marked the start and end points of your run. All you need is something suitable to calculate how long it takes to travel the distance. A stopwatch is ideal. The time taken to travel the distance is your **dependent variable (DV).**

The time taken to do the running *depends on* how many bags you are carrying. The dependent variable in a project is the thing you, the observer of the behaviour or performance, record for later. Sometimes sophisticated software or automatic measuring devices might be employed that record the information for you, but it's all the same thing really. Infrared devices that record when someone starts and finishes a run are not very easy to obtain, and when they are they are expensive and prone to failure. A simple stopwatch will do just as well here.

The thing to try and remember is that the dependent variable *depends on* the independent variable. In this case your dependent variable (the time taken to travel the measured distance) depends on how many bags of shopping the person is carrying.

Where will we do the running?

We could use a bus, and a known bus route, but this adds another level of complication. We would have to control the speed the bus driver opens the doors and boards passengers before driving off. We'd also have to control the speed that the bus driver approaches the bus-stop in the first place, and a host of other factors, so let's simplify the problem even further. How about a running track, or, better still, a nice long corridor in your department? This ensures a regular temperature, regular wind-speed and regular weather conditions. What we're trying to say is that you must try to ensure the *only thing*

that influences your dependent variable is your independent variable.
In your case you need to do your best to ensure the only thing that
influences the time people take to run the standard distance is the
number of bags of shopping they are carrying. The wind or temperature may have influenced your results, and anything that *may* influence your dependent variable other than your independent variable
is called an **extraneous variable**.

Many a well-laid plan has been ruined by an extraneous variable
that has been overlooked, and not controlled for. A project perfect in
almost every way can be spoiled by a stray extraneous variable making the whole procedure a waste of time and often a waste of money.
Imagine setting up a weekend project employing 25 data gatherers
and observers in a busy town centre only to find when you get there
that the rain has arrived and the usual 20,000 visitors to your data
gathering area have been reduced to approximately 1,500. Your gatherers must be paid, and their expenses accounted for, but you are left
without enough data and your weekend has been wasted. All because
of the rain. If you had chosen a covered shopping centre, this might
not have been such a problem. In this case we can say that the extraneous variable has *confounded* your project. It has stopped being an
extraneous variable and has turned into a **confounding variable**.

This is an important point. Extraneous variables are not a problem, and will not become confounds, if you know they are there and
your design is careful enough to deal with them.

In our bags example, potential extraneous variables might include
the type of bus being used. The new 'Super-Turbo Speedybus' is likely
to cause the runner more problems than the older 'slow and steady'
bus, for instance. Also, the driver of the bus could cause problems.
Crazy Dave, for instance, may pose more of a challenge to the runner than Gently-Gently Stan. If you change the type of bus used, or
the driver, your data will not be much use to you as the dependent
variable may be influenced by more than just how many bags your
runner is loaded up with.

How far will we run?

Does it really matter? Obviously you need to run a distance that can
be timed sensibly, so a few metres may be too short, and a kilometre
is likely to be too far for your runner. As long as you clearly mark the
start and end points it shouldn't make any difference as long as you
make your runner travel exactly the same distance in the same place
on each occasion. What you don't want to do is make the measurement in a nice quiet gym or corridor for one level of your independent
variable (carrying two bags) then take them outside for the measurement with another level of your independent variable (carrying one

bag). This introduces atmospheric conditions, and a different running surface, that may influence the speed at which the runner travels. You would have introduced an extraneous variable that may well have confounded your project.

Shall I use three different runners?

You might decide to use three different runners, one carrying one bag, one carrying two bags and one carrying three bags. This is known as an **independent-samples** design, where each level of your independent variable is accounted for by a different person.

But there is a problem with this, easily illustrated by a suitable bizarre example. Let's say you choose your runners as carefully as possible, but from the people you normally find standing at your local bus-stop: the old lady with the walking stick, the pregnant woman, and the 25-year-old world indoor sprint champion. It might happen – you never know! The point is that, even if you find triplets of exactly the same physical build, you cannot be sure they have had the same running experience. These *individual differences* can be a serious problem, and are a kind of extraneous variable which may confound your project. Even if you managed to find triplets of identical genetic make-up you could not be absolutely sure that individual differences may not arise because of different life experiences. It could even be that one may be suffering from a medical problem such as a virus which could influence their running.

Ok, three people aren't enough – how many should I use?

The best way to try and control for these individual differences is to make three large groups of people. If you have 50 people in each group, even though you will still have quite different people in each group, the chances are that you'll have a similar range of differences in each group also. The rule is that the larger the groups are, the better. The larger the group, the more chance there is of matching people in each group by chance and the less chance there is of one group accidentally looking completely different from the others.

In an extreme example, you could put 10,000 people in each group. If you took one person in group 1 at random, let's say a 35-year-old male who takes on average 2 hours of exercise a week, the chances are you'd find similar males exist in groups 2 and 3. The best way to maximize your chances of finding matches like this if you decide to use different groups is to use as large a group as possible, although, as we mentioned in Part 1, you could choose to reduce group size by introducing a matched-pairs component to your design.

In a matched design, each person in each group is 'matched' with as similar a person as possible in the other groups. If your design had two groups, and it was an ideal world, you could consider using sets of identical twins, allocating one of each pair to a different group. Either way, be aware of individual differences: even twins have different experiences, motivation levels and abilities! Individual differences can really cause problems with an independent-samples design. Sometimes, of course, you just have to choose this type of design. If you are interested in gender differences, for instance, or the behaviour of different age groups, one single individual cannot be a male and a female at the same time, and they cannot be different ages at the same time. Your only option here is to choose an independent samples design.

Couldn't I use the same runner?

Yes, you could certainly do that. It would eliminate the individual differences issue but would also bring different problems which you need to consider. Here you are designing a **repeated-measures** design. It's called that because each individual repeats the task for each level of the independent variable. If you imagine what might happen in your study, some of the problems you could encounter will become clear...

Your runner arrives, and you give them a bag. They run the distance, and you record their time. Next you give them two bags and they run the distance again. You carefully record the time. Finally, three bags. You thank them, pay them and turn to your data. It does indeed seem that the runner got slower when they carried more bags. It is just as possible, though, that they got slower because they became more and more exhausted in successive runs. **Fatigue** is a serious extraneous variable associated with repeated-measures designs.

You need to control for this. You could allow your runner to have a nice long rest after each run, but can you be absolutely sure that the runner is fully rested? In any case, you need to be aware of another important problem: **practice effects** are also extraneous variables that might confound your project. It could be that the runner actually improved because they worked out how best to carry the bags or how to alter their running style to help them run better when laden. If this were the case then any influence of the weight of the bag could be hidden, or at least reduced, by the runner's improved technique. What you need to do is get a number of runners. One starts with one bag, then two and finally three. The next runner starts with two, then runs with three and finally one bag. You continue like this until all possible **orders** have been completed. This is called **counterbalancing**. You can now take an average for each number of bags carried. Taking an average is a really good idea. It means all the data are boiled down into a single number, making it much easier to see what is going on overall (if anything).

But doesn't that mean that I'm introducing individual differences again?

It does, but, because each individual is providing you with data in each level of the independent variable, the differences are not a problem. Your clever design has eliminated them as possible cause of confound. We can say that, with a counterbalanced repeated-measures design, *each participant acts as their own control.*

By this we mean the individual characteristics (height, weight, gender, fitness, running experience, etc.) are exactly the same for 1 bag as they are for 2 and 3.

So how many people do I need for this kind of project design?

That's the great thing: because you have controlled for individual differences, you need far fewer people. You should try to fully counterbalance if possible, which means that you need enough people so each can provide data in every possible order. The way to work this out is relatively simple. Let's say you have three levels of the independent variable, as we do with our bags. We'll call them A, B and C. There are six possible orders of these three levels, and they are as follows.

1. ABC
2. ACB
3. BAC
4. BCA
5. CAB
6. CBA

This means that to fully counterbalance you need at least six people, or multiples of six people (12, 18, 24, 30, 36, etc.). If you use seven people, you'll end up with one of the orders being done twice, which could bias your results. So you should really use multiples of six in this case.

In mathematical studies (now don't panic!) the number of possible orders can be easily calculated and described as '3 factorial' which is written as '3!'. In longhand it is written as 3 x 2 x 1, which equals 6. If you have three conditions, as we do in our example, then there are 3! possible orders, which is 6 in total. If you have four different levels or conditions then the number of possible orders is 4!, which is 4 x 3 x 2 x 1, which equals 24. With five levels, you have 5! orders, which is 5 x 4 x 3 x 2 x 1, which equals 120. As you can see, the more levels you have, the more complicated your design, the longer it will take you to collect the data you need and the more it will cost. Another very good reason for keeping it simple!

That's fine for this project, where the number of independent variable levels is low, but what if I have a project that has to have more levels, six perhaps?

That's a good point. It's worth pointing out that a fully counterbalanced design like this is the ideal way to manage orders and control for any order effects, but this is not always convenient or possible. If, as you say, you had six different levels of the independent variable, then fully to counterbalance you would have to ensure all possible orders were run. Using the calculation above, you can see the number of different orders for six different levels of the independent variable is 6!. This is 6 x 5 x 4 x 3 x 2 x 1, which works out as 720. That is, there are 720 different possible orders if you have six levels of the independent variable. To fully counterbalance this design, you would need to run multiples of 720 participants. That's 720, 1440 or 2160 participants at least! Not only would you find that extremely difficult to do, you'd find it unbelievably boring, and research should never be boring if you can possibly help it.

In a situation like this, then, it is acceptable to **randomize** the orders you present. This is an acceptable alternative to a fully counterbalanced design when you are faced with a large number of possible orders. What's important is that you are aware of the issues involved in choosing a randomized order. Be upfront about it when you write up your work, and make sure that the reader knows that you have chosen this method of presentation for a sensible reason.

OK. What's next? My runners are coming in tomorrow

That's great. Getting people to help with research is part of the problem, and finding participants and helpers can really be frustrating and slow things up. The best thing to do now is to clear a little time and test your procedure, to make sure that things will go to plan when all your runners arrive. Imagine what a disaster it will be if you get them in only to find out your design is dreadfully flawed in some way. A run-through like this, as an investigation of how your variables are set up, and to see if the procedure is viable, is a **pilot procedure**. You'll only need a couple of runners for this. We usually ask each other to try out new ideas and procedures, or our long-suffering office-mates and PhD students! You might ask your housemates or loved ones to join in.

The kinds of things you are looking for in your pilot study are problems like, in our example, the size of the bags being carried. They may be too large for some people. Or the place you have chosen to do the running might be inappropriate, perhaps because people use it as a route through your building, spoiling your measurements with regular interruptions. In one embarrassing personal example of a procedure rather similar to this, we designed a project to measure how fast cars travelled along a stretch of country road. We drove there, all prepared with sandwiches and coffee for a good day's researching. It was a fine spring day, and we were looking forward to it, only to find out that *both* of our stopwatches didn't work properly! Best to check before you start.

If you find that anything needs changing, you should alter your design accordingly and try it again to make sure all is well. Finally, draw up a suitable response sheet. For our project it might look something like this.

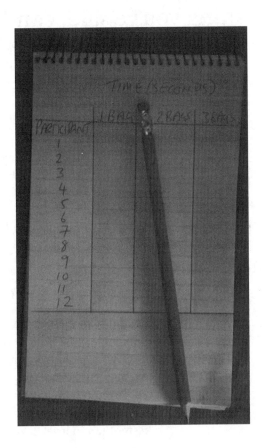

If you do this, your data will be perfectly organized. It makes the post-data-collection tasks very much easier than writing down numbers of scraps of paper that make no sense a day or so after you have made your careful measurements.

Let's take this opportunity to take a break at this point and check that you've done everything you need to before you begin collecting the data proper.

Summary and check points

1. Decide what to investigate.
2. Formulate a hypothesis.
3. Decide on the design.
4. Think it through.
5. Run a pilot study.
6. Alter the design if necessary.
7. Organize yourself – design a results sheet.
8. Collect your data!

Right. Enough already. I've done everything you've said, can I get on with it now?

Yes, you're ready. You should have a set of runners, some bags, a pen, a response sheet and a stopwatch that works. Get to work! Allocate each of your runners an order. If you have six runners, each order will be carried out once (as there are six possible orders in which three conditions can be tested). If you have twelve runners, each order will be carried out twice, and so on. Take your time, be organized and businesslike, and write down your data carefully. Once you've done all that you should end up with a data sheet that looks something like the one overleaf. *We've included some sample data in the web-companion to this book, so you can practice with it. We'll use the data shown on the data sheet here.*

Great, all done, I'm off to the bar to celebrate now that I am an expert researcher

Hold it. There are still a few things to do just yet. We need to take a look at the data you've collected and think about what they tell us. The first thing to do is summarize the data in some way. At the moment we have three columns of numbers that don't really tell us much at all. If you take a look at the numbers it seems clear that the running speeds in level 1 of the independent variable (one bag carried) are faster than in level 2, and these in turn are faster than in level 3, but this is not the case for all participants.

For some reason, participant 4 ran faster while carrying two bags than while carrying one bag. Similarly, participant number 9 seemed to run faster with three bags than with one or two bags. You often find this. It's the wonderful thing about research with people: the amazing, and often unexpected, variation between us. Whereas these variations may cause our hypothesis and predictions some difficulties, they are the result of a carefully designed procedure, so we cannot ignore them.

Summarize the data you say. So how do I do that?

First of all you will want to calculate the average time taken to run the distance used. Specifically, you will want to look at the mean running time for each condition, or level of our independent variable. You saw how to do this in Part 1, but we will spell it out one more time because we know some people are rather good at remembering the complicated things but for some reason forget the simple things like calculating a mean.

Step 1: Add up the times taken in each condition
Step 2: Divide the number by how many runners you have (in this case 12)

Your results sheet will now look like this. Notice the totals and means for each condition at the bottom.

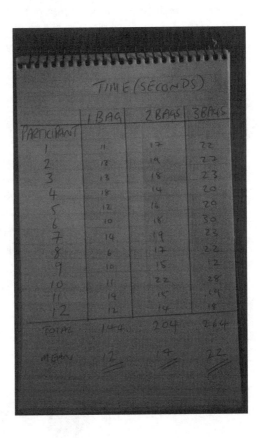

Most spreadsheet software can do this calculation for you if you ask it nicely, as well as other more complicated calculations, but a calculator is just as good, especially if you are in the middle of a field, or on a beach, or standing next to a country road without a laptop!

Well, that's pretty clear then. Can I go now?

Feel free, but you can't accept or reject your hypothesis yet. There's more to do. Looking at the numbers like this is called *eyeballing the data.* When you become really experienced you can sometimes draw accurate conclusions simply by the way the data feel, but this is not recommended. You can often miss things if you don't do it properly. Eyeballing the data is the first thing you do. It can give you an idea of what to look for, or if something really is going on.

The next thing to do is simplify the data further. Imagine you are looking at someone else's data. Your friend has completed some research, and wants to show you the results, for example. Unless you are very experienced with data, a page full of numbers is not the most obvious way for them to show off their findings. The best thing to do is draw a graph. There are plenty of ways of graphically representing data, and we discussed them in Part 1. So, decide on which graph to draw and plot it, either on paper or using some of the software available for job.

OK, I like drawing graphs. I can draw loads of them. How many do you want?

Yes, that's not an unusual question. We've often seen work from students with hundreds of graphs, most of which are completely irrelevant! One graph will do nicely thanks, but make sure it's the right one. The type of graph you draw depends on the type of data you have and the point you are trying to make. In this case a bar-chart is perfect. It allows us to show mean scores in each of the three levels of the independent variable. Make sure you label the axes correctly, and give the graph a title. Something like Figure 5.1 is the sort of thing you are aiming for.

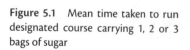

Figure 5.1 Mean time taken to run designated course carrying 1, 2 or 3 bags of sugar

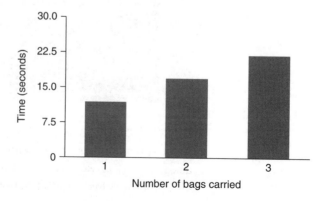

One glance at Figure 5.1 shows us that on average, people carrying one bag of sugar ran faster than those carrying two bags, who in turn ran faster than those carrying three bags.

I get it now. The graph helps us 'visualize' the data. What else do we need to do?

That's the spirit. You're on the home strait now. The next thing to tackle is another descriptive statistic which will give us some idea of how varied the data in each condition were. If you look at the raw data it's clear that some people ran reasonably fast and others not so fast. In Part 1, when we discussed the ages of two groups of people, we described the perils of only using a mean to describe a set of data. We'll not go over it all again, but essentially the problem lies in the fact that one large or small value can have a very big effect on the mean. For this reason it is important to show how varied the data that went into each mean were. In this case you should probably calculate a standard deviation for each mean. It's a pretty simple thing to do. Just remember to do one thing at a time, and try not to ask questions like 'Why do I take the square root of this?' You don't ask questions like that because the answer, while interesting to some people, is extraordinarily dull to nearly everyone else and not at all important to the end result. Just do what you're told and calculate the standard deviation for each of the three columns of numbers. If you are using the values in the example here, you should come up with the following values.

9	10	15	12
10	11	22	28
11	14	15	19
12	12	14	18
TOTAL	144	204	264
MEAN	12	17	22
ST DEV	2.89	2.37	4.86

That's really it for descriptive statistics. A mean and the appropriate measure of dispersion, which in this case is a standard deviation, and we're all done with describing the data.

I can see this coming. You're going to make me do hard calculations now aren't you?

Never. We're not hugely fond of sums, and you'll have noticed all we've done so far is add things together, do a spot of dividing, and take the occasional square root. That's hardly tricky analysis. It's true, though, that even though the data look pretty clear in your beautifully drawn and labelled graph you can't say for sure whether the numbers in each condition are *significantly* different from one another. By this we mean that, even though the means look different, that doesn't necessarily mean that there is a statistically significant difference between the different conditions. We need to perform inferential statistics on the data to allow us to see whether there really is a difference. In this case, we have three groups, each of which has produced a mean score. As you will learn at some stage, the most appropriate test for seeing whether the three groups differ from each other is something called one-way analysis of variance.

There's no need to worry about the details of this just yet – as we said, you'll probably learn those soon enough. What we want you to focus on for the moment is what we said in Part 1: all inferential statistical tests do the same thing, which is to produce a p value. This was, we hope you remember, the probability of seeing results like yours if the null hypothesis is correct. That is, it's the probability of seeing your results just by accident, if nothing interesting is really going on. More informally, it's the probability you will be wrong if you say you've discovered something.

In this case, when we did all the analyses of our runners' data, we got an end result of $p = .01$. This means there is a .01 – a 1% – probability of seeing this effect of carrying different numbers of bags if the number of bags people carry doesn't really affect how they run. In other words, there is a 1% chance of seeing this difference between one, two and three bags just by chance – or, in other words, there is a 1% chance we would be wrong if we said we had discovered that the number of bags makes a difference to how people run.

This 1% chance is nice and low: there's a 99% chance that the opposite is true, that the data we collected *were* affected by the number of bags people were carrying, and so a 99% chance that we will be right if we say we have discovered something. We said in Part 1 that the usual cut-off used in research is .05. Our p-value of .01 is comfortably below this, so we would almost certainly take this as a positive result. We would conclude that carrying more bags did indeed alter how fast people can run for this bus, which was exactly what we wanted to know all along.

chapter 6

designing a study: the best way to manage people

Ian:	What do you mean you're not going to do it?
Nigel:	I think it's pretty simple actually, Ian. He told me to do it but I'm just not going to.
Ian:	But he's your boss! If you don't do it you might get into trouble!
Nigel:	If he had asked me to do it and explained why he thinks it's a good idea and let me have some input then I probably would have, but as it is, it's a ridiculous idea and I absolutely refuse to lecture wearing a chicken outfit.
Ian:	You're just being argumentative. Get the chicken outfit on, and get in the lecture theatre. Do as you're told, or you'll be sacked and I'll never get that money back that I loaned you.
Nigel:	No, I will not, I will not, I absolutely refuse.
Ian:	So you're telling me that if your boss had treated you differently you'd have done it?
Nigel:	I might have done.
Ian:	So what is the best way to get things done in an organization then?
Nigel:	I'm not sure. How do we find out?

It is reasonably unlikely that you have been asked to give a lecture dressed as a chicken. It is, however, extremely likely that you have worked for people, or studied under teachers and lecturers, who have required that you do certain tasks in certain ways. Management is rather tricky to define actually. One phrase that often gets used is 'management is what managers do', suggesting the mercurial nature of the art. When faced with a problem of clarity, a 'back to basics' approach usually works for us. Our trusty dictionary tells us the word management finds its origin in the Latin word *manus* meaning 'hand', and subsequently the Italian word *maneggiare* which means 'to handle'. So management is something to do with the skill of handling people and things.

A little further investigation brings us to the Mary Parker Follett (died 1933) foundation. This organization, named after an extraordinary woman, is focused on supporting Follett's ideals, which include ideas on education and learning, and community and social support and development. It was Follett, writing at the beginning of the twentieth century, who coined phrases like 'win-win situation' and 'conflict-resolution'. She was clearly a person before her time and must be identified as a great pioneer and thinker, not least because she was a woman pioneering thinking in a very much male-dominated sector of a male-dominated world. Her definition of management was 'the art of getting things done through people' and we rather like that. It is a great skill and the best managers are creative and artistic in their approaches.

I read somewhere that Richard Branson is a natural leader of men, a born manager. I'm not a born manager, I'm a born 'sleeper' and 'stroller to the refrigerator'. If people can't learn how to do this, what's the point?

Just because someone is naturally brilliant at something doesn't mean others cannot learn from them. Wouldn't you just love to sit down with Richard Branson and learn his secret spell for making tons of money? The thing is, there isn't a secret spell, it is a skill like any other. It's just that some people are better at it than others.

We often hear that being a manager requires charisma (whatever that is!) and a natural ability with people. We are certain everybody who has had experiences with management would agree with this. There are some managers who just exude some sort of authority, not in a frightening bullying way, but in an almost magical way. This must be the charisma thing people talk about. There are also some managers who are extremely good at resolving conflicts, and making staff feel good about the job that they are doing in a way that encourages hard work and loyalty and a real desire to succeed and come to work each day. This must be the great ability at handling people and situations we have heard about. There is a flip side to the coin though. The managers who bully their staff and make them unhappy, who force changes through without discussion and explanation, who manage by intimidation and threats. Many have had this experience, and it is not a nice way to spend your working life.

In fact, good management is not always very obvious. Sometimes people respond extremely well to being left alone to get on with their work. These people are capable and self-motivated, and can be left to their own devices to come up with solutions and good ideas. Some people need a more hands-on approach from their managers, and these people respond better to positive reinforcement. This phrase comes from the psychology of learning, and work in the area was done by Burrhus Skinner, who investigated how different types of tasks are best taught to animals, particularly rats and pigeons. Skinner found rewarding an animal when it did something right was a strong incentive for it to do that thing again. However, he also found that punishing it when it did something wrong could also be a useful teaching tool. In schools and colleges, teachers are encouraged to reward good behaviour and performance rather than punishing bad behaviour, suggesting that positive reinforcement might be used as a useful management technique. Some people, though, respond very well to criticism and we must not rule this out as a technique that can, and does, sometimes encourage people to work hard towards their goals.

Yes, yes, but I'm not a manager, and I'm not in the least bit interested in becoming one. Why am I here again?

Ah, we see what you mean. You're having trouble finding your motivation for this bit of the book, yes? Well, use your imagination! A rather significant part of learning is the idea of 'transferable skills'. If you learn about something in one area of your education, you can apply it in another. In fact research design, which this book is all about, is one big collection of transferable skills. An ability to apply the techniques and methods we are addressing in this book *anywhere* will be extremely useful to you. Thinking about the best way to get things done through people (as Follett would put it) is something that you are certain to bump into in your lives, so why not use this as a way of honing your research skills? Let's have a think about it a little further.

It's not just in the working environment that we find authority figures, and a need to balance your aims and goals with the opinions and skills of others is common. Parents are often juggling busy jobs and households, and management policy and technique is something they often try to employ in an attempt to make things go more smoothly. If done correctly, 'conflicts' between work and home can be carefully 'resolved' with the minimum fuss, and the occasional 'break-down in relationships' between parents, and within families, can be brought to a 'satisfactory win-win resolution'. You see? This management speak is actually relevant to all sorts of things! Let's try it again with a university or college environment.

Students are required to attend seminars and classes, manage their time correctly and deal with their financial arrangements in as mature a fashion as possible, often adding to the money available to them through paid work. Writing papers and reports for lecturers who demand them on time and in certain formats often requires management-like skills. These may include managing your time correctly, and dealing with people who require your attention, such as family, friends and colleagues. The more successful students are often those who know their limitations; they know when, and, perhaps more importantly, how to ask for help from friends, colleagues, lecturers and professors. We always introduce 'working as a member of a team' into our course designs because we think it is a vital transferable life-skill, and a student's ability to do this is often a reflection of their management and workplace skill set. Getting things done with and through people is also, then, a rather important part of life as a student in whatever discipline they are engaged.

You've made your point. It's not all about 'learning to be a good manager'; it's about how you go about investigating it also

Let's start to think about what exactly it is that we are investigating here. How about the idea that 'some people are better managers than others'? In order to test this idea, all we would have to do is give two people a management test of some kind. One is certain to be better at it than the other person, even if it is by a small amount, showing us clearly that some people are better than others at managing. Yes?

No! This is the wrong approach. It would be a much better idea to take it slowly, and see whether one method of management is better than another. We have already said that some managers are fierce and forceful, and some are more encouraging and positive in their approach. Which of these is better? And how might we go about testing it?

The first thing to do is to make sure that you have your research idea in place, and the best way to do this is to take some time to think about a hypothesis. How about this:

'The best kind of manager is one that praises you all the time.'

Right, that's it then. That's my hypothesis, and I'm going to get on with it. I'm ready to make with the researching...

You are, of course, joking. This statement is really not at all sufficient. A good hypothesis clearly sets out what the procedure will address. A good hypothesis allows the reader to know what the variables are and gives a good idea of what to expect from the article or paper that they are reading. We need to say something about the type of management styles we will be comparing, and how we will go about comparing them. So a better hypothesis would be:

'A manager who provides regular positive encouragement to staff during a task achieves better results than the manager who regularly provides staff with negative criticism during the task.'

Now that's more like it. Here we have generated a 'one-tailed' or 'directional' hypothesis. This is because we have decided to anticipate what will happen in the task. We might decide to choose such a hypothesis if we had reason to believe positive encouragement was more successful than criticism as a management technique. For argument's sake, let us assume that we have some reason to believe this would happen – perhaps from other people's work that we have read – and as such we have chosen this one-tailed hypothesis.[1]

In this hypothesis we have something that we can identify as an independent variable and also something that gives us a clue as to the dependent variable. In this case the 'type of management style' is the thing that we are varying, so this is the independent variable. The thing it is influencing is the 'ability to perform a task'. The skill of the researcher is to ensure as best as they possibly can that the only thing influencing the dependent variable is the independent variable. In other words, the only thing that influences the outcome you are measuring is the thing that you are varying or altering in some way. In this case we now need to design a watertight procedure, so we can be absolutely sure that the method of management (in this case **operationalized** as whether the manager gives positive encouragement or negative criticism) is the only thing that influences how well the task is performed.

There is something else to consider, however. What if the method of management makes no difference at all? What if those carrying out the task respond better to a completely hands-off management approach, so that they perform better on the task if they are left

---

[1] Whether we choose a one-tailed or two-tailed hypothesis can influence our statistics later on, and can affect how likely it is you will find a significant result. We'll talk about that when we get to it.

completely alone to get on with it? This sets up another management style, which we can call a **control** condition.

What's a control condition and what's it for?

A control condition is an additional condition where the control group does not receive the 'treatment' or 'intervention' that your independent variable involves. In this case we are looking at whether different types of management intervention can influence performance of a task. So the control condition in this case would involve no management intervention at all. Performance in a control condition like this provides us with a baseline against which we can compare performance on the other levels of the independent variable. Control conditions are often used because they allow us to comment on whether our 'intervention' has done anything at all.

We now have three levels of our independent variable. and these are as follows:

Management Level 1 (ML1) – No management at all (Control)
Management Level 2 (ML2) – Positive Encouragement
Management Level 3 (ML3) – Negative Criticism

I can see how you are 'operationalizing' the independent variable, but what about the task? What am I going to get people to do exactly?

You are absolutely right: the independent variable is operationalized as ML1, ML2 and ML3. What we now need to do is have a think about how we might go about operationalizing the dependent variable. In the hypothesis we said something about a task of some kind, didn't we? What we need to do is arrive at some sort of task that allows us to measure how well someone, or a group of people, is performing. A creativity task of some kind is often a good plan here. This is where people are encouraged to identify as many uses for a selection of objects as they can. We've used this type of task in a practical later in the book, so let's use another one here. How about making words out of a selection of letters? This could be a little like one of those word games where letters are provided to participants and the task is to rearrange some or all of the letters in different ways to form as many words as possible.

Another task that would do very well is a word-search puzzle, where a number of words are hidden in a grid of letters. The task here is to identify the words by placing a line through them in the grid. With a word-search puzzle as your experimental task, you could give your participants the list of words they are to search for or you could, to make it harder, not give them a list at all, simply leaving them to identify words within the grid of letters. If you gave each participant a fixed amount of time, such as 1 minute, to do the task, you could then count up how many words each of them had identified. This would provide a way of *quantifying* how well they have done. In this case the dependent variable has been operationalized as 'number of words found in 1 minute'.

Summary

1. Decide on your research question
2. Turn it into a hypothesis
3. Identify how the independent and dependent variables will be operationalized

Ok, I've got it now. Before I start, though, what statistics will I need to do?

You see, that is *so* not the right question to ask right now. The real art of research is to be found in the design[2] – the statistics are used at the end of the process and, as long as you've designed your study well, choosing appropriate measures and collecting data properly, the eventual analysis will be easy. So let's not worry about this just now.

I've got the idea about the hypothesis, and operationalizing the variables, but how am I going to actually do the research?

What you are getting at here is the overall design of your project. Are you going to choose a repeated-measures design or an independent-samples design? We'll not spoil the surprise for you as to which one is appropriate here just yet, but in general there are good and bad points with both. We've already discussed them elsewhere in the book, but it would not hurt to go over this a little here in the context of this particular project. Essentially, the major problem with an independent-samples design is that individual differences can influence your dependent variable. In a repeated-measures design we find that order effects may become an issue. Before we go on, though, let's make sure

---

[2] It is probably sad to have to admit it, but when we read a report or paper where the researcher has taken great care to design an elegantly simple solution to their design problems we get rather excited. It's rather like reading a wonderfully phrased poem, or a carefully twisted and untied plot in a short story. It is something to admire and feel ever so slightly jealous that we did not think of it first!

we are absolutely clear what the research question is, and what the variables are.

In this project we are investigating whether different styles of 'management' influence a person's ability to carry out a task. The independent variable is 'different styles of management' and it is operationalized in three levels as 'providing positive encouragement – ML2', 'providing negative criticism – ML3' and 'no interaction at all – ML1'. The dependent variable is the 'ability to carry out a task' and it is operationalized here as 'the number of words correctly identified in a word-search puzzle in a given period of time'.

Let's say I choose a repeated-measures design. How would that work?

In a repeated-measures design each participant experiences every level of the independent variable. We have identified three levels, ML1, ML2 and ML3. There are six different orders in which these levels can be presented[3], and each order needs to be presented for you to fully counterbalance. This means you need to locate at least six different people, and probably 12 or 18 or more, so that all possible orders are presented equally often, countering the tendency for people to improve with practice. This practice effect would influence their performance on the task, which is your dependent variable.

Conversely, the opposite may happen. If everyone does the task in the same order they may get worse at it each time they do it. This might happen because they become tired. This fatigue effect would also influence your dependent variable. In each case (practice and fatigue) we have introduced a confound into the procedure. Each is an extraneous variable that has been allowed to become a confounding variable. That's why you need to counterbalance.

There are also other issues to consider in this case if you choose a repeated-measures design. Think yourself through the procedure and see what comes to mind.[4]

You turn up to the room in which the procedure is to take place, you are given a word-search puzzle, and you do as much of it as you can in the time given. Then there is delay while you have your all-important cup of coffee, and are set off on the next level of the independent variable, this time doing the task with a person looking over your shoulder telling you how well you are doing. You then take another break, and some more coffee, before doing the final level of the independent variable, where the word-search puzzle is accompanied by someone pointing out how badly you are doing and how you really need to try harder and do better. When you're done, you are thanked, and shown the way to the exit.

---

[3] Have a look back at the 'running for the bus' example for an explanation of why there are six orders.

[4] We do this kind of thing all the time. Thinking it through, and acting it out like this, can be a really useful way of identifying problems that might otherwise not occur to you.

Is there anything in this that you are unhappy with? There should be. The most obvious thing here is the coffee issue. We know that caffeine takes some time to reach its optimal effect on alertness but we also know from experience that there is an immediate feeling of alertness when drinking coffee, albeit psychological, that may well influence your performance on the task that follows it. This means the act of drinking a cup of coffee between levels of the independent variable has, possibly, influenced your dependent variable – your performance on the task. It is very important to do our best to keep everything as consistent as possible if choosing a repeated-measures design in an attempt to avoid issues like this.

Also, what about the word-search puzzles themselves? You can't give people the same puzzle three different times because they are very likely to get better at them on each occasion, because they will remember the answers. You'll need to locate three different word-search puzzles which are equally difficult to do or you will have another *order effect*. On that point, you may become tired and less alert as you move through the different levels of the independent variable and as such your performance on the puzzles may get worse as a result.

Finally, what about the type and frequency of 'management intervention' you will receive? You have to think carefully about how often a person will be praised or criticized, and train those giving the feedback very carefully to do it the right way. The coffee issue is very simple to control, you just need to be stern and tell the participants as firmly as possible that they are not allowed to have coffee until the end of the procedure. The other issues are not easy to control at all, particularly the point about the level of difficulty of each word-search puzzle.

The real nail in the coffin of a repeated-measures design for this particular procedure is the problem of identifying word-search puzzles with identical levels of difficulty. The effect if you could not do this (and we suspect that you most certainly cannot do this) would be very significant indeed, and really would confound your results.

Would an independent-samples design be any better then?

In short, for this particular project, yes, an independent-samples design is probably better. If you are asking whether independent-samples designs are better than repeated-measures designs in general, though, it all depends on what you mean by 'better'. If by 'better' you mean 'will it make for better results?' then probably not, because a result is a result, and as long as you have controlled your design properly one result is no 'better' than another.

Let's go through the thought process again and see what crops up if you imagine that you have chosen an independent-samples design. Remember, an independent-samples design is one where different people experience each level of the independent variable. In our case there are three levels, so we'll need three groups of people. Imagine the scene…

Arriving at the offices where the data are to be collected, you are greeted by a formally dressed woman, clearly part of the research team, and shown into a large room with three big tables. You take your place at the table indicated, and are joined by five others, In the middle of the table is a sign reading ML2. You have no idea what this means, but notice that the other tables have signs reading ML1 and ML3. At this moment, 12 well-dressed and official-looking men and women come into the room and stand at the front. An announcement is made, indicating that in front of everyone sitting at each of the three tables there is a piece of paper, on the other side of which is a word-search puzzle. Each also has a pencil. When instructed, everyone should turn the paper over at once and complete the puzzle as best they can. One minute will be allowed for this, at the end of which time everyone will be required immediately to put down their pencils. Each person on tables marked ML2 and ML3 will have one of the research team standing behind them throughout the process, and on occasion this research team member may comment to the person in front of them.

After a short delay the command to 'START' is given. Almost immediately, people began to find words in their puzzles. Those on table ML3 seem to be receiving rather critical comments about their performance. The person behind you is very complimentary about how you are doing, however, congratulating you and saying how clever you are. Those on the table marked ML1 have no one behind them, and so complete the puzzle in silence. After the minute has elapsed the command 'STOP NOW' is given. You stand, are thanked by the person behind you, leave the room and go home.

Nothing wrong there. I'm happy with that

We're not happy with it and neither should you be.[5] We've summarized some of the issues on page 126, but it's worth going over them in a little more detail here. First, the word-search puzzle. It is not clear from this whether everyone received the same one. If they did not, then a confound may have been introduced. If different groups are given a different word-search puzzle then any differences in performance between groups cannot be attributed entirely to the type of management feedback the participants were being given.

Second, everyone was in the same room, and everyone was, therefore, aware of what was going on around them. If those receiving negative criticism could hear that others on a table nearby were receiving positive encouragement they may have responded in a way

---

[5] It is fair to say that we've done this sort of thing before so problems are clearer to us. Do forgive us for coming across as being a little critical occasionally. Indeed, positive encouragement may well prove to be a better approach, in which case we'd like to rephrase this as 'Clearly the errors were far too obvious for you to waste time identifying explicitly, so well done for not pointing them out.'

not anticipated or controlled for by the researchers. It is possible their self-esteem may have suffered with the belief others were doing better than they were: they might have tried even harder if they knew others could hear the comments they were receiving. Anything like this, that is not controlled for but which may influence the independent variable, is a possible confound and must be carefully designed out of the procedure. The way to do this, of course, is to test each individual separately, in the same room, with the same surroundings. This way they would be unaware of the different groups and how different people were receiving different comments from the researchers, or indeed that some people were not subjected to any comments at all.

This brings us to another issue with the design as indicated in our 'think-through'. Twelve different researchers were used. Presumably each was carefully trained in the procedure, and how to go about providing the type of comments they were giving, but how can we be absolutely sure their comments were consistent? One researcher may have been harsher than another in giving negative criticism, or, similarly, one may have been much nicer than another in giving positive encouragement. We are also told that the 'official-looking' researchers are 'men and women'. This may also be an issue. Men may be perceived as more aggressive than women and so this may be a factor in the effect their comments may have. The best thing to do would be to use the same researcher each time, thereby keeping 'presence' and 'charisma' and 'natural authority' exactly the same for each participant.[6]

How about the number of people in each condition? In our example we had six people in each level of our independent variable. Are six really enough? The major problem with independent-samples designs is that individual differences might affect the dependent variable. How have the researchers controlled for the possibility of the world word-search puzzle champion finding their way into the ML2 group? Their world-class word-search puzzling would make the ML2 scores look very good indeed. When you design the procedure you need to do your best to control for such issues, and we've described how you might go about doing this elsewhere in the book. In short, you can either match people in each group (you'll need sets of three similar or identical people, with each allocated to a different level of the independent variable) or, more simply, you can minimize the influence of individual differences by using large groups. How large? As large as possible. Large enough that having one particularly good word-searcher wouldn't throw your results off completely.

---

[6] We have no idea what these things really are, but if they may be a factor in the procedure it's best to make sure you control for them!

You could also screen people for their experience with word-search puzzles, excluding anyone who does more than five a day, perhaps. That said, with large enough groups an addiction to word-search puzzles should not be a problem at all since large groups will hopefully provide similarly addicted people in each.

Problem	Solution
Participants may have received different puzzles. If this is the case, the results may be confounded.	Ensure each participant gets the same puzzle.
All participants completed the task in the same large, noisy room at the same time and were aware of feedback on other tables etc.	Test each participant separately in the same, quiet room.
Twelve different researchers were used to provide the 'Management Level'. Influence on the participants and 'severity' of 'feedback' may not be consistent.	Use one researcher to provide the positive and negative comments.
Relatively small groups were used, so individual differences between the groups may have influenced any differences found between groups.	Use big groups.

You see? If it's laid out like this, the solutions to the problems are relatively straightforward.

Both designs have their problems then. Does it really matter which one I choose if neither is much good?

It's not really true that you must always choose one design over another, but in some cases your choice is made for you. For instance, if you were interested in gender differences then you would select a task and see how well men and women complete it. You could not possibly choose a repeated-measures design in a case like this, because someone cannot be male for part of the procedure and female for another part of the procedure.[7] In many cases, though, you could choose either design, just as long as you are aware of the issues this raises and how you can avoid or minimize these. The most important thing is to make an informed and careful decision. In this case, for the management styles study, it is probably most appropriate to choose an independent-samples design.

---

[7] Please do refrain from sending emails pointing out this all depends on whether gender can in some way be reassigned between conditions. We know there may well be some sort of expensive, time-consuming, painful and ethically questionable way around this particular sticky issue, but we thought it best not to complicate matters any further.

Summarize all that for me will you?
It will save me reading it all again

No problem at all. It's always important to make summaries as you go. There can be a lot to take in.

- Identify your research question.[8]
- Turn it into a hypothesis.
- Identify your independent and dependent variables.
- Work out how to operationalize your variables.
- Decide on an overall design (independent- or repeated-measures).

I've advertised for participants on my department 'wanted' bulletin board.
I have 60 participants signed up for different
5-minute slots during the week. What now?

We're presuming that it is you who will act as the 'manager', providing comments to the participants. Make sure you know exactly how you are going to behave towards your participants when providing encouragement or negative criticism. The best way to do this is to run a short pilot procedure where you try out your 'nice friendly positive manager' persona with your 'not so nice critical manager' persona. It's also important to decide at which points, and also how often, you are going to respond to your participants. When we tried this on each other we found it easiest to make a response (either positive or negative) each time a word was found, and, on top of that, every 10 seconds. You can time this using a stopwatch, or a watch with a second hand. Don't set an alarm, though; this would provide the participant with a cue to what is coming and may change the influence any comment may have.

The last thing to do is assign each participant randomly to one of your three groups. It's simple enough just to assign the first 20 to group 1, the second 20 to group 2 and the last 20 to group 3, or you could get adventurous and use a hat or a 'random number generator' on your computer if you are really flash. Choose a suitable room; a small quiet room where you will not be disturbed will be ideal. Make

---

[8] We know this sounds terribly basic, but honestly, you'd be amazed at how many people either don't bother to do this, or forget it when they are writing up their work. These are invariably the people who lose their way and get confused. We advise students to write their research question down on a sticky-note and attach it to the corner of their computer screens so they do not forget what it is that they are doing. These students are more likely to remain focused.

sure that you write the group (management level) on each word-search puzzle, so you don't mix up your data when you are done (but write it as 'ML2' rather than 'Lovely positive feedback condition', as that's sure to tip the participant off!).

What do I do once I have all the data?

Once you are all done, add up the number of words identified on each of your completed word-search puzzles, then tabulate the data. You should end up with something like this: (we've only given five in each group here, you'll have more)

ML1 (control)	ML2 (positive)	ML3 (negative)
8	7	2
9	8	3
6	7	3
7	9	5
8	6	2

Next, produce some summary statistics. Calculate a mean and a standard deviation for the performance in each independent group. You'll get something that looks something like this:

	ML1 (control)	ML2(positive)	ML3(negative)
Mean	6.85	4.95	3.05
Standard Deviation	6.21	3.91	2.86

The numbers in the tables suggest that no management intervention (ML1) is better than either positive encouragement (ML2) or negative criticism (ML3), although we can't say this for sure just yet as we'll need to run some statistics to see if the difference is large enough to get excited about.

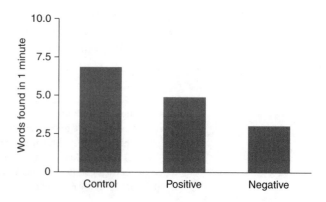

Presenting the data graphically helps make it clearer for people to see any possible relationships quickly. You might construct something like the graph above.

What's the point of descriptive statistics and graphs if they don't actually tell us whether we've found something or not?

It's not so much that they don't tell us whether we've found something or not, it's more that they help us talk about what we have. Descriptive statistics on their own do not answer research questions, but they are a very useful way of turning a lot of data into a few simple and manageable numbers. A graph[9] allows readers of your work to get quickly to the point and see what you have found.

Am I reading this graph wrongly? Doesn't it suggest that no management is best?

No, you're not wrong. It appears from our graph that the performance on the task in ML1 (that is, no management intervention whatsoever) is better than in either of the management levels. This is something of a surprise, but when conducting research you always have to be prepared for something like this.

This shows what a good job it was that we ran a control condition: without it, we would have made a mistake and simply assumed positive feedback is better than negative. Of course, in a study like this the implications of getting the wrong conclusion are not terribly serious. The worst that might happen is that a workforce gets annoyed at the constant management intervention they may begin to receive as a result. But imagine what might happen if a clinical trial had been designed badly, without a control condition! This issue appears regularly in debates of whether alternative therapies really do work. Providing the therapy may well be followed by an improvement in the person's condition, but without a control condition we are unable to say whether the condition might have improved all on its own with no treatment at all.

Hard sums next I imagine. Go on, just tell me, I'm ready for it

Hard sums indeed. Really, that's not the point of this book. Statistics are certainly a part of researching people but they're not really

---

[9] When we read new research, the first thing we look at is the results section, even though it comes later on in the paper. A well constructed graph is often worth a thousand words. There's another reason for using a graph then...It saves you writing more words!

central. As we said earlier, doing the right statistics to allow us to infer things from our findings is definitely something you will want to consider, but for now we want to take this opportunity to remind you they are simply a tool used by researchers in their work. The fun, engaging and really interesting bit comes in planning solutions to problems and carrying out the plans.

That said, we did run an analysis on our data to see how likely it was that what we saw in our sample – that no management was better than praise, which was better than criticism – would also be true in the wider population. You might have noticed that this study, like the study in the previous chapter, gives us three scores which we need to compare. In the last study we used a technique called analysis of variance, and because the overall task is the same now – comparing three scores to see if they are really different or not – we will use the same technique. It will be a slightly different version of the technique, as this time we have independent-measures data rather than repeated-measures data, but the end result is the same, a p-value.

In this study, the output of our analysis tells us that $p = .24$. This means there is a 24% chance of seeing the data we obtained just by chance, if management style really makes no difference to how people do word-search puzzles. In other words, there's a 24% chance we would be wrong if we said we had discovered something about our independent variable. This chance of being wrong is too large for comfort! We don't like to see p over .05, so in this case we would conclude that the different management styles do not really affect people's scores, and that the differences we saw in our graph just arose by chance – we probably wouldn't see the same thing if we tested other people.

As a final note, have another look at the table with the mean values in it and see if you can guess why the differences between the groups were not significant in the analysis.

Did you spot it? We did. Our experienced eyes immediately noticed that the standard deviations in all three groups were quite large compared with the means. This tells us that although, on average, the ML1 group got the highest score and the ML3 group got the lowest, the scores in each group must have varied a great deal around the mean. The differences between the groups were not consistent, and were probably just an illusion caused by some outliers – individuals getting particularly high or low scores.

Some things to think about

Before we set you off on your own to cut your teeth on some workshops, there are two important and useful things that you should be aware of. The first of these is to be aware that conducting research with people always carries some risk of causing you or your participants harm, and we need to be sure that we avoid this as much as possible. The second thing we want to mention is that forewarned is forearmed, and investigating what other people have already done, before you set off on your voyages of discovery, can save you an awful lot of trouble, time and money. Searching the existing research literature, in libraries or, most commonly these days, electronically, is advised. We'll describe how to go about that in just a moment.

Carrying out research ethically

One of the problems of doing research with people is that people are not necessarily as robust as you think they are. You may say something or do something that causes offence, or you may manage to physically harm people in the course of your research. This is to be avoided at all costs. The best way to do this is to think carefully before you begin collecting any data at all. Let us give you an example.

The 'management' workshop we have just discussed involves three levels of management. Let's just imagine that we had included a fourth level, let's call it 'hyper-aggressive management'. Your managers in this condition would be instructed to scream at the participants, poking them with sharpened sticks when they complained and abusing them verbally – calling them names, making up hurtful jibes. Overall, your managers in this condition would be instructed to give their participants an extremely hard time.

The idea here might be that pushing people around, possibly even making them frightened of their management, may encourage more work from them. It's not such a crazy idea: some managers thrive on inducing fear and discomfort in their staff, and management have been known to make staff so unhappy that they find themselves working so hard that they burn out, and suffer all sorts of problems directly as a result of their job.

It might be fine to study a workplace where such appallingly aggressive management tactics are already being used. However, it would be unethical to manipulate your carefully constructed investigation of management styles to include such a management type, because this is very likely to cause your participants considerable discomfort.

'Ah,' you might say, 'but I am a scientist, and it is not my problem if a few people get harmed along the way. I shall pursue the truth whatever the cost!' And to this we say, 'Ah yourself, you are no scientist if you act that way. You are bringing this beautiful pursuit into disrepute and you should be ashamed of yourself and banned from practising research with people at all costs.'

The thing is, it's not that we, your authors, are particularly soft about research. Many of our students would tell you that we are just the opposite. It is more that we are of the mind that research should be carried out with no harm to those who take part.

And this is above all the key principle which should guide all research with humans: *you should aim above all to cause no harm to your participants.*

Of course in some circumstances a form of 'harm' might be called for. For example, Ian has colleagues who study people's responses to pain. In their experiments they have no option but to make people suffer pain temporarily.

In situations like this, it is your duty to instruct the participants exactly what will happen to them and why, and make absolutely certain that you have their permission before carrying anything out. This process is called getting **informed consent**: the participant agrees to take part, knowing what is involved. For instance, we work at universities in Northern Europe. For this reason there is no need at all for our tiny offices to be air-conditioned. On the two or three hot days we experience every year, appropriate comfort can usually be found by opening a window and turning on a fan. However, we are aware that heat is often a real problem in many offices worldwide and air-conditioning is often used to provide a more comfortable working environment. Imagine you were employed to see whether turning off the air-conditioning really made any difference to people's output. It's expensive to run, after all, so a company may stand to save a lot of money by doing away with a/c. Imagine now that you want to run some controlled measurements before setting off to Dallas to test out your ideas on a real workforce.

How hot is too hot for a person's workplace, do you think? Let's say, 43 degrees Celsius (110 degrees Fahrenheit). You heat up your testing room to the required temperature and set your participants off on your chosen task. 30 minutes later three have melted entirely and one is crawling for the door in search of water. You have physically caused your participants harm, which is not something you should do. Not only have you assaulted them, but your science is of no use to you or anyone else as your findings do not tell you anything much about your research problem. All you know is that this temperature is enough to make four people very unhappy indeed.

Let's take another example. Let's say that a local television company has received complaints from viewers about a series it is showing late at night on different weapons and the damage they can do to the human body. Graphic images of animal carcasses and soldiers cut down during war are shown and people have felt the need to complain. The television company is being taken to court with a possible view to prosecuting them for doing harm to viewers. It is your job to see whether the types of images shown really do cause people to be upset, and if so how upset and whether it constitutes the kind of harm that the law would regard as unacceptable. How you go about this involves a delicate dance between the law, scientific pursuit, moral values and participant consent. Informing the participants what they might experience is vital, but informing them may prime them and influence your measurements of their 'distress'. In cases like these think very carefully before embarking on your research. The first thing to do with all cases like this is to consult your professional body.

Professional Bodies

A professional body is an organization that oversees your particular line of work. For instance, if you are a sociologist working in North America your professional body will be the American Sociological Association (ASA). In the United Kingdom it's the British Sociological Association (BSA). If you are working in media or communication studies in the UK you might consider talking to the Media Communication and Cultural Studies Association (MeCCSA). Notice that international bodies do exist but you must also look to the 'local' national bodies for judgements of what is acceptable in your profession in your country, as it is usually in individual countries that legal action would be taken if something went wrong. For instance, there is an international association of applied psychology but in the United States the APA (American Psychological Association) has certain rules of conduct that are slightly different from those of the BPS (British Psychological Association). You may be required by your professional body to ensure an ethically correct approach, for instance by carrying out certain checks and gathering a signed consent form from each of your participants.

In all cases where you may be unsure, professional advice is to be strongly recommended. The first person to ask is a member of staff at the organization you work or study at. If you are reading this book at a university or college then you will have access to tutors who will be able to guide you. If you are using this book in your workplace and no-one can help you, then your relevant professional body can be contacted directly.

Even if the field in which you work does not tend to focus on ethical considerations as a central foundation (television production comes to mind!), you are strongly advised still to work from an ethical approach in which the wellbeing of your participants comes before anything else, such as viewing figures or advertising revenue. It not only protects your participants from you, but protects you from your participants. If you are clear what will happen, and they have agreed, then there is an understanding and you are less likely to experience complaints or any other problems following your work.

We always find it useful to use the following checklist and ask ourselves these questions before we begin collecting data of any kind.

- Has your participant provided informed consent? To do this you need carefully to inform your participants of what will happen, make sure they understand and have had the chance to ask you any questions. They should then indicate their consent clearly. The best way to do this is to construct a consent form of some kind, indicating the participant's name, details of your research and their signature. The consent form should also contain all the details of your study, written down, so it is clear exactly what you told your participants they were agreeing to. (We have included one of our consent forms on the website, so you can see what we mean.)
- Do you need to deceive your participants? Sometimes you just have to be economical with the truth about your research. For instance, if you are investigating whether tourists prefer one brochure or another, and you have manipulated the number of tanned beautiful bodies to see if this influences them, pointing this manipulation out in advance may spoil your research as their answers may be coloured by this prior knowledge. You should be very careful to deceive your participants as little as possible and only if the research calls for it.
- Have you made it clear that they can leave at any time? You should not restrain your participants in any way. If they are unhappy or uncomfortable and want to leave at any time you must let them. You must also point out to them that they are free to leave if they wish, whenever they wish, and that there will be no penalties or come-backs if they do – for instance, if they are being paid for taking part, they get the money even if they want to leave half-way through the procedure.
- Have you made it clear that the information you collect will be confidential? There may be implications for people who provide opinions or information on, say, gender in the workplace, religious views, etc. To ensure a candid response and to make the participant feel comfortable about providing any information, you should always make it clear any information, be it the data provided or the name and address of the participant, will remain confidential. This will often involve storing all the participant's data in a way where they cannot be identified – no names, addresses, etc.
- Are you sure of the protection of your participant and yourself? If there is any chance of you or your participant being harmed then think again. If ethical concerns are too great, and you do not have an amazing justification for your research, clearly showing it to be in the public interest, you may simply not be able to conduct the study you are planning.
- Have you prepared a debriefing procedure? At the end of the procedure you should always explain to your participants what was done and why. Any deception should be revealed at this stage. The participant should be given the time to sit with you and talk it through until they are content. After a debrief, a participant should be exactly in the same state they would have been in (same level of anxiety, etc.) if they had never done your study.

As we said above, specific ethical standards can vary from discipline to discipline, and here we have identified those which are common to most. You should make sure you read more about any ethical procedures and standards that apply to your specific field before conducting your own research.

What's already been done?

It's just possible that the idea you have for your research has already been done at least once before. It's also extremely likely that there is research already out there that you might find useful and informative in your design. Why reinvent the wheel? If it's already been done, save yourself time, trouble and effort by looking it up.

It is unlikely, though, that any previous research in the area that interests you has been done exactly as you would like. It may employ different variables, or operationalize the variables differently. Knowing these things can be really useful and informative.

The facilities you will have for searching through existing research will depend on where you are working. In companies, for instance, you may well have access to internal, private and technical reports that may be extremely useful. If you are working at a university or college you may well have access to a number of electronic resources and search engines for which your institution pays (and which require licence codes and passwords). We all have access to the wonderful Internet, though, and it's a good place to start searching for what has been done before, just to give you an idea of what is available.

Ultimately, however, looking further than a search engine on the web is strongly advised. You can do this at libraries and often through portals to indexes that look at how often a paper has been cited by someone else and who they themselves cited in their work. A day or so researching the existing body of work is strongly advised. At the beginning of this management practical we started by describing what management is, and a brief history to set the scene. This is the kind of thing you can do, using existing literature, when beginning to report your work. It adds context. A search through the Internet will provide this sort of information. More specific research will involve a more concerted and exhaustive search.

chapter 7

practical: it's a matter of taste

Here we use a simple procedure, which involves people trying two drinks and deciding which they like best. Because the experiment is so simple you will easily see the need for extremely tight control in a study of this sort. Thinking about how you would control this procedure is a really good exercise in spotting potential confounds in your studies.

Topics covered: variables, repeated-measures design, extraneous variables, confounding variables, experimenter effect, experimental method, blind testing, double-blind procedure, two-alternative forced choice, binomial test.

You will need: some drinks, two identical containers to serve them in, a blindfold (possibly).

Background

When we were youths (and the diligent Internet researchers amongst you can probably use what we are about to say to discover how old we are), a well-known cola company used to run television adverts in which suspiciously good-looking people would drink two different brands of cola without knowing which was which. They would say which they preferred and then the presenter would whip off the covers to reveal the best-tasting cola had been the brand paying for the advertising. Shocking! Everyone would smile a lot and reflect on the importance of avoiding rival brands of cola.

This procedure, although devised by advertisers, is perfect for considering all sorts of interesting experimental design issues, especially the need to be really careful about controlling everything when planning a study. Keeping control during an experiment is essential in order to make sure no **extraneous variables** – things you are not interested in – can affect your results. Extraneous variables in this study could be things like the shape of the glass the person drinks out of, or the temperature of the drink – anything that might affect people's responses but which you are not interested in. If an extraneous variable does affect your results it becomes a **confounding variable** and your findings are no longer reliable: any discoveries you make *might* be interesting, but they might instead be caused by the confound, and so you can reach no firm conclusions. So before you carry out your own version of the cola challenge, let's think about some of the ways it could go wrong.

Let's say you have a participant about to sample two different drinks and say which they prefer. What you really want is their unbiased opinion about which drink is best, but there are lots of possible confounding variables – in other words, there are lots of ways their answer could be affected by more than just the drinks' flavours. First, the drinks might look different. If a person is tasting a glass of red wine and a glass of white wine, then, as long as they can see the glasses, it is immediately obvious to them which drink is which. In this case their decision might be influenced not just by the taste, but also by their knowledge or opinions – perhaps they think 'I know I prefer red wine to white' and so say the red is best without really thinking about how the two samples taste. Or perhaps they believe a preference for red wine is in some way 'classier' and so choose it for this reason.

This wasn't a problem with colas, which all look the same, but in a situation where the drinks look at all different you would need to stop people seeing them. You might not be surprised to learn that if you stop people seeing the drinks, this is an example of **blind testing**! Blind testing doesn't necessarily mean not being able to see something (although it does in this case), but rather means the participant cannot tell which **condition**, or which level of the independent variable, they are taking part in – they are 'blind' to the condition. In this case they will take part in a condition where they taste drink A and a condition where they taste drink B. We want them not to know which is which: we want them blind.

In fact, blind testing can take two forms. You can make people blind to the condition they are in by not telling them which condition they are in, and taking steps to prevent them discovering it – in this experiment, for example, you might make them wear a blindfold when they drink. Keeping them blind in this way will stop their decisions being influenced by what they see or what they know.

But even if you keep a participant blind to what you are testing, it is still possible they will be influenced by what *you* see or know. Imagine *you* own the drinks company that is carrying out this experiment, and are doing the testing to see whether people prefer your product or your arch-rival's product. In this case, where you would obviously want people to prefer your drink, it's entirely possible the testing process would go something like this:

You:	Here, taste this one.
Participant:	Mmm, nice.
You:	What?! Oh. Well, now taste *this* one!

In this case, it would be pretty clear to the participant, even if they were wearing a blindfold, that you expected them to like the second drink more than the first. This could easily influence their responses. This would be an example of an **experimenter effect**, where the person doing the testing affects the participants' responses.

But I don't own a cola company ...

Even if you don't really care either way what the participant says, it is always possible that something in your manner will alert the participant to which condition they are taking part in, meaning they are no longer blind. A really good way of controlling for this possible experimenter effect confound is to ensure that both the participant *and* the experimenter don't know what condition the participant is experiencing. This is known as a **double-blind** procedure, since both people do not know what condition the participant is in. (The first example, where the participant didn't know what was happening but the experimenter did, is known as a **single-blind** procedure.)

You could arrange a double-blind procedure in your drinks test by getting another person to prepare the drinks and give them to you labelled simply A and B, before you give them to the participant.[1] All you know is that the drinks have different names – you don't know what they are and so cannot possibly alert the participant to what they are drinking, even with subtle, subconscious clues. The double-blind method gives really tightly controlled designs and is normal in drug trials, where the person who gives the medicines to the participants does not know whether each participant is getting a real drug or a **placebo**, and so cannot possibly alert the participant through their manner.

Anything else I need to control?

Why, yes. There are plenty of other possible confounds we would need to consider in this drinks test. The two drinks would need to be presented in exactly the same type of container, or else this could

---

[1] Ideally, you would want your helper to label the drinks then leave them somewhere for you to collect: if they handed the drinks to you, you might pick up clues from them as to which drink is which.

affect people's responses, and the drinks would need to be at the same temperature. Try to think of some other possible confounds before going further.

What did you get? Some more possible confounds we thought of included the size of the drink (if participants swallow a huge amount of one drink and a sip of the other, this might affect their responses) and familiarity with the drinks (if your participants know one of your drinks well, they might recognize what they are drinking). We also thought of various possible confounds related to the participants: some may smoke and have a poorer sense of taste; some may have colds, which affect their sense of smell. A woman's sense of smell can be dramatically heightened by her hormonal levels. And finally, taste is the sort of ability that varies over the course of the day, so ideally you would test all your participants at around the same time. All these things would have to be controlled in your study, otherwise whatever results you find might be the result of a confound, rather than a difference between the drinks.

All this comes down to one simple principle: in an **experiment** *nothing* should vary except the thing you are interested in. In this case, the thing you are interested in is 'type of drink' and the measure you are interested in is how often each drink is chosen as the best. Nothing else should vary, and your task as an experimenter is to do everything you can to ensure only your independent variables change during the course of the experiment.

Method
Design

We are going to recommend you carry out this study like the original commercial, where people taste two drinks and choose the one they prefer. As such, this is a procedure that *must* use a **repeated-measures** design – everybody tastes both drinks. Your **research question** will simply be something like 'Do people prefer one drink to the other?'

Incidentally, it *would* be possible to address this same basic question – which of two drinks do people prefer – using an **independent-measures** design, but this would be more complex. If each participant only tasted one drink you would need to get them to make some sort of rating: for example, each person might taste a drink and give it a rating of 1 to 10. You would then compare the average rating for the two drinks. This would work in principle, but not only would you need more participants than in a repeated-measures design, you would also have to start worrying about whether everybody was using the rating scale in the same way. A repeated-measures design avoids all these concerns and so is greatly to be preferred in this study. Each person tastes both drinks and picks the one they prefer – this is much simpler and has far less to go wrong. *Simplicity is good.*

There is a technical term for the method you are using to look at people's preferences, which is the **two-alternative forced-choice** technique (or 2AFC to its friends). That's because you are giving people two options and forcing them to select just one. We should say that by 'forced choice' we don't mean you threaten the participants with weapons or blackmail (tempting as this may be sometimes). What this means is that you don't let the participants say they like both drinks equally; instead they *must* choose one or the other as their favourite – that's the forced bit. The 2AFC technique only works with repeated-measures designs.

You could, if you wanted, choose to carry out this procedure with more than two drinks. For example, you could give people three or four different drinks and ask them to choose their favourite. However, this becomes a great deal more complicated than two. Let's say you taste drink A, then drink B, then drink C, then make a decision about which is your favourite. At this point, drink C is fresh in your memory. When you tested drink C, you had just tasted drink B and so could easily tell if it tasted better or worse. But you never tasted drink C next to drink A, and so never made a direct comparison. So you are welcome if you like to use more than two drinks, but you would need to think very carefully about exactly how you would make this more complex design work. (Hint: if you wanted people to select their favourite of three drinks, you would probably need to let your participants drink more than three times.)

So, to summarize, the **independent variable** in this study is 'drink type' and the **dependent variable** – the thing you are measuring, which might depend on the independent variable – is people's drink preference. As a true experiment you are hoping to keep everything constant except the drink, which will vary between two **levels** – two different types of drink. If people's preferences change whenever the drink changes, you can know that people prefer one drink to the other.

pedant point Pedants like us take an almost obscene delight in knowing that the word 'alternative' should only be used when there are two options. So it is okay to say 'The alternative to being male is being female' but it is not correct to say 'If we can't visit France next year, what alternatives are there?' As such, some people prefer to use the term 'one-alternative forced-choice' to describe the process of making people choose one alternative out of the two available. This is, we admit, rather confusing, but at least you are now warned if you ever see the term.

ALTERNATIVES

Design checklist

■ Decide on a single-blind or double-blind procedure. If using double-blind, decide how you will make sure the person speaking to the participants does not know what the drinks are.

■ Decide on a repeated- or independent-measures design. (Hint: choose repeated-measures as it is much better for this research question.)

■ Decide whether you will use a two-alternative task or a task with more than two drinks. (Hint: keep it simple and choose two!)

Participants

As with almost all studies, you will need to run this test on more than one person – there is very little useful information to be learnt from knowing a single person's opinions. In fact, as with most research, the more people you can study the better, but if you are doing this as a demonstration, rather than genuinely to explore people's taste preferences, you should be fine with as few as 20–30 people.

You can run this practical on almost any **opportunity sample**, although you would probably want to avoid groups of people who might have particularly high levels of skill or experience in tasting things – wine waiters, chefs, brewers, and so on. Just remember to think about how your results might be generalized: if you do your study on a sample of students, you may only be able legitimately to generalize your findings to other students.

Materials

You need two different types of drink. It doesn't really matter too much what these are – cola versus diet cola (of the same brand), red versus white wine (at the same temperature), coffee versus tea, or whatever.

Oh, and as an ethical point you might want to avoid choosing any drinks that might make people ill, violate their principles or the law (e.g., avoid alcohol with people who might not drink it, or be too young to drink it), and so on.

Data collection

The main thing to watch out for whenever you use a repeated-measures design is to avoid any **order effects**. Let's say you have two drinks labelled A and B. If drink A is always tasted first and has a really startling or disgusting flavour, people might never really pay full attention to drink B. Or if drink A always comes first, people would always taste drink B with the taste of drink A already in their mouths but never vice versa. So you would want to make sure you **counterbalanced** the order, such that half the participants taste drink A then drink B, and half taste the drinks the other way round. By counterbalancing, you guarantee any order influences will be cancelled out: half the people taste drink A having just tasted drink B, and exactly the same number have the opposite pattern. We'll leave it to you to choose a method of counterbalancing you are happy with.[2]

If your drinks don't look identical, you might want to use opaque containers, or blindfold your participants when you test them. Brief each participant using some **standardized instructions**. These should tell the participant they will taste two drinks and that at the end they should say which they like the most. You should also give them some idea of how much you are expecting them to swallow from each drink! Then give them the first drink, then the second, then ask which they preferred. Note their response.

Procedure checklist

- If using a double-blind procedure, have somebody else randomly allocate the title Drink A to one drink and Drink B to the other. If the drinks don't look identical, they should be put into containers where the participant and the tester cannot see the difference.
- Brief each participant with your standardized instructions.
- Blindfold them if necessary.
- Let them taste one drink then the other, counterbalancing the order. Keep everything constant except the type of drink (drinking vessel, amount drunk, temperature, etc).
- Record their preferred drink.

Results

Looking at your data

The data from this study will be very simple. For your two drinks you simply need to count up how often each was preferred. For example, let's say you tested 50 people with ordinary cola and diet cola. You might find 36 people preferred the ordinary cola and 14 the diet cola. In this case you wouldn't just want to write '36 people preferred the ordinary cola' because that tells us nothing on its own: saying '36 people preferred the ordinary cola' means one thing when you have tested 36 people and means something *very* different when you have tested 800 people! So you need some way of showing not just how

---

[2] One possible method is to create tokens that indicate the order. So if you have 30 participants you would want 15 tokens (e.g., slips of paper) which indicate A then B and 15 which indicate B then A – you draw one at random for each participant. Or you can toss a coin for each participant. The first method *guarantees* half the participants get one order and half get the other and so is probably better for small groups.

many participants preferred each drink, but also how many participants there were in total. One way would be to do something like this:

Number of participants, out of 50, who preferred each drink

Preferred ordinary cola	Preferred diet cola
36	14

However, a more elegant way of doing this is to divide each number by the total number of participants to get the *proportion* of participants who preferred each drink. 36 people out of 50 preferred ordinary cola. 36/50 = .72. 14 people out of 50 preferred diet cola. 14/50 = .28. If we put these values in a table we get:

Proportion of participants who preferred each drink

Preferred ordinary cola	Preferred diet cola
.72	.28

As well as being more elegant, using proportions is also more consistent, and makes it easy to compare studies with one another. Imagine you found the results we've shown above. And imagine also that your friend Dr Crumplezone carried out the same study and found that, out of 124 participants, 88 preferred the ordinary cola. Using raw numbers you would have to write something like this:

'In our study, 36 out of 50 participants preferred the ordinary cola. In Dr Crumplezone's study 88 out of 124 participants preferred the ordinary cola.'

Did your studies agree, or did they find something different? It's really difficult to tell. But using proportions it becomes simple:

'In our study, a proportion of .72 preferred the ordinary cola. In Dr Crumplezone's study a proportion of .71 preferred the ordinary cola.'

You can immediately see that the two studies found almost exactly the same result. You can also multiply each proportion by 100 to make them into percentages if you prefer – which in this case would give 72% and 28%. One more advantage of proportions is that they can be nicely presented using **pie-charts**[3], which almost everybody understands.

---

[3] The French call the pie-chart 'Le Camembert', after the famously delicious circular cheese. There is no reason for this footnote other than that we rather like this fact. Oh, and if you happen to be passing through Normandy, Ian can recommend a visit to the Camembert Museum in … well, Camembert.

When you calculate proportions, you divide the number of people in each category by the total number of people you tested. This means proportions *always* fall somewhere between 0 and 1. If this doesn't make sense to you immediately, imagine all 50 of your participants preferred diet cola. This would mean 50 out of 50 preferred this drink, and 50/50 = 1. If *none* of your participants preferred diet cola, this would be 0 out of 50, and 0/50 = 0. So there is no way for the proportion to get higher than 1 or lower than 0.

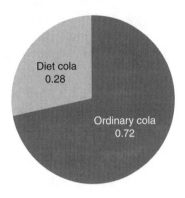

With proportions, it is always a good idea to check they add up to 1 – or to 100 if you are working with percentages – to help spot any mistakes you might have made. In our example .72 + .28 = 1, so we know we haven't made any obvious errors when processing our data.

pedant point

LEADING ZEROS

Proportions are a type of number that can never go above 1. Some people (including us) prefer to write numbers that can never go above 1 without a zero at the beginning. So it would be '.72' rather than '0.72'. This also applies to probabilities – you'll notice we don't have zeros on our *p*-values in this book.

Finally, when using proportions, there is no need for any measure of **dispersion**. This is because proportions are simply a number of people (36 out of 50), rather than averages.

Statistical thinking

At the end of this study, you will have two proportions: the proportion of people in your sample who preferred one drink and the proportion who preferred the other. These two groups are *mutually exclusive*, meaning a person can only contribute to one proportion or the other. You cannot like ordinary cola best *and* like diet cola best, no matter how indecisive you are![4]

The research question you will be interested in is whether, overall, one drink is more popular than the other. Let's say the proportion preferring drink A is .50 and the proportion preferring drink B is also .50. In this case, it is clear both drinks are exactly equally popular. It is a 50:50 split.

What if the proportion preferring drink A were .48 and the proportion preferring drink B were .52? In this case, although drink B was chosen slightly more often, it is unlikely you would get very excited by such a small difference. A difference this small could easily arise through chance – it might only take one person to move from preferring drink A to drink B to give you a difference of this size, and you really don't want to base any conclusions on one person's opinion.

But what if the proportion preferring drink A were .21 and the proportion preferring drink B were .79? In this case, there is a much clearer preference for drink B. Indeed, this difference is so large it is unlikely to have arisen in your sample just by chance. You wouldn't expect to get a difference this big just because you were unlucky with the people you sampled, for example. Instead, a 21:79 split almost certainly tells you drink B is genuinely more popular than drink A.[5]

Whatever you are researching, the **null hypothesis** always states there is nothing interesting happening. So in a study like this, the null hypothesis would say there is no preference for one drink over the other. In this case, because we have two mutually exclusive proportions, we look in a statistics book and learn that the appropriate analysis is a **binomial test**. This tells you the probability of any preference you might have seen in your sample for one drink over the other arising purely through chance.

For example, let's say ordinary cola and diet cola are really just as popular as each other – meaning that, if it were somehow possible to test the whole population you are interested in, the two drinks would be chosen equally often. If the two drinks are equally popular in the population, you would expect to see the same in your sample: roughly half the sample should prefer each drink. Indeed, if the two drinks are equally popular in the population, it would be pretty odd if they were not equally popular in your sample. What this means is that, if the two drinks aren't equally popular in your sample, you need to consider the possibility there is something interesting going

---

[4] Our procedure ensured the groups were mutually exclusive by using the forced-choice technique.

[5] And the larger your sample, the more you can be certain about this.

on. Perhaps the reason one drink was more popular in your sample is that it is more popular in the population.

This might be a little abstract, so as an illustration we have just carried out a quick binomial test on the numbers we have used here. This test revealed that if ordinary cola and diet cola genuinely are equally popular, the probability that 36 people in a sample of 50 would choose one over the other is $p = .003$ – in other words, there is only a 0.3% chance of this happening in your sample as a fluke event if there is no real preference for one drink over the other.[6]

What this means is that, if the drinks are equally popular in the whole population, it is *really* unlikely that 36 people would prefer one drink over the other out of a sample of 50. As such, if we found a preference in our sample that was this strong, we'd reject the idea that this is a coincidence and decide instead that the population probably has a preference, like our sample did. The two types of cola are not equally popular. And this would be the answer to the research question.

Discussion

When considering the lessons learnt from this study, you will probably want to focus on what you did and did not control. Even though this was a very simple experiment, there was a big list of things you had to do to avoid any biases which might make your results untrustworthy. You ensured the participants included no professional tasters; you hid any visible differences between the drinks. You presented the drinks in identical cups, at the same temperature, and had each person drink the same amount of fluid. You counterbalanced the order in which the drinks were sampled. You may even have hidden the identities of the drinks from yourself.

This level of control – which, we admit, can look obsessive to an outsider – is essential if you want to carry out good experiments. If you can manage this level of control, your findings will be **robust**. This means you can have a lot of confidence in them and can know it is unlikely that anybody will show you made mistakes.

If you had not taken such care over the control in this experiment, your findings would not be robust. Let's say you had done almost nothing to control your study – you told your participants what the

---

[6] The binomial test is a really useful one to know for everyday life. We have to confess that when we see commercials making claims like '65% of women said the cream make their skin feel softer*', with a microscopic footnote saying something like '*Out of 40 women tested', we run off and use a binomial test to see whether the advertisers are blowing hot air. (If they claimed a 65% preference was interesting in a sample of 40 people, they would indeed be pulling a fast one: $p = .37$.)

two drinks were going to be, you gave everybody drink A before drink B, and so on. In this case, it really doesn't matter what you find. You might find something really amazing, like 99% of your sample preferred drink B. But if you tried to conclude that drink B is better, we would just point out that your findings aren't robust and that there are any number of other explanations.

So the idea of the experimental method is to *rule out any other explanation for what you find.* For this reason, it is good to get into the habit of questioning yourself when you plan an experiment. Indeed, it can be a good idea to practise being your own worst enemy! Say to yourself 'What am I expecting to find? Okay, now what if somebody I hate found that? How would I try to show they were wrong? How else might I explain their findings to make them look stupid?' If you think like this, scary as it sounds, you will learn to spot possible mistakes early on, before you have collected any data and when it is still early enough to do something about it by improving your design. With practice, this all becomes second nature and you start to spot possible problems automatically – and with other people's work as well as your own.

So, in the interests of fairness, we have to point out a possible problem we have spotted with our own study as we have described it here (as you should always do when writing about your research[7]). We suggested that if people know what they are drinking, their knowledge or opinions about that drink might affect their judgement. Even in a careful double-blind version of the procedure we have given here, it is possible that some participants would recognize the flavour of a drink. For example, if you compare ordinary cola with diet cola, you might have some participants who recognize the flavour of diet cola (which is, after all, fairly distinctive), and deliberately choose it because they prefer diet drinks.

Alternative versions

There is a lot of scope to vary this procedure. You can use any pairs of drinks you like (within reason!). You can also do it with food: you could give people two different types of bread, two different types of cake or whatever. You could even do it with music: you might let people listen to two pieces of music and say which they prefer. Just remember that they might recognize the performer, or the musical style, and be swayed by what they think about those subjects.

As we mentioned above, it is also possible to do versions of this design where people choose from more than two options. This gets a

---

[7] If you don't point out any problems you spot, somebody else will.

lot more complicated, and you will probably need to allow people to make multiple comparisons before choosing a favourite. For example, if there are three options you should probably let them compare A with B, A with C and B with C before making a choice. You might even let them sample the three drinks as often as they like before they decide. Note also that, if you have more than two options, you can no longer use the binomial test, as this only works with two mutually exclusive categories. When you have more than two categories, you need to use a **chi-squared** test instead. (Specifically, you would probably need a *goodness-of-fit chi-squared* test.)

chapter 8

practical: abnormal cells on a slide – how people search for things

Here we will use a simple procedure to look at some experimental design issues such as counterbalancing and the choice between repeated- and independent-measures designs. We will also show you an interesting example of mental chronometry, where the time people take to complete a task can reveal how they are doing it.

Topics covered: variables, order effects, counterbalancing, repeated-measures, independent-measures.

You will need: a timer (a stopwatch is best, but an ordinary watch or clock is okay), target sheets (we'll tell you how to make these), paper for recording people's scores.

Background

People who work in medical laboratories commonly need to search microscope slides, looking for abnormal cells which might indicate conditions like cancer. Think, for a moment, about how difficult their task is: they need to look at thousands of cells to spot what might be just one or two subtle signs of abnormality. The thing is, with each slide they look at, they don't know in advance whether or not there are any abnormal cells there to be found. It would be one thing if we handed you a slide and said 'There are some abnormal cells on here – find them.' In this case you would pore over the slide until you spotted what you were looking for. But it would be quite different if we said 'There may be some abnormal cells on here or there may not – let us know what you decide.' You look over the slide and don't see any sign of an abnormal cell. But you know the abnormal cells are really difficult to spot so you don't feel comfortable about concluding the slide has no abnormal cells on it just yet. Probably best to look over it again, just to make sure…

How many times would you search the slide for something you know is difficult to spot before you gave up looking and decided there was nothing there to find? That is the decision facing the laboratory workers, and it raises some interesting questions we can look at here. What we will do is use a task that is a lot like scanning a microscope slide to explore how people search for difficult-to-find targets when the target may or may not be there. You will see how the time people take to do a task can give you clues about how they are doing it.

Method
Participants

If this were a genuine study of how medical laboratory workers examine slides, it would make sense if the sample were a group of laboratory workers, as that way we could have a lot of confidence when we generalized from the sample to the population of interest. This would be especially important as professional laboratory workers have not only training in examining slides but also experience of the task, and a sample of non-laboratory workers might therefore be particularly unrepresentative. However, for the purposes of this demonstration you will be fine with any willing **opportunity sample,** since we are just exploring the skill of visual searching in general.

As usual, the more people you can test the better, but as a demonstration this practical tends to work with just a handful of people (in a repeated-measures design) as the effects are so strong.

Design and materials

What we need for this practical is something that works like the laboratory slides, with lots of distractors and a subtle target for the participant to find. However, we also want something easier and more convenient than real slides: we don't want to have to worry about training participants to use microscopes and briefing them on the safety regulations concerning tissue samples! So we suggest using sheets of paper with letters printed on them. Half of these sheets will be printed so the letters are all identical, with no different letter to spot – the equivalent of a clear slide with no abnormal cells. The other half will have a single letter that differs from the rest and this is what the participants need to find – the equivalent of a slide with an abnormal cell.

So the first manipulation in this experiment – the first **independent variable** – is 'target type', which has two **levels**: 'target present' (the sheet has a target on it) and 'target absent' (the sheet does not). Even on its own, this would be quite an interesting study: we could see how long it takes people, on average, to find the target when it is there and how long, on average, they spend searching a clear slide before giving up and deciding there is no target to find (as you can see, search time is the **dependent variable** in this study).

If your study just had this one independent variable (target present or target absent), you would only need to worry about two things in the procedure. First, you would need to ensure every slide has the same number of letters on it – if the number of letters differed, any differences in search time could be caused by the independent variable but could instead be caused by some grids being bigger than others (so grid size would be an **extraneous variable**). Second, you would need to ensure the target is fairly difficult to spot. Look at the two small samples below: in the first, the letter O is really easy to see amongst the Ls. This is thanks to a phenomenon called *pop-out*: because the letter O is fundamentally different in shape from the Ls, you spot it almost instantly – no matter how many Ls there are nearby.

```
L  L  L  L  L  L        L  L  L  L  L  L

L  L  L  L  L  L        L  L  L  L  L  L

L  L  L  L  L  L        L  L  L  L  L  L

L  L  L  O  L  L        L  L  L  L  L  L

L  L  L  L  L  L        L  T  L  L  L  L
```

This is no use for our demonstration – the pop-out effect would make the task far too easy, so we need to use a target that doesn't show this phenomenon. As you can see from the second grid, the letter T works quite well. Because it is has a lot of features in common with the letter L – both of them are made of a horizontal line joined to a vertical line – T doesn't pop out, which means that the larger the number of Ls the harder it is to find the T.

Having now decided the stimuli will be grids of Ls, sometimes with a single T present and sometimes not, we can move on to the second independent variable, which will be the number of letters in the grid. We suggest using three different sizes of grid – for example a 10 × 15 grid, a 20 × 30 grid and a 30 ×60 grid (we have suggested rectangular grids simply because most paper is this shape – the shape of the grid really isn't important). Three different grid sizes will let us see how people's performance changes as the search task gets more and more difficult.

So we have one independent variable with three levels and another independent variable with two levels, giving us a total of 3 x 2 = 6 conditions. These break down as follows:

1. Small grid, target present
2. Small grid, target absent
3. Medium grid, target present
4. Medium grid, target absent
5. Large grid, target present
6. Large grid, target absent.

The next decision is whether you will conduct your study using a **repeated-measures** design, where each person is tested in all six conditions, or an **independent-measures** design where each person is tested in only one condition. As usual, there are advantages and disadvantages to both approaches. The repeated-measures design, where everybody takes part in all six conditions, means any differences in search times you see between conditions could not be explained by differences between people, as the same people are in each condition. However, there may be some issues with the numbers needed if you want to counterbalance your design, as we will see in a moment.

An independent-measures design, where each person is tested in just one condition, raises the possibility that any effects you find are the product of differences between people rather than differences between conditions. This is because the independent variables *and* the people change as you go from condition to condition, unlike a repeated-measures design, where the people stay the same. On the other hand, in this particular study an independent-measures design might make life easier with counterbalancing (see below).

You can create the search sheets yourself, and it is very easy to do this with a word processor or a spreadsheet. Or, if you prefer, you can print the sheets we have provided in our on-line resources.

Design checklist

- The independent variables are grid size (three different sizes) and whether or not there is a target (yes or no). This gives us six conditions.
- Decide whether to use a repeated- or an independent-measures design.

Data collection

With this search task, it is possible that people will get better with practice. As such, if you are using a repeated-measures design, where each participant does all six tests, there is a risk of **order effects**, where people perform better in some conditions than others not because the conditions are different, but simply because one came before the other. Imagine for a moment that people's searching is not affected by the size of the grid, so that they take the same amount of time to search a large grid as a small grid. If we gave people one grid then the other, they might be faster on the second grid because they have got used to their task; or they might be slower on the second grid because they have started to get bored. They would be faster or slower not because the grids are different but because one came first and one came second – this would be a difference in speed that we are not interested in: an order effect.

The two main methods for dealing with order effects are to **randomize** the order in which each participant completes the six conditions or to **counterbalance** the order. The difficulty with counterbalancing six conditions is that if you do it properly there will be 6!, or 6 x 5 x 4 x 3 x 2 x 1 = 720 possible orders. This means you would need a multiple of 720 participants: 720 people, or 1440 people, or 2160 people...! Unless you happen to be the ruler of a country, you probably don't have access to these sorts of numbers, but this is a really good illustration of what it can take to counterbalance a design properly. This study has only two simple independent variables, but counterbalancing is already hugely difficult: another illustration of why it is so important to keep things simple when planning your research!

So, given that counterbalancing is going to be so difficult, you'll probably want to combat any possible order effects by giving each participant the six tests in random order. A way of doing this that gives you some of the benefits of a counterbalanced procedure would be to write out the 720 possible orders[1] and then pick one of these randomly for each person. This is perhaps the tightest procedure you could use, ensuring no two people get the same order, in the absence of having 720 people or more.

On the other hand, order effects are not a concern if you use an independent-measures design. The only issue in this case is that, as

---

[1] The spreadsheet experts amongst you will be able to do this in seconds. The rest of you... well, this might be a good time to learn how to use a spreadsheet.

there are six conditions, you need a multiple of six people – 12, 18, 24, 30 ... – so each condition is tested equally often.

If you decide to use an independent-measures design, testing each person takes the following form. First, explain the participant's task to them using a set of **standardized instructions** (to ensure all participants get the same information about what they need to do). You might want to use some instructions a bit like this:

You are about to see a sheet of paper with lots of letter Ls on it. There may – or may not – also be a letter T somewhere amongst them. You need to search for the letter T. AS QUICKLY AS POSSIBLE, try to find the T. If you see it, point to it on the page; if you cannot find a letter T on the page, say 'Not there'. Remember, you are looking for a letter T and it may be there and it may not.

Place the participant's test sheet on a table in front of them, face-down. When you and they are ready, turn the sheet over and start the timer. Measure how long it takes them either to find the T (if it is there) or to give up and say 'not there'. For each test you then record (a) the grid size, (b) whether there was a T in the grid or not, (c) their response (finding the T or giving up searching) and the time it took them to respond. For example:

Participant 14   –   small grid   –   T present   –   Found it   –   8.7 secs

If you are using a repeated-measures design the procedure is exactly the same except that you repeat it six times for each person (although you should only need to read the instructions once).

Participant 14   –   small grid   –   T present   –   Found it   –   8.7 secs
Participant 14   –   medium grid   –   T absent   –   gave up   –   16.4 secs
Participant 14   –   small grid   –   T absent   –   gave up   –   12.1 secs

And so on ...

Procedure checklist

- Present the instructions to the participant.
- Place the search-sheet face-down in front of them.
- Turn it over and start timing.
- When they respond, note the condition details, their response and how long it took.
- Repeat, if using a repeated-measures design.

Results

Looking at your data

These data can be displayed effectively on a **scatterplot**, with the mean time for each of the six conditions plotted as a single point. A scatterplot is a good choice because we are interested in the relationship between two measures: grid size and response time. The scatterplot we have drawn here is what we found when we ran this practical using a repeated-measures design. As you can see, in our data, as the size of the grid increased, people tended to be slower to make a decision. This is logical, since as the grid gets larger the participants have to do more searching.

Completely separate from this grid-size effect, participants were overall faster at searching when the T was present in the grid than when it was absent from the grid. As such, the time people take to search a grid is separately affected by our two independent variables – people are faster when the target is present and also faster with smaller grids.

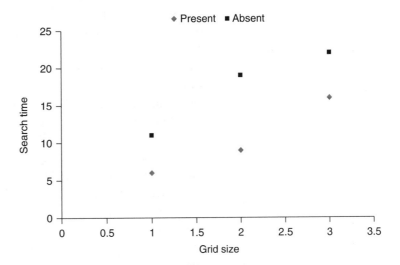

Statistical thinking

These data would probably best be analysed using **regression**. This will give you a description of how search time changes as the grid size changes. Simple linear regression, which is what you would use to analyse the data here, gives you two key numbers. The first is the **slope**, which is a measure of how the dependent variable changes as the independent variable changes. If your data look like ours, you will find the Present data and the Absent data give very similar slope values – this reflects the fact that the two sets of dots *slope* up in a similar way as you move from the left-hand side of the plot to the right-hand side. In the case of our data, the slope for the occasions when the target was present is 5.0 and when the target was absent the slope was 5.5. These are really similar values, showing that the decision time tends to change in a similar way for both.

The second number you would get from a regression analysis would be the **intercept**. This is a measure of where, overall, the points tend to lie on the graph. If your data look like ours you will find that, whereas the slopes were similar, the Absent data have a higher intercept (in our example, the Present data have an intercept of 0.33 and the Absent data have an intercept of 6.33). This reflects the fact the Absent data lie higher up the plot, and so were slower overall. When two lots of data have similar slopes and different intercepts, this shows that they tend to lie parallel to each other on the plot.

Discussion

The amount of time people spent searching the grids will give you some idea of *how* they were doing the searching. With our data, we first saw that the average amount of time to search the grid increased as the grid got larger. What this tells us is that people must be *searching* the grid – because the amount of time to make a decision went up when the grid got larger, people must effectively be spending a certain amount of time looking at each letter. Their searching must be systematic, moving over the grid, rather than seeing the grid as a whole, in a single glance. We learnt this simply from the time people took to respond. You may well have found the same thing. Of course, if you didn't see any evidence of search time increasing with grid size, your participants must have been searching in a different way from ours. What might explain this difference? Different participants alone? Perhaps we printed our letters in a different font, and yours caused pop-out?

Our second finding was that people took longer to make a decision when there was not a target in the grid. There are actually a couple of possible interpretations of this. First, it could simply be that, when the target is present, people stop searching when they find it. Let's assume people search the grid by looking at one letter at a time. If this is the case, when there is a target present they will, on average, reach it half-way through their search (sometimes it will be one of the first letters they look at, sometimes one of the last, averaging out in the middle). At the point they reach the target they will stop searching, as it doesn't make sense to keep searching further. As such, trials where the target is present might be shorter because people only search half the grid, on average, whereas when the target is absent they have to search it all before they can be sure the target is not there.

Alternatively, people might spend longer searching the grid when there is no target because, having scanned the grid and found nothing, they tend to go back and have another look, to make sure they didn't just overlook the target.

It is also possible that *both* these mechanisms are operating. If you found similar results to us, you might be able to get an idea if either of these two explanations is correct by looking at the errors people make. We'll leave it to you to work out how the errors might tell you this!

Finally, what we learn from this study could be applied back to the examination of slides in the laboratory. If we knew what proportion of cells tend to be suspicious in various types of sample, we might be able to use what we learn from studies like this to estimate the ideal size for a search sample, and to guess the likelihood of various targets being overlooked. What else might this experiment tell us about how people search in the real world? What might it say about radar operators? Or policing?

Alternative versions

A really good alternative version of this practical is to explore the pop-out effect, like the original studies by Treisman (1982). Instead of half the grids having a target and half the grids having no target, you can arrange your study so some grids have the target T (which is difficult to find amongst Ls) and some grids have the target O (which pops out from the Ls). What you should find is that the grids with Ts give you a scatterplot that rises as the size of the grid increases, just like the plot we have shown here. The grids with Os, on the other hand, should give you a strikingly different pattern, with the points all lying on a flat line which does not change with grid size: people take the same amount of time to spot the O regardless of how large the grid is. This is another example of how the time taken to carry out a task can reveal something about how people are accomplishing the task: in this case, the different patterns – one horizontal, one rising – show that people must be using fundamentally different techniques to find the target when looking for an O and a T.

Another version – which we have not even tested ourselves, so you would be out on the frontiers of knowledge here – would be to have more than one target in the grid, and see how people's search times vary when the grid size stays the same and the number of targets changes.

Test yourself

1. You carry out a study to measure how many eggs people can eat in 3 minutes. You have two independent variables: gender (half your participants are men and half women) and age (half are old and half are young). What is the smallest number of people you would be able to test if you wanted to use a fully counterbalanced repeated-measures design?

Reference

Treisman, A. (1982). Perceptual grouping and attention in visual search for features and for objects. *Journal of Experimental Psychology: Human Perception and Performance, 8*, 194–214.

chapter 9

practical: constructing memories

When carrying out any experiment on people, we have to make a fundamental choice early on in our planning: do we use a repeated-measures procedure, where each person is tested more than once, or an independent-measures procedure, where each person is tested only once? Each method has good and bad points, and it's important to get used to weighing these up. Here we use a psychological experiment to explore the issue of how we decide on a design when, as is often the case, both are feasible options. Don't worry if you're not a psychologist! We're just using this subject because it's interesting, and good for illustrating the point we want to make.

Topics covered: repeated-measures versus independent-measures designs, variables, sampling, logistic regression.

You will need: print-outs of the supplied story, pieces of paper for people to write responses on, a pen or pencil per participant, watch or clock.

Background

Think back to the last journey you made. As you remember that journey, the experience is probably a lot like watching a video recording taken from your point of view whilst you were travelling. When we remember things we have experienced, we often feel as if our memories are like recordings of those events which we can watch back and analyse if necessary. However, this impression is misleading, and what really happens when we remember things is that we are reconstructing the memories from really quite sparse bits of information that we have stored in our minds. That is, when you remember walking or driving down a street, a lot of what you see when you imagine that journey was not stored in your mind at the time; rather, your mind adds it in at the time of remembering because it thinks that this detail belongs there.

Because remembering is a process of working out what you experienced from incomplete memories, the process often makes mistakes during recall, and can be biased by things you experience between the original event and the time you try to remember it. This practical involves having people read a passage of text and then recall it afterwards. The experimental manipulation, inspired by the classic work of Bransford and Johnson (1972), involves giving people different titles for the text after they have read it, and seeing whether changing the title leads to people tending to remember different parts of the text. If hearing different titles leads people to remember the same passage of text differently, this tells us that remembering must be an active process, capable of being affected by experiences after the original event, and not really like a recording at all.

Method
Participants

Experiments on basic mental processes like problem-solving and memory tend not to be affected much by many participant factors. As such, you don't need to worry all that much about carefully balancing your sample to ensure exactly equal numbers of male and female participants, as you might when studying some other questions, and don't need to be very concerned about the ages of your participants either; in fact, most opportunity samples are fine for this sort of work. The only real concern, given that this test involves reading a passage of text, is that your participants will probably all need to have English as their first language.

As a rule of thumb, we recommend having at least 40 participants for this practical, but it may work with fewer if that is all you have access to.

Design

You are going to get people to read a short passage of text and then, after they have read it, tell them the title of the passage before asking them to remember as much of the passage as they can. There will be two different titles in the experiment and our hypothesis is that each will lead people to remember different parts of the passage. You need to decide if you will use a repeated-measures design, where everybody reads the passage twice, once with each title, or an independent-measures design, where you split your participants into two groups with each group getting a different title. This is a key decision, so think about which design you would use before reading further.

The repeated-measures design has the advantage that you can do the study with fewer people. Because each person takes part in both conditions, in principle you only need half the participants that you need for an independent-measures design (so, say, 20 instead of 40). And the really big advantage of repeated-measures designs is that any effect you see cannot be explained away by the idea that the people in one condition may be different somehow from the people in the other – tending to have better memories, say.

However, although repeated-measures designs have a lot of good points, there is a big problem with using one for this particular experiment. If everybody does the procedure twice, the second time they do it their ability to remember the story may well be affected by the experience of previously having heard (and remembered) the story. This risks introducing a bias into the results, such that everybody tends to perform differently (either better or worse) the second time round. You could try to eliminate the bias by using counterbalancing, in which half the participants get title A followed by title B and half get the opposite order, so that there can be no systematic effect of hearing one title before the other, but, as we're interested in how experiences distort memory, it would be much neater to be sure each person who recalls the story is doing so for the very first time, with no previous experience of seeing and recalling the story at all. As such, we recommend an independent-measures design in which half the participants read the text then hear one title and half read the text and then hear the other title. Aim for equal numbers of people in each group.

Data collection

Before collecting your data, you need to make a decision about how long you will give each participant to read the passage of text. You might want to give each person as much time as they want to read the text, or you might want to give people a fixed amount of time. We leave this choice to you, as there are advantages to each method: giving people as long as they want allows for the fact people read at different speeds, which means that, if the reading time is fixed, faster readers will be able to study the text more than slower readers; but on the other hand, giving everybody a fixed time makes it easier to test a group of people all at once, and makes the procedure more consistent. It's your choice – just pick the option that you think is best.

The passage of text you will have people read is below. You need to copy this onto a piece of paper (or print out the pre-prepared file *memorytext.pdf* from the web resources) and give each person a copy. Alternatively, you might project the text onto a screen if you are testing people as a group.

Every time I see it, I'm sure it has grown some more. I can see that she thinks the world of it and it looks like having it around gives her a lot of pleasure. It's sleepy a lot of the time, but plays with its toys whenever it's awake. It's covered in dark fluffy hair.

After each participant has read the text, you give them a title. For one set of participants, the title is:

My neighbour's new baby

And for the other set the title is:

My neighbour's new kitten

If you are testing people in groups, you will probably want to send half the participants out of the room for a moment whilst the first group is tested. An alternative method, which allows you to test both conditions at once with a large group, is to print or write the titles on slips of paper and give these out for the participants to look at only after they have read the passage.

After participants have heard or read the title, have them wait one minute and then write down the passage of text as best they can remember it. When you have collected the responses, we are interested in whether participants remembered that (a) 'it's covered in dark hair' (or similar words) and (b) 'it plays with its toys.' Count up, in total, how often the dark fluffy hair and the toys were mentioned by each of the participant groups.

Procedure checklist

- Decide how long participants will have to read the text.
- In each condition, have participants read the text and, after they have finished, give them the title.
- One minute later, have the participants write down the passage of text as well as they can remember it.
- Count how often each of the two key ideas appears in each participant's remembered text.

Results
Looking at your data

The data you are collecting here are known as categorical data, which means you are counting how often people fall into various categories, rather than collecting scores of some sort. Categorical data are usually best seen in a contingency table like the one shown below:

	Number mentioning hair	Number mentioning toys
'kitten' title	17	9
'baby' title	5	14

You can see that in our sample data there was a definite tendency for people given the 'kitten' title to remember hair more than toys, and people given the 'baby' title to show the opposite pattern – it seems our experimental manipulation did have an effect on people's memories. See if your data look similar to ours.

Statistical thinking

The task we have here is essentially the same as something we often need to do in research: we have to predict an outcome from some other measure. Usually, in research statistics, this takes a slightly more obvious form. We might, for example, predict whether people get sick or not as the result of some lifestyle factor. Do they get sick (outcome 1) or not (outcome 2) given how much garlic they eat (the measure)?

Here, what we are doing is conceptually similar (choosing statistical tests is all about seeing what the underlying concepts are, regardless of where your numbers come from). For the hair measure, we are looking at whether people mention it (outcome 1) or not (outcome 2) depending on which title they were given; the same goes for the toys measure.

We know from looking at our statistics books that there is more than one analysis we could use for data like these, but that the most common is *logistic regression* (and if we are being really clever, *multinomial logistic regression*). Logistic regression tests tell us whether knowing the title somebody was given allows us to predict, better than guessing alone, whether they mentioned hair or toys. (In short, it works like this: imagine all the people with the 'kitten' title mentioned hair and none of the 'baby' people mentioned it. Knowing which title a person was given would allow you to know whether they mentioned hair with 100% accuracy; if you didn't know the title you'd only be able to make a 50:50 guess.)

When we did the analysis for the 'hair' outcome, we found knowing which title a person heard dramatically increased our ability to predict whether or not they mentioned hair. Knowing the title a person was given, you could predict whether they mentioned hair or not with 80% accuracy; if you didn't know the title your accuracy would drop to 55%. Clearly, the title makes a difference to whether people mention hair, and this is reflected in the data table above: people who had heard the 'kitten' title mentioned hair far more often than the people who heard the 'baby' title.

This table also shows that, in contrast to the 'hair' outcome, the title seems to have had less of an effect on whether people mention toys. Sure enough, when we analysed these data we saw that knowing which title people were given only increased our ability to predict whether or not they mentioned toys by a small amount: it went up from 57.5% to 62.5%, which isn't much of a difference.

Discussion

Memory and the way we process information in our minds are peculiar things. We all know people who are amazing at remembering numbers and routines involving numbers. An accountant friend of ours, for instance, can glance at a balance sheet and see errors and inconsistencies as if they were written in a different coloured ink. This is because reading a balance sheet is a great skill. In writing this section we called this accountant friend of ours to discuss this. He tells us that the format of the values and numbers, and how they are placed on the page, makes a big difference. If the page is altered in some way he has to read the balance sheet again to gather the information he'd previously gathered. It seems the way in which things are formatted or written can influence our information-gathering skills quite dramatically.

In our practical we manipulated the title of the passage to investigate whether this influenced people's memories of the text. The idea is that memory is an active process, and we can guide it, or drive it, with the title, manipulating what people are looking for as they search through their memories. It's an interesting idea, and perhaps the same sort of thing happens outside memory as well. Let's go back to the example of accountancy and think about someone reading a balance sheet who is not experienced, or not terribly vigilant. What would happen if the report promised hugely positive values, and the title of the accounts page is something along the lines of 'This year's fabulous figures' rather than 'Unfortunate accounts of this banking year'? Directing attention, and aiding a person's reading of some text, can be misguiding just as directing their memory searches can be.

Of course, in our practical we were looking at how memory for something might be influenced simply by altering the title of the text. The possibilities here are endless. We could have called this 'You can't judge a book by its cover' and investigated whether your opinion of a story is influenced by the picture on the front of the book. What's important is that you carefully manipulate one thing and see what happens. This is the basis of the experimental method and it is a powerful tool for investigating how people behave in different situations, given different information.

Something we often find is that people battling with how best to do research with people often hit a brick wall, and decide it's easier to sidestep it and make a few mistakes in their research design than it is to work out the best way to do it properly. The mistake they are making here is that a small mistake, or a small compromise in research design, can have disastrous effects on the usefulness of their findings. This is why we spend quite a lot of time on details. The problem with this is that focusing on the details can often lead people to lose the will to live! They often forget the bigger picture and get stuck not being able to see the wood for the trees. What we do at *this* stage is remind them there may well be a practical use for their research, and this really helps them keep focused. If the small investigation you are doing does not at first seem relevant to your discipline, then *make* it relevant. Use text that is important to your work or study. Next, if you are having trouble seeing how this can be of any use in the real world, and so you are having motivation problems, then *make* it relevant. Really think up a way in which this kind of research can be *applied*. In the case of this practical we are hoping to investigate whether a title can guide us to remembering certain details from the story. Imagine you wanted people to read important information on a drugs bottle, or the instruction leaflet that comes with some medication. How might you really direct a person's reading? Or imagine you were in the business of offering financial advice, and reading matter is constructed in such a way as to help people gather the most important facts about your many products. Might you see how this kind of research could help in those areas? You see, research does not exist in a vacuum. Your wit and imagination allow you to investigate how best to do things when you interact with people.

Let's think a little more about our practical for a moment. You should always think about how your research has enlivened debate, or how your results fit in with existing findings. It's a good way to really focus your work. So in this case you should ask what your results say about memory and how it works. This practical says something about how we imagine things and how we generate images from information being presented. In this case we are framing the image, guiding it with the title. When we come to recall the information later on, the picture that we see (the memory) has a shape at least in part guided by your title. So memory, and how people deal with new information, can be guided. This is an extremely useful finding for anyone in the business of information delivery of any kind.

Alternative versions

You might want to analyse the data you have collected further, by identifying other ideas in the text and seeing whether there are differences between the conditions in how often these are recalled.

Reference

Bransford, J.D. and Johnson, M.K. (1972). Contextual prerequisites for understanding: Some investigations of comprehension and recall. *Journal of Verbal Learning and Verbal Behavior, 11,* 717–726.

chapter 10

practical: I'm trying to concentrate!

Have you ever had someone talking to you when you've been attempting to do something that required you to concentrate? In this practical we look at how you might go about investigating what constitutes 'distraction' and what kind of tasks you might use when investigating whether distractions can cause problems for different work practices, such as navigating, finding information, or working on a document or presentation. This will let us look at a few issues of design that you need to know about.

Topics covered: Variables, independent samples, standardized instructions, practice effects, independent variable, dependent variable, repeated measures design.

You will need: a sample of people, a maze printed on some paper, a pencil, something to record sound on and play it back with (a computer is ideal) and some headphones.

Background

Governments appear to be waking up to the idea that doing more than one task at once can be a problem for people. For instance, having a conversation on a hand-held telephone while driving is now illegal in many countries. This is because there is a belief that not having both hands on the wheel is dangerous. It could, of course, be that it is the conversation itself that is the problem. Common sense suggests that completing a task, even a relatively simple one, can be made significantly more difficult with the intervention of a friend intent on describing the plot of a movie they went to the night before, or, even worse, attempting to reproduce the jokes of a comedian who they obviously found hilarious.

The implications of research like this are rather wide-ranging. Let's think about the telephones in cars problem for a moment. Next time you are a passenger in a car, watch the driver for a few minutes. Do they really keep both hands planted firmly on the wheel? Usually it depends on how long ago it was that they received their driving licence! A few weeks of freedom from an instructor telling them what to do and you'll soon find that one hand strays to the controls of the stereo, or an elbow finds its way onto the sill of an opened window. So what is the issue with people using a hand-held telephone? Well, it might be that having a conversation is distracting them from their ability to concentrate on the road. If that were the case, then perhaps all conversations in cars should be banned? Passengers would be banned from 'speaking to the driver' as they are on many buses around the world. Or it might not just be speaking: it could be that having any kind of distraction is a problem. If that was the case, listening to music or the radio while driving should be banned as well.

How about another example that those of us who work in offices are becoming more aware of? The larger institutions get, the more staff they employ, and these have to be put somewhere. Offices are expensive places to buy or rent, and heat, and so more desks are crammed into smaller and smaller places to accommodate the increasing workforce. Eventually, there is no more room for desks, and managers try and come up with solutions to the problem. One glance around a busy office will usually reveal an empty desk or two, vacated briefly by a colleague at a meeting or symposium out of town perhaps, or someone unfortunate enough to be sick and unable to attend work. 'Aha!' says the manager, 'I spy a solution!' and so 'hot-desking' is born – a (some would say) elegant solution to a busy open-office environment. However, is it? Does a 'different' environment alter the way we work? If it does, and people work better, longer and more efficiently in familiar surroundings, then the concept of the 'hot desk' is not really the good idea people thought it was.

Let's go one step further since we're on the subject of offices. Many of us now work in open offices, separated by low walls into workspaces where we are allowed to bring personal items such as photographs and sometimes plants to make the space our own. Open environments like these are extremely busy and often quite noisy places. Workers there are carrying out their tasks while bombarded with information from screens and their surroundings. It could be that the level of distraction is damaging their concentration and their ability to do their task. There is research showing memory can be significantly influenced by different types of sounds (Beaman and Jones,

1998), and so any task that involves dealing with information may also be affected by a noisy office. If this really is the case, then open office spaces (even though a suitably inexpensive way to accommodate many workers) may not be the best way to achieve high standards of work.

How about anther example? Have you ever had to learn information for a test or an examination? Of course you have! Have you ever had to run through an important presentation for a seminar, conference or meeting? How annoying is it when your careful preparations are interrupted by the family pet, or the television or radio in another room? Many of our students tell us that they revise with a personal stereo on, or, worse, the television! Whereas it may well be true that some lucky people can indeed develop an understanding of information under very distracting conditions, the majority of us, alas, cannot. Or can we? Perhaps you could think about how you might go about finding out?

You see? We're thinking here about relatively big and important questions. What kind of office environment is best, what kind of legislation to pass ensure the safety of your car-driving population, and how best to learn material in order to get the job at interview, or pass your examinations.

Method
Design

The *keep it simple* rule is in play, as usual, so have a think about how you might best begin to answer the question of whether being distracted influences your ability to do a task. We'd like you to develop your own plan for this project, but you should be aiming to test a hypothesis something like:

'Performance on a task will be affected by the level of simultaneous distraction that is experienced.'

It's pretty clear, then, that *level of distraction* will be the thing that you vary. That's the **independent variable** and *performance on the task* will be the **dependent variable** you will measure. The next thing for you to decide is exactly how you will operationalize these dependent and independent variables.

What constitutes 'distraction' depends at least in part on the person being distracted. Our example of studying for a test in front of the TV or while listening to music shows that rather neatly. However, for the purpose of your investigation you need to decide on something you can sensibly identify as a 'distraction'. A word of warning here...

There will be a temptation here to complicate the design of your study to investigate whether one thing is more distracting than another. That's not really the question, though, and, whereas it is an interesting problem to try and solve, there are issues you will have to consider in the design that would be best left until you have addressed the more basic matter of whether distraction matters at all. We recommend you at least think your way through a very simple design first before complicating it with more questions. Keep it simple, remember?

So have a think about things that people might find distracting, and write them down. We've just done the same and have come up with a few options. Our list includes the following: *Conversations, television, noises like car-horns, flashing lights, cats sitting on keyboards, crying children, music in the room next door, the sound of a kitchen appliance rumbling away downstairs, barking dogs, the ringing of an unanswered telephone.*

With the need to keep things simple we can choose two conditions, one with 'no distraction' and one with 'distraction'. The distraction condition will involve listening to one of these noises; the no-distraction condition will involve silence.

The next thing to decide upon is the study's design. The choice of independent measures or repeated measures is central again, and each brings with it its own positive and negative aspects. It's worth talking through the two possibilities here as this practical is rather a good one for showing up the various issues in this particular design choice.

What if I choose an independent-samples design?

If you choose an independent-samples design you'll have two groups of people doing your task. One group will do the task under distracting conditions; the other will do the task in silence. The issue you now have is the people in each group. A suitably ridiculous example will highlight the major problem here. Let's say you choose 'listening to a recorded conversation' as your distracting stimulus, and 'watching out for red cars in a film of a busy road' as your task. As a good researcher you fill up your two groups, in two trips to the park, approaching people to help you with your carefully designed project. Your results, though, gathered over several days of testing, seem a little odd. Some investigation reveals that Monday is the day that the local colour-blindness support group take their weekly stroll in the park, and Tuesday is when the local deaf football team train. You have, inadvertently, filled one group with people who have problems seeing colours, and the other group with people who have difficulty hearing. Your procedure has been confounded by a very significant extraneous variable.

We know the odds of this kind of thing happening are rather slim, but the point is, an independent-samples design is prone to the influence of individual differences. If there are more highly vigilant people in one group than another then your results will be misleading. Similarly, if there are more people with uncorrected visual problems in one group than another then their ability to spot red cars will be influenced by that as well as the variation of distracting stimuli.

If you do choose an independent-samples design, the best way to deal with these individual differences is to have large groups. This is not so much avoiding the effect of individual differences, as minimizing or limiting their effect. With a very large group, each individual should find a similar person in the other group, just by chance. How large do the groups need to be, you ask? As large as possible really. A group of 20 people in each group is good, a group of 100 in each group is better. Either way, you'll need plenty of people for this type of design.

What if I choose a repeated-measures design?

If you decide on a repeated-measures design, each of your participants takes part in the whole project, providing you with data for the 'no distraction' condition as well as the 'distraction' condition. If you were to choose this type of design you would be removing any effects of individual differences because if any participants have weak eyesight, or slightly damaged hearing, this will be just the same in each of your conditions. As such, you don't need to choose quite as many participants to limit the influence of individual differences as in an independent-samples design.

Of course, the price you pay is that you now have to deal with order effects. Since each participant will be doing the task in both conditions they may get systematically better at it the second time they do it. This is a practice effect. Similarly, if you choose a task that takes a while, or that involves quite a lot of concentration, when they do it for the second time they may be tired, and not perform as well. This is a fatigue effect. You can control for order effects by counterbalancing your procedure.

Design checklist

- ■ Think about which is best: a repeated-measures design or an independent-samples design.
- ■ Rough out the pros and cons of each design, and run through a 'thought' version of each procedure to see if that illuminates any problems.
- ■ Either decide on how you will put participants into groups (for an independent-samples design) or identify how you will counterbalance the procedure (for a repeated-measures design).

Participants

We will assume we are using a repeated-measures design for the rest of this practical, so we need to locate some participants. Where you locate your participants will depend on where you are. A conveniently placed poster requesting that participants volunteer to help you, perhaps, for the reward of coffee and cake. In some university departments at which we have worked, students are obliged to help researchers with their studies and receive credit for participating. These students form a 'participant pool' upon which you may be able to draw. You may work for a company or organization which has a budget available for research. Whichever way you get people, it is likely that you will engage in opportunity sampling of some kind, so be aware of sampling bias. It is possible that people who sign up to help with research have a more 'helpful' personality than those who do not. If this is likely to be a factor in your research, or if you think that it may be, then you should consider it when locating your participants.

How many participants do I need for a repeated-measures design?

That's the beauty of a repeated-measures design: you need fewer participants than in an independent-samples design because you do not have to limit the influence of individual differences. Because each participant provides data in each condition they are 'matched' to themselves. They are their own 'control'. Obviously, you need more than one participant, but you don't need too many. In this example we have two conditions, and so there are two ways in which the different conditions can be presented. For this reason you would need to use multiples of two participants (4, 6, 8, 10, 12, etc.), although, as usual, the more the better. The reason for this is that the **power** of the experiment increases quite significantly with sample size: if there really is something going on in your investigation, and if distraction really does have an influence on performance of a task, then you are more likely to see it with more participants, even if the effect is relatively small. For now, however, let's choose 24 participants. That seems like a sensible number.

How will we distract the participants?

You'll have come up with the same kind of things. For argument's sake, let's choose barking dogs as an example of a distraction. This is a handy one for us to choose and we have at hand a decent microphone, a laptop computer, a squeaky toy and (importantly) a handy dog. While one of us winds Baxter up into a frenzy of barking the other can record a suitable amount of 'barking sound' onto the computer for use in our project. Our independent variable is whether people are distracted or not and we have operationalized the distraction as hearing a recording of a dog barking (distraction condition) or hearing no noise (control condition).

What task shall we use?

There are countless tasks that you might use. One could be completing simple mathematical problems involving adding and subtracting numbers. Another possibility is a simple task where participants read a page of text and are required to identify all incidences of the letter 'e' with a highlighting pen. The task that worked best for us when we were trying out all these practicals was a maze completion task.

Find yourself a simple pen-and-paper maze and print it out onto paper. If you can't find one you can use the one we used when we tried this out, and we've included it in the electronic resources for the book. The task is simple enough to understand: you measure how many mistakes a person makes as they complete the maze. We did it by measuring how many times either of us touched the edges of the maze. Our dependent variable (the thing that depends on our independent variable) is the participant's ability to complete the task, and we have operationalized it as the number of times their pencil touches the edges in a maze completion task.

The next thing you need to do is decide on some standardized instructions. This helps you to avoid any bias that you may inadvertently introduce into the procedure by using different instructions with different participants. Your instructions may look something like this:

Thank you for agreeing to participate in this procedure. In front of you there is a sheet of paper and a pencil. When I say 'go' please turn the paper over. You will see a maze. Using the pencil, please solve the maze doing your best not to touch the sides. You will be required to do the task twice, once while listening to some sounds over headphones and once in silence.[1] On this occasion you will be presented with sounds / working in silence (delete as appropriate).

Make sure that each time you give a participant a maze to complete you write on it the participant number and whether it was completed in silence or with sounds.

Collecting and collating your data

After your participants are finished, take their completed mazes and work out how many mistakes they made by counting up how many

---

[1] Even though the person is not listening to any sounds, you must still have them wear headphones. This ensures that the only thing you are varying is whether they are listening to distracting sounds. Keeping the headphones on maintains the 'feeling' of wearing headphones.

times they touched the edges while completing the task. Draw yourself a table, and fill it in. You should end up with something that looks like the one we have shown here. We've only given the results of four participants here; you will have 24 in total if you have followed the procedure we have decided upon.

Participant number	Silence	Distraction
1	4	9
2	2	7
3	8	8
4	6	10

Procedure checklist

- Decide on how many participants you will need and locate participants.
- Counterbalance, if you are using a repeated-measures design. Decide on the order in which each participant will complete the procedure (distracting sound first or second).
- Operationalize your variables (decide on a task and how you will distract people).
- Read out standardized instructions to each participant, or give written instruction for them to read.
- Have participants complete the task.
- Collate and tabulate your data.

Results

Looking at your data

First of all, calculate some descriptive statistics to help you decide what your data are telling you. You'll need a mean value for the number of mistakes made in each condition, which will tell you whether, overall, distracting sounds affected people's performance. You'll also need a measure of dispersion for the data to show you how people's scores tended to vary. A standard deviation will do nicely. Put your descriptive statistics in a table for your own reference. You'll hopefully end up with something that looks a bit like this:

	Silence	Distraction
Mean	6	8.8
Standard deviation	2.6	2.3

Draw a graph to help yourself and others see as clearly as possible what you have found. A single graph will do. Two conditions, and one data point for each, lends itself to a barchart of the type shown here:

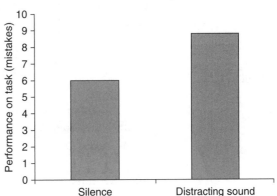

Performance on a maze completion task

The graph really helps us see what appears to be going on in our version of the procedure. From the mean performance it would suggest that people make more errors when distracted than when they are allowed to complete the task in silence. Of course, that's not the end of the story at all. We now need to see if the results of your small sample can be said to appropriately reflect the behaviour of the population from which it was drawn, so we'll need to do some analysis.

Statistical thinking

What we want to know at the end of this study is whether the number of mistakes in the 'silence' column of our results sheet is reliably different from (smaller than) the numbers in the 'distracting sound' column – is the difference in our graph large and consistent enough that we can attribute it to the effect of distraction rather than chance? The analysis we would use for this is of a very common type, where we want to compare two mean scores to see if they differ. There are several tests for this, depending on whether you are using a repeated-measures or an independent-samples design, and depending on whether your data meet certain assumptions. In this case, where we used a repeated-measures design, we would test the effect of distraction using a repeated-measures t-test or, if the assumptions for this test were not met, with a Wilcoxon[2] test.

After we ran this study we used a repeated-measures t-test which provided us with a t-statistic, from which we could calculate a p-value. In our data, the p-value was .006. This tells us there is only a .006 chance – a 0.6% chance – that the effect in our graph just

---

[2] A Wilcoxon matched-pairs signed-ranks test, to give it its rather grand full name.

arose by chance, and so means nothing. This is a nice small p-value, well below the usual criterion level (α) of .05. As such, with this low p-value we would reject our null hypothesis: these results almost certainly didn't arise by chance, and this is what we will conclude – they almost certainly arose because distraction affected people.

Discussion

This practical has used an extremely simple design that can be manipulated and added to to suit your needs. It rather nicely illustrates a point in research design that never ceases to surprise those new to the art. That is, even the simplest of designs with very few conditions and manipulations can become very seriously complicated unless you are methodical and careful about your choices.

When you are thinking about reporting your findings and discussing your results you should always have a think about how your procedure might have been improved. Use part of your write-up's discussion to be reflective and self-critical. That is not to say you should spend all your time saying how awful your ideas were and how much better they might have been if someone who was any good at research design had done the work for you[3], but there is a place for some sensible and carefully placed comments on your own work that will have occurred to you while you were carrying out the procedure.

For instance, has it occurred to you that the way in which we decided to measure an 'error' might have been a little misleading? Just because you touch the edge of a path on a maze does not mean that you have made an error on a maze completion task, really, does it? It just means that you are a little clumsy. It could be that more errors were made in the distracting sound condition because the sound simply made people more clumsy for some reason. The other problem we spotted with our error measure is that it does not take into account different strategies people might use. Some might try to complete the maze as quickly as possible, and so touch the edges often, whereas others might be extremely cautious, never touching the edges but also taking 20 minutes to complete each maze! If we repeated the procedure we would probably include a measure of how long people took, or at least give them a time limit, and this insight is something we would mention in our write-up.

---

[3] Yes, odd as it may sound, we have both read discussion sections that spend nearly all their time indicating how much better it would have been to test more participants or how a completely different design would have been more appropriate. It rather makes us want to write 'Well WHY didn't you test more participants then, and why didn't you use the better design?!'

The choice of maze completion task may also have been a little peculiar. We rather liked it because it was convenient and simple, but is it an appropriate task? Does it sensibly operationalize your dependent variable? In the 'alternative versions' section of this practical, below, we describe some ideas for other tasks you might consider that might suit your needs a little better. It all rather depends on why you are investigating the problem. Those of you working in an office may be more interested in using a task that better reflects their line of work, so you might choose a task that suits your particular needs better. Those of you who are students might choose to look at the ability to study material whilst being distracted, to investigate the sorts of task you face regularly.

It is entirely possible that you will have found completely different results from ours, and you should be prepared for that. We often hear the phrase 'My research project didn't work' from students who found unexpected results, or no effect at all. This is disappointing to the student, who has slaved away as carefully as possible just to be faced with either very confusing or extremely dull graphs and results. They usually perk up a little when we explain to them that it is not really the result that matters, it is knowing that you have designed the procedure properly and carried it out carefully. If you have done that, then, whatever the result is, this is absolutely acceptable. More than that, an unusual result can be more interesting than an expected one as it allows you to refute evidence provided by other researchers in the field. This can lead to a very lively discussion section indeed.

Alternative versions

Think about the type of task you have used to operationalize your dependent variable. We used maze completion, but you may like to use something else that is more relevant to your line of work or enquiry. 'Proof reading' might be a good one. Reading a document for errors is a regular task in a busy office environment, and you could deliberately insert a number of mistakes into a series of documents and use this as a means of calculating how a means of distraction influences performance of a task.

You might also like to think about how you could vary the means of distraction. We have used the sound of a dog barking, as it is something that annoys us when we are trying to work. You might like to engage in a less serious investigation, perhaps as a pilot procedure. We did think about 'tickling' as a means of distraction, but you'd need to be sure that you were amongst friends to try this one out. Again, the method you employ to operationalize your independent variable of distraction might depend on your environment and the focus of your investigation. You might like to investigate whether people listening to music are more distracted than those who are not, directly investigating the claim of many people who say that they are completely unable to work in silence.

Further investigations of whether people's performance on a task is influenced by some sort of distraction may take the form of a direct comparison of the types of distractions used. For instance, what is worse, a person speaking directly to you over a telephone, a person speaking directly to you whole sitting next to you, or some sort of speech-based radio show? This kind of procedure relates to the issue of the use of telephones in cars and might be of interest to you.

Test yourself

1. What are order effects and how do you avoid them?
2. In an independent-samples design, individual differences can be a real problem. How can their influence be minimized?

Reference

Beaman, C. P. and Jones, D. M. (1998). Irrelevant sound disrupts order information in free recall as in serial recall. *Quarterly Journal of Experimental Psychology, 51A*, 615–636.

chapter 11

practical: what do you think? attitude research

Here we look at some of the issues involved in measuring fairly intangible characteristics of people, such as their attitudes. We look at ways of measuring such characteristics, and in particular look at how you can aim to be as objective as possible even though you are looking at something totally subjective.
Topics covered: Rating scales, Likert scales, Thurstone scales.
You will need: paper, pen, imagination.

Background

What's the best way to show how you feel about something? We have both been known to get up and walk out of a cinema because the film was so dreadful that we could not bear to sit through it. These actions express our opinions very clearly. We've also both been known to send food back at restaurants because the meal did not arrive in the form that we had ordered it, or because a vegetarian dish had arrived with meat hiding in it. This isn't hard for the restaurateur to understand. We didn't like something so we sent it back. *How* unhappy were we though? Were we *just* unhappy enough to send it back or were we absolutely furious? How do you go about measuring how pleased, or unhappy, people are with something? You could ask them, that's always a good idea.

Nigel:	I ate at that new pizza place yesterday		
Ian:	I went there last week. I hated it.		
Nigel:	Hated it? That's a strong response. Hate? Really?		
Ian:	I despised it, I loathed it. I hated it.		
Nigel:	Calm down man. Didn't you say that you hated that Italian place too?		
Ian:	I did. I didn't hate it as much as the pizza place though.		
Nigel:	So you hated both, but you hated one more than the other?		
Ian:	I guess so…		
Nigel:	It's not easy to measure, I think. Perhaps you need a scale of 0 to 10, where 0 means you didn't hate it at all and 10 means you hated it a lot…		

The point here is that measuring attitudes is something that we all try to do naturally all the time. You make a meal for people, slaving over cookbooks and the stove for hours, and then try and gauge whether your guests appreciated all your hard work when they begin to eat your food. Wouldn't it be much easier simply to cut to the chase, and hand out a questionnaire after each course? This saves your guests the trouble of having to say how much they liked something, and saves you the problem of having to keep asking them. It does tend to spoil the ambiance a little, however.

Measuring opinions is very difficult. When conducting research with people there are a number of options open to us as to how to go about it. Rating scales are a favourite. More and more these days you are asked to complete a survey following any kind of service that you have received. This involves you indicating whether the company that fitted your new heating system did a good job, whether the experimental theatre you went to see by mistake met with your approval, or whether the services provided by your local government authority are acceptable. More often than not, we are asked to indicate our opinion with a Likert scale. Developed by Rensis Likert in 1932,[1] the Likert scale can take a number of different forms. In each case, though, opinions of something are recorded. The Likert scale is used to measure along a range how much people like something, or how much they agree with a statement. For instance, you might use a Likert scale like this:

Question: How much did you enjoy your meal?

Not at all!	Not much	Can't decide	It was OK	Hugely!

---

[1] Likert, R. (1932). A Technique for the Measurement of Attitudes. *Archives of Psychology, 140.*

Or you might use a Likert scale like this:

Question: How much do you agree with this statement: 'My meal was fabulous!' (1 – Disagree completely, 5 – Agree completely)

In either case, opinions are indicated by placing a mark in the appropriate box. You'll know from your careful reading of this book that Likert scales are examples of an ordinal scale of measurement. You'll also know that when data from Likert scales are analysed they are treated as interval data. This always happens. It's wrong. It really is, but it's the done thing.[2]

Just as with other things, Likert scales have their strong points, but they also have their limitations. If Ian filled in a series of Likert scales on the culinary merits of the tomato, and one on the culinary merits of cheese, then comparing his opinions of these two very different items is problematic. For instance, if he rated the tomato with a 1 on a scale of 1 to 5[3] and cheese with a 4, you cannot say that he liked cheese four times as much. You can probably say he liked cheese more than tomatoes, but what if Nigel also rated cheese with a 4? Does this tell us he likes cheese exactly as much as Ian? This is the sort of problem we have when dealing with low levels of measurement in our numbers. Had we been dealing with interval or ratio measures we could answer questions like this. Because Likert scales have lower levels of measurement, we have a bit of a problem.

Perhaps as a result, the Likert scale is only one of a number of methods of gathering data on attitudes. A cocktail of data from a number of different sources is generally a good way of ensuring that you have done everything you can to take as reliable a picture as possible of the attitude in question.

Another option open to you is a Thurstone scale. These were developed by Louis Leon Thurstone in 1928[4] as a means of measuring people's attitudes to religion. A Thurstone scale involves a series of statements and the participant indicates whether or not they are in agreement with each. The pattern of responses allows researchers to assess the participant's opinions on the subject under scrutiny. Part of a Thurstone scale can be seen below; it's the kind of

---

[2] Have a look back to Chapter 3 to remind yourself why.

[3] He would have rated it a −20 given the chance.

[4] Thurstone, L. L. (1928). Attitudes can be measured. *American Journal of Sociology, 33*, 529–554.

thing you might see in a study that investigates people's attitudes to immigration:

> Immigrants are very hard working
> There are too many immigrants these days
> Immigrants should learn the language of their adopted country

We may use 20 or 30 statements like this. The first step here is to have a group of participants organize the statements. They do this by scoring them from 1 to 11, 1 being classed as 'least favourable to the concept of immigrants' and 11 being 'most favourable to the concept of immigrants'.

Once we've done this with a number of people we collate all the data and see how often each statement is rated at each level. This allows us to plot a distribution. Each item will have its own distribution, so each item will have a mean rating, a median rating and a modal rating.

The next thing to do is to choose some of your items for the final stage, the data collection. Each item used will hold the score given by the median value it inhabits. So, for instance, the item 'immigrants are all lazy' will have a very low score (a modal value of 1), indicating the raters all saw this as an anti-immigrant statement. The statement 'Immigrants should learn the language of their adopted country' may have the score of 6, indicating that the raters felt that this was more favourable, or at least more neutral. The statement 'Immigrants are wonderful people' would be likely to gather a score of 11, as it is clearly favourable.

The final stage is to list each of your chosen items (statements), and have new participants indicate whether they agree or disagree with each. In doing this we can calculate a score for each participant. Each time the person agrees with a statement the score for that item is added to a total. Once the list is complete each participant has a total which can be averaged. This shows us where they sit in their attitude to the concept under investigation. The higher their average score, the more favourable is their attitude to the concept under investigation.

This sort of scale can be used to measure people's attitudes to all sorts of things. We both work in universities and we are constantly asked whether we think something is a good idea or not. Generally, being in the trade, we have an idea just by looking at the measurement tools used whether our opinion is important or not! The more serious people are in their data-gathering, the more seriously they want to know what you think. A Thurstone-type scale is a relatively long-winded thing to try and organize, so when we spot one of those we know that those doing the survey mean business.

Here's a good example: what do you think the role of education is? Do you think it's to make people clever? Do you think it's to measure people's cleverness? Perhaps you think it's the role of education to get people into jobs, or onto further education at university or graduate level. In the good old days all you needed to get into university was a decent pipe, a nicely cut suit, an improbably long hyphenated name and a good honest private education.[5] These days, however, universities cater for a wider clientele, and so too do high schools, and the world is a better place for it. Those of us who have had any experience of education from either side of the desk (that makes all of us) will often wonder what it did for us, so how about formalizing your wondering a little? How would you go about organizing a study into people's attitudes to education?

Method
Stimuli

We're suggesting here you have a go at creating your own Thurstone-style measurement scale as a way of investigating what people think about education. This will give you an idea whether people's attitudes to education are favourable (they think it is a good idea), whether their attitudes are not favourable (they do not necessarily think it is a good idea), or whether their attitudes are neutral. In summary the project looks like this:

Step 1: Arrive at as many statements about education as you possibly can.
Step 2: Have a number of participants sort the statements into 11 piles, from 'Unfavourable to education' to 'Favourable to education'.
Step 3: Look at the distributions for each statement, and sort into median values (see later for more on this).
Step 4: Choose 11 items from your list.
Step 5: Collect the data.
Step 6: Analyse and present the data and draw conclusions.

A little help here? Can you give me a little more of a hint?

Of course! Let's take each step in turn.

---

[5] We think it sensible to point out that this P.G. Woodhouse-esque stereotype does not fit either of us; we are just extremely jealous that neither of us attended university in a time of valets, smoking pipes in the library and where the only sensible vehicle for the young boulevardier about town to drive was an Aston Martin Lagonda.

Step 1: The aim of this step is to arrive at a list of attitude statements that you can sort into 'favourable to education' through to 'unfavourable to education'.

We'll start you off with a few. You need to identify as many as you possibly can. 70 or more is ideal. That seems rather a lot, but thinking up these statements is perhaps the most time-consuming part of the whole process. Experience has shown us that the more you use at this stage, the more accurate and consistent your measurements of attitudes will be.

Examples

'Education is a complete waste of time'

'Education is the most important thing in the world'

'Education is useful for some people'

'You can do anything if you put your mind to it, so why bother with education?'

'I left school at 14 and wish I had spent more time in education'

'Education can't teach you street-sense'

'If only I had spent more time working in school I would not be stuck in this dead-end job'

'One way to improve yourself is through education'

Step 2: Locate some participants. We'll call these your 'judges'. What's important here is that you try and use a good cross-section of people, and the more judges you use the better.

Write each statement on a piece of paper. Find a decent-sized table and tape 11 pieces of paper along the edge marked 1 to 11. Under 1 write 'favourable attitude to education', under 11 write 'unfavourable attitude to education'. Each participant now sorts each statement (item) on your 11-point scale.

After each judge is finished, mark down on a table where each statement was placed and start again with a different judge. Eventually you will have a graph of rating frequency for each statement. For instance, the graph for the item 'Education is a waste of time' will look something like this if we had used 48 judges:

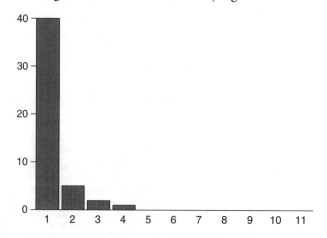

The graph for the statement 'Education is the most important thing in the world' might look like this:

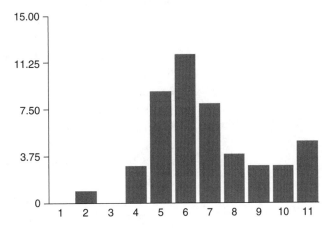

The graph for the item 'Education is useful for some people' might look like this:

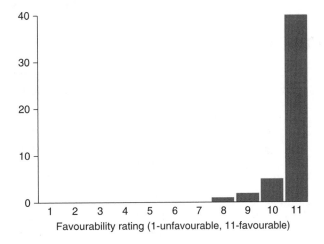

For these statements we can see that the modal scores (the most common scores) are 1, 6 and 11 respectively.

Step 3: Once you've done the judging and got the frequencies, you need to identify the median score for each. That's the score in the middle if you arrange them all from highest to lowest (or, in other words, it's the score above and below which 50% of the ratings fall). You'll end up with a table like this.

Statement	Median score	Interquartile range
Statement number 1	1	3.4
Statement number 2	5	2.7
Statement number 3	9	6.2

You'll need to do this for each of your statements. Notice, it's also very useful to calculate an interquartile range which tell us how spread out the judges' ratings were. This is useful for the next step.

Step 4: Choose one statement with a median at each value, 1 to 11. If there is more than one statement with the same median value then choose the one with the smallest interquartile range, because this will be the one the judges most agreed upon. If, for some reason, you do not have a statement for one of the median values between 1 and 11 then you should choose two more statements from the selection which, when averaged, provide the missing value. For instance, if you are missing a statement at level 6 then choosing one at level 4 and one at level 8 to replace it will provide an average score of 6 for this pairing.

Step 5: Place your items in a list and have a new set of participants indicate whether or not they agree with them.

Step 6: Calculate a score for each participant. Each of the items you chose had a median value associated with it. If the participant 'agrees' with this statement, then add this median value to their total. Once you're all done, take your total and divide it by however many questions there were. Simple.

Participants

The regular 'how many people do I need?' comes here. The answer is as many as you can find. The judging is relatively time-consuming depending on how many items you have to sort. Typically 100 items takes less than 10 minutes. The data collection from the final set chosen from the original pool of items takes even less time. It's exactly the kind of thing you see people with clipboards doing around town every weekend.

Essentially you will be using an **opportunity sample**, certainly for the data collection in the final stages. You can see the problems already, I imagine. If you choose to station yourself outside a university cafeteria full of people who have chosen to be in education you may get a biased view. If you situate yourself outside the unemployment office you may also get a biased view. However, this may be part of your research. It may be that you are interested in seeing what university students think of education, or whether those currently seeking work feel that education would be beneficial to them. In this case a scale like this can be very useful indeed.

Another thing to consider is the make-up of the sample you chose as judges. This is a good lesson in why size matters when it comes to samples. The point of the judging process is to get as balanced and agreed a view as possible. The larger your group, the more likely it is that a balance would be achieved. The problem with the judging process is that you are not really interested in the judges' opinions of education: what you are interested in is their judgement of how favourable the statement in their hand is towards education. You need to do your very best to get them to be as objective as possible, and try and keep their own opinions out of it.

Data collection

It's really important that you take the time to do this properly. Cutting corners with the judging, sorting or choosing which items to use will cause you problems in the end. It's also really important to explain to all the judges and participants that their opinions are useful in your research, but that they themselves are not being judged. Education is not such a controversial topic, but imagine the difficulty a scale like this could cause if it were concerned with homosexuality, the police, animal rights, hunting or, as Thurstone originally had in mind, religion. Be aware of what you are doing and disclose the purpose of your work.

Procedure checklist

- Choose up to 100 attitude statements about your topic.
- Write each on a separate slip of paper.
- Find some judges, and have them rate the statements.
- Calculate medians and interquartile ranges for each statement's ratings.
- Choose 11 statements to use and write them down to give your questionnaire.
- Find your participants and have them agree or disagree with the statements.
- Calculate a single score for each participant.

Results
Looking at your data

How you display your data will depend in part on what it is that you are trying to communicate with your reader and what was the motivation for your completing the project. Let's imagine, for instance, you were involved in an advertising campaign aimed at altering people's attitudes to education. This is just the sort of thing a university, school or indeed a government may find themselves involved in. How do you know whether attitudes have changed at all following your concerted advertising campaign? Measuring attitudes to education before the campaign and after it could give you some reason to think that your campaign has or has not been successful.

Or perhaps you decide to plot the mean score for your participant group against the mean score for a different participant group. This kind of thing is often useful when you want to look at attitudes held by different sectors of society, or different demographics. For instance, opinions of teenagers compared with opinions of older people, or opinions of people in cities compared with those of people who live in less urban environments.

Analysis

Your analysis can take a number of forms. Again, it all rather depends on what it is you are investigating. It may be, for instance, that your project is concerned with seeing how attitudes to management in a workplace change over time. To do this you might split your work-force in two, comparing the attitudes of one group at the start of the project with the attitudes of the other group after a period of time has passed, as an independent-samples design. The danger here, of course, is that any changes in attitude may in fact be an artifact of your having used two different groups. You'd need to be careful to match the groups, or safer still choose two very large groups.

An alternative might be to measure the attitudes of the entire work-force at the start of the project, storing each value with each employee's identifying number. After time has passed you could again measure every member of the workforce. In this way you could see how each individual's attitude has changed. This way you could analyse your data as a repeated-measures design, comparing the scores of one participant in one 'condition' with their score in another 'condition'.

Statistical thinking

The type of analysis you do here will depend on exactly what you are trying to achieve with the rating scale. The rating scale you are creating in this practical is a tool which you use to answer other questions – do attitudes to education change over time? Do university students differ from workers in their attitudes to education?

If you decide to use your questionnaire to answer this sort of question, you are doing a comparison of two groups. The standard way of doing this is with a t-test, which takes two groups and asks whether they are, on average, different from each other. The t-test makes various assumptions about your data, however: it assumes your data are normally distributed and that the spread of scores in each group is similar. If you can't meet these assumptions then you should really use a similar test which makes fewer assumptions. There are two of these: if you are using a repeated-measures design then the non-parametric equivalent of a t-test is called the Wilcoxon test; if you are using an independent-samples design then you want the Mann-Whitney test. These, or a t-test if you can use one, will simply tell you whether your two sets of attitude scores are different or not.

Discussion

Attitude research is an area that seems to sneak in all over the place. Magazines seem to measure attitudes all the time, in questionnaires and surveys. You may have experienced calls from agencies or market researchers who ask your opinions of things. When implementing a policy change, the sensible political party will employ a measurement scale like this as a yardstick, or a benchmark, to test the pulse of a demographic, to see if there is need for change or whether change would be well received.

In your research into attitude research make sure that you consider all the options. As we've already noted, a Thurston scale is just one of many ways to investigate opinions of things. In fact, the example we have employed here is only one form of a Thurstone scale: there are more! The one we have used is a method of equally appearing intervals, where attitudes are scored using intervals on a 1–11 scale. Our advice is to shop around: see what other attitude research is available as well. In fact, that's often a rather good way to proceed. Why trust one scale and not another? Why not see if different measurement tools provide you with similar answers? They should, after all.

The last thing to say is really the first thing to remember, as it is with all research. Be absolutely clear what it is that you want to measure and why you want to measure it before you even start choosing statements to judge. This will really help you focus, and can provide much-needed motivation during the process.

Alternative versions

This is exactly the kind of procedure you might use to investigate attitudes to all sorts of things. Wherever people may hold an opinion about something a scale like this can be employed to help investigate it.

Test yourself

1. Why use a large number of statements and judges in the judging process?
2. What is the point of calculating an interquartile range for each statement's ratings?
3. What do you do if you don't have an item for a particular median value when choosing items for your survey?

chapter 12

practical: something's not right

Topics covered: variables, sampling, experimenter effects, correlation, data assumptions, scatterplots, p-values, linearity.
You will need: paper, pen, imagination.

Background

Have you ever recommended a book or film to someone, one you've really enjoyed, but the other person didn't like it as much as you did?

The reason for this difference of opinion is because we live in a world populated by very different people, and that's why it's such an interesting place. One reason the other person might not enjoy a story which really spoke to you is that they have different experiences, expectations and knowledge from yours; it was your particular life history which made the story speak to you; their different experiences didn't 'click' with the story, and it left them cold. These life experiences we all carry around with us are what we are going to look at in this practical. In particular, we're going to look at the 'stories' or 'scripts' we all carry around with us. Think about what usually happens when you go to a shop. The fact you can know what 'usually' happens is because you have remembered the sequence of events – the script – for shopping.

Black and Bower (1979) said these scripts guide our expectations of how conversations work or how different activities, such as going to the supermarket, or taking the car to a filling station, work. They provide us with an order, telling us what to expect next and helping us operate efficiently. Think of them as a route to a goal: you know what you want and the script helps you get there. For example, you know you want a cup of coffee and the 'cafeteria script' you have in your head helps you get it.

You know from experience that sometimes these scripts don't quite run to plan, especially when something unexpected happens. Many of the more forgetful amongst us have shown up at the filling station only to discover that we've left our money at home, interrupting the usual flow of events we were expecting. Similarly, some steps in the script can be left out or skipped over. For instance, a trip to the supermarket usually begins with collecting a basket in which to hold your goods. However, occasionally, you may just need one or two things, and so a basket is not required − not typical for a trip to the supermarket.

Research (in Galambos, Abelson and Black, 1986) suggests we use these scripts − these mental guides to how events unfold − when we read stories. If the character takes a trip to the supermarket, or to a cafe, we have a ready-made script which helps us understand how things will progress. We can formalize this a little and think of it in terms of a memory for an event. Because we have a script for a particular event, unusual aspects of that particular event will be coded separately from usual aspects. Forgetting your money at the filling station for instance will be unusual or *atypical*, and as such will be stored separately in memory. But *typical* parts of the scripts, such as pulling up next to a fuel pump and selecting the correct hose, would be coded together. We might expect that, because all the usual events get stored together and the unusual events get stored separately, the unusual events are easy to remember and the usual events aren't. The workshop here looks at whether this really is the case.

Method
Stimuli

Begin by writing a series of short scripts or stories. You should choose a subject matter that is relevant to you. For instance, if you are studying business, or advertising, then your story should refer to the type of data a typical business or advertising student might have. Your script needs to have clear events, some typical and some atypical. How about this for an example? Here the events in the script are identified in bold letters, to show you what we mean by 'events'.

Jon woke to the sound of his old alarm clock. ***As he reached for his glasses*** *the world came into focus.* ***He got up, struggled to the kitchen*** *and* ***boiled water*** *for his morning coffee, returning to his bed to* ***wake up to the morning news*** *on the radio while he* ***drank his coffee.*** *Finally he stirred himself and got up, entering the bathroom where he turned on the shower,* ***glaring at the buffalo which had been sleeping in the shower cubicle and which now obligingly moved out of the way.***

Now, obviously, we're not being terribly subtle about things here: most of the events are very typical and one is quite clearly atypical. You make up your own stories with a mixture of typical and atypical events. You can write about anything, or you might decide to write more about Jon's day: small episodes relating to his trip to college, etc. Shape the story to your own circumstances. Jon may be a medical student, for instance, and he may have a physiology class at 11, meeting his friends for coffee and to discuss a project. You can fit this to your own needs and environment.

Take your stories and photocopy them. They should not be too long, because you don't want to fatigue your participants. Now before you can get on with data collection there are two more things you need to do. First, simply identify the actions in your story, perhaps by numbering them or using colour to identify each event (as we used bold letters). Second, have a panel of friends read through your scripts and indicate on a scale of 1 to 5 how typical each action is. (So drinking coffee is quite typical; finding a buffalo in the shower is very atypical.)

Next, take a piece of paper for each script and write down each of the actions you have identified and rated. Now make up some similar actions (*distractors*), and write these down also. Muddle up the real actions with these *distractor* actions.

You now have a series of events and each has been identified and has a typicality rating. We can now get down to business and think about collecting the data.

Participants

A frequently asked question in these sorts of things is 'how many people do I need?' The answer, typically, is that your sample needs to be 'as large as possible' but in reality it depends on how many stories you use, and how many events each story has. We've done this a few times, and it makes sense to pick four or six people to provide data per story. Power analysis is an extremely useful tool here, but think of where you get your sample from. If you are working in a medical school, perhaps training to be a nurse, then four people you met on the beach in the summer may not be from the population you are studying, and rating events as typical or atypical may be impossible for them if your scripts are about a day in the life of a nursing assistant at a busy city hospital.

If you are doing this practical as part of a workshop or a seminar session then the obvious thing to do is to use the people you find around you to provide data. This type of opportunity sample is very traditional when doing research with people, but you should be aware of some of the issues we covered in Part 1 about the problems you may encounter with this method of choosing your participants. There is a good chance, for instance, your classmates have a good idea of the content of your stories and scripts, so they may not be the best people to ask.

Data collection

Tell your participants they will be asked questions about a story you will give them to read (you can read it to them if you like). You don't have to be too specific here, but should give them an idea of what is about to happen. There is an issue about disclosure. You must not lie to your participants, and must not mislead them, but you do not have to give them all the information about the experiment. We have covered this elsewhere in the book in a section concerned with ethics. Finally, give your scripts to your participants and ask them to read through them once (or read it to them once). Now send them away, and meet with them 2 days later.

The original experiment was done by Graesser et al. (1980) and they used a number of methods to see what the readers remembered after hearing their stories. For the purpose of this practical we suggest you give half your participants the sheet you created with lists of actions and distractor actions, and ask them simply to indicate with a *Yes* or *No* after each item on the list whether it occurred in the story or not. With the other half of the participants, simply ask them to repeat the story back to you. This will give you data which will allow you to look at recognition (whether they recognize an action they have already seen) and also recall (whether they can remember an action they have been exposed to).

Procedure checklist

- Create several short stories, each describing a series of events in a recognizable setting.
- Have judges rate how typical each event is.
- Create a list of the events in each story, mixed up with similar events which were not in the story (distractors).
- Find several participants per story (say four or six).
- Give them the story to read (or read it to them).
- Wait for a while; 2 days is ideal.
- Half of each group writes down what they remember, half use your 'action lists'.

Results

Looking at your data

First of all, score your data. Score each action on the action lists as right or wrong. In the free recall groups, identify which actions have been recalled in each typicality level (remember, each action was given a rating on a 'typicality scale' before you began collecting data). For each typicality rating (1 to 5) you need a score of how many actions were remembered. Don't worry about word-for-word accuracy here; it should be clear enough whether the action has been recalled or not.

The next thing to do is plot the data on a graph. This is the best way to see if anything is going on. A scatterplot will give you an idea of whether a relationship, or correlation, might be seen between typicality rating and number of events recalled. For example, perhaps there is a positive relationship such that the more typical an event is, the more likely it is to be recalled.

With the event lists, you can use signal detection theory to see how your participants have managed to separate the real events from the distractors, which were not in the stories. What you're looking for is the accuracy with which the real events have been identified or recalled.

Statistical thinking

Your scatterplot gives you an idea of the relationship between how typical each event is and the likelihood it will be remembered. But remember, the graph only gives you an idea: you'll need to do some statistics on the numbers to provide a more accurate picture of how typicality is related to remembering. Correlation is covered elsewhere in this book and there is no need to repeat it here, but be careful about a common mistake people make. They regularly use the words 'prove' and 'cause' in their analysis of correlation data. Just because you get a positive correlation does not' 'prove' that one variable 'causes' another to increase: if there is a relationship between how typical an event is and how often people remember it, this does not tell us that typicality caused people's memories to work better.

The other thing you need to do here (as with all correlations) is check your scatterplot carefully to make sure it doesn't show any curved relationships. The correlation test can only handle relationships which look something like a straight line when plotted on a scatterplot. Sometimes, however, we see scatterplots where the points fall on curved lines. This is quite possible in this practical. Perhaps people are good at remembering very typical and very unusual events, but are bad at remembering events in the middle. In this case, you'll end up with a U-shaped plot, and you can't use correlation to measure the relationship.

Discussion

We've mentioned signal detection here. Signal detection analysis is an extremely powerful technique. It relates closely to this workshop but can be applied in many areas. You might be a town planner, whose job it is to make sure road signs and warnings are seen by motorists and pedestrians. You might be a doctor, checking slides for abnormal cells which may indicate the need for important treatment. In both these examples, and countless others, identifying the signal (road sign, abnormal cell) in amongst the rest of the visual scene is very important. How would you make a warning signal stand out? How would you test whether it really does the job?

Alternative versions

There are lots of changes you can make to this practical to suit your own needs or ideas. For instance, you may be interested in seeing how the length of the narrative influences how people remember it. Or you could restrict the amount of time people have to read the script, perhaps. This could be a useful study, as there are many situations where preparation time is limited (perhaps a tight meeting schedule, or a busy court case) and it may be useful for you to know how best to construct information to ensure optimal readability. Remember, where there are people involved, and information to be delivered or acquired, it benefits you to know how to construct your information to ensure optimal performance.

References

Black, J. B. & Bower, G. H. (1979). Episodes as chunks in narrative memory. *Journal of Verbal Learning and Verbal Behavior, 18*, 309–318.

Galambos J. W., Abelson R. P., Black J. B. (1986). *Knowledge structures.* LEA.

Graesser, A. C., Woll, S. B., Kowalski, D. J. & Smith, D. A. (1980). Memory for typical and atypical actions in scripted activities. *Journal of Experimental Psychology: Human Learning and Memory, 6*, 503–515.

chapter 13

practical: too many cooks or not enough heads?

In this practical we will look at why choosing an independent-samples design is a good idea and why it is a good idea to use standardized instructions. We'll also comment here on the importance of simple designs, and how varying more than one thing at once can cause confusion and mistakes in interpreting results. The type of project we describe here is flexible and can be adjusted to suit your needs, whether in the classroom or in a more professional setting where assessors may like to see whether people can work alone to achieve goals, and whether they can work as a member of a team to develop solutions to problems.

Topics covered: variables, practice effects, independent-samples design, group design, standardized instructions, practice effects, independent variable, dependent variable, confound.

You will need: some friends or volunteers, some paper and pencils, a stop watch (if you don't have a stopwatch, an egg-timer or a regular watch will do just as well; you just need something that can time a consistent period.) You also need some amusing 'items': you'll see why!

Background

What is the best way to solve a problem? That's a bit like asking 'How long is a piece of string?' It's a ridiculous thing to ask, you might think. But it all depends on the problem you are trying to solve. You might also think there are just as many ways of *solving* problems as there are problems that need to be solved! You'd be correct, up to a point. Of course it depends in part on the problem you are working with. After all, you'd not apply the same method of problem-solving to the question of how to be happy in your life as you would to decide the best way to move a chess piece from one side of the board to the other in the fewest moves: that would be ridiculous.

When we were growing up, food came from the kitchen, every evening, like magic. We just sat in front of the TV watching cartoons, getting hungrier and hungrier, when, as if by magic, a plate of wholesome food arrived, carried by our loving mothers. At that time, it never occurred to us that food might be prepared by someone other than our mothers; in fact, it came as a surprise when we realized every professional kitchen has many chefs and cooks, each preparing a small part of the dish for final construction right at the end. So what is it with this phrase we hear so often? Is it really true that 'too many cooks spoil the broth'? If it is, then surely all these professional kitchens could be so much more successful if they downsized to one competent chef rather than half a dozen 'competent' chefs. How might we go about investigating this? It's clearly a problem crying out for the 'research with people' treatment, and we think the principles you need to apply to solving this problem can be used in solving any number of issues you might encounter.

So let's think about what the phrase 'too many cooks spoil the broth' actually means. We could approach it by trying to make soup, or a cake, or we could approach the problem in the spirit in which the phrase is meant. What it actually means, of course, is 'When lots of people work on a project the result is inferior to that which might be achieved if fewer people worked on the project.' This is an issue managers of people must consider on a daily basis. How many people would it be best to assign to a project to achieve optimal results? A brief survey of management personnel in the business department of one of our universities reveals that, as we expected, management is a great skill, and good managers assign people to jobs almost intuitively. That's not much use to those of us beginning our journey to management stardom. We are trying to learn how best to manage a group of workers and we want to know how best to do it and why certain things work in different circumstances.

By this stage in our academic careers we have both attended many training events that are carefully designed to help us become better teachers, or better researchers, or more aware and sensitive tutors. At these events we are put into small groups, to talk over problems together, to work towards a common goal. At whatever stage you are at in your education or career you will undoubtedly have had exactly the same experience. In a classroom environment, tables are rearranged and six or seven people sit in groups to discuss something relevant to the topic in exactly the same way as we do with our colleagues at our training days. Why do you do this, though? Is it just 'received wisdom' that this is the best way to solve a problem?

We think it's about time that those interested in research with people, and working with people, really questioned their beliefs and 'received wisdom'. Do 'too many cooks spoil the broth', or are 'two heads better than one'?

Method
Design

The design is always terribly important. For this project we need to be sure to choose groups with different numbers of people in them, since this is really the focus of the investigation. (This is quite unusual: in nearly all research designs you will want to keep the number of people in each group the same; this is only an exception because the number of people is the very thing being studied.) You could approach this in a number of different ways, but three groups would seem like a manageable number.

Group A	Group B	Group C
One person	Two people	Three people

We suggest for this study you use an independent-samples design, where each participant only takes part in one group. Can you see why we suggest this? If we tried to use a repeated-measures design, for example testing a person working alone, then working with a companion, then working with two companions, the participant will be building experience of the task as they go, and this will affect their later performance. As such, an independent-samples design is almost certainly better.

So each 'group' carries out the same task, and we compare each group's performance. This way we should be able to see whether one person, two people or three people are best. In this case our independent variable is 'number of people in each group'. This is the variable that we are in control of. It is the thing that we, the researchers, are manipulating.

Do I only need three groups then? That's only six people in total, are you sure?

Good point. The danger is you may well find a result that you are happy with, but it won't generalize. What we should really do is carry out the procedure a number of times. We could, for instance, have five Group As, five group Bs and five group Cs. In fact, the more of each group you have, the better. This is because your sample becomes more representative of the population from which you are sampling as more of them partake in the procedure. Really, the best thing to do would be to get absolutely everyone in the world involved in the procedure, but that's not practical really; the fun of the research would be very short-lived, as would your bank account if you were paying people to take part. You also need to think about the impact an individual might have on the overall results if you choose to use a very small sample. We'll talk about this a little more later on, in the discussion, but take a moment now to have a think about it. Imagine, just by chance, the five most brilliant people in your opportunity sample were randomly allocated to Group A. How might this influence your results and conclusions?

Design checklist

■   Decide on a design (repeated-measures or independent-samples).
■   Spend a moment to think through the alternatives (pros and cons of each design).
■   Go back and reassure yourself that you have chosen the correct design.[1]

Participants

OK, we've decided on a general design. Now we need to fill up the groups with willing participants. Where we get these participants from will depend on a number of things. If you are reading this book in your study at home, and you feel the need to carry out the procedure right away, then you will need to rush out into the street and find some people who are prepared to help you. This would be an opportunity sample. A nice long bus queue maybe, full of people not in a hurry to get anywhere.[2] If you are reading this in preparation for a class workshop or practical demonstration then you are likely to be surrounded by people who will constitute your opportunity sample. It's worth mentioning a rather general point here: think about the overall make-up of your sample. The problem is that you are likely to be sampling from a rather restricted population. What you'd really like to be able to say is that your results reflect the behaviour of the general population. By limiting your sample to university students, for instance, you are only really able to say that your results reflect the behaviour of students. Similarly, if you are carrying out this sort

---

[1] Yes, we know we are making a big deal about this, but the design option is very important indeed. Spending more time at this stage will save you so much trouble later on.
[2] If they are catching public transport in the United Kingdom they couldn't possibly be in a hurry to get anywhere.

of procedure at a workshop as part of a management training seminar, your sample may be heavily biased towards white, middle-class men. The best thing you can do is be completely upfront about what you are doing and be aware there may be an issue with your sample and how well it generalizes; think about it very carefully before getting too deep into your project.

Each person you choose (from your group at university, from a volunteer sample who may have signed up upon a sheet you posted on the department notice board, from your management seminar, or from your bus queue) is allocated randomly to a group. You continue to allocate in this way until the groups are full. Now you are ready to begin.

What task will we use?

We now need to decide on a task that will provide us with our dependent variable – the thing being measured. What you choose for a task is really up to you. Try and choose something manageable that provides you with a really clear and quantifiable result. When we were trying this out we used a number of different tasks, but our favourite was what we call a 'creativity brainstorm'. The task here is to come up with as many uses for an object, or a collection of objects, as possible in 1 minute. You can choose whatever you like as objects: it rather depends on what kind of mood you are in. We used an ice-cream cone and a fish-slice. Research is a serious business after all. Your dependent variable is the number of uses for the item(s) chosen each group can come up with in 1 minute. The number of uses identified *depends* on the number of people in each group. The *dependent variable depends on the independent variable.*

Give each group a piece of paper and a pencil. You'll need a stopwatch or an egg-timer or something similar. Put the object(s) they are to use on the tables and conceal them beneath a sheet or napkin, to ensure that the members of all groups only have sight of the objects for a fixed period of time which is under your control. Make sure you give them standardized instructions. The reason you do this is that the only thing you want to influence the dependent variable is the independent variable, and giving each group different instructions may well influence their behaviour, and therefore taint your results. The best way to do this is to read out the same printed page of instructions to each group. Your instructions might look something like this:

'Thank you for agreeing to participate in this procedure. You will be given two objects[3] which are currently beneath this sheet on the table. When I say 'GO!' I will reveal the object(s). Can you please use the pencil

---

[3] You might not, of course, choose to use two objects, you could use any number. In fact, this would make an interesting twist to your project, and could form an independent variable in itself.

and paper provided to write down as many uses for the object(s) as you can. You will be given 1 minute[4] to do this. When I say 'STOP!' please put your pencil down immediately.'

You should also be extremely careful of how you address the participants before the procedure. If you are more enthusiastic with one group than another, this may influence their behaviour, so it's best to give the instructions and attempt to keep your approach as neutral as possible.

Collecting and collating your data

After your participants are finished, take their response sheets and count up how many uses were identified for the object(s). You need to collate the data on a single response sheet rather like the one below. In this example we have five of each of the different groups. We've started filling in some results for you so you can see how it might work.

Group ID	Group A	Group B	Group C
1	4	6	9
2	2	2	5
3	8	4	
4			
5			

Procedure checklist

- Randomly allocate participants to groups.
- Decide on a task.
- Read out standardized instructions to each group.
- Allow each a fixed amount of time to complete the task (using stopwatch or egg-timer).
- Collate and tabulate the data.

Results

Looking at your data

The first thing to do is to engage in a little simple mathematics. You need some descriptive statistics to help you decide what your data are telling you. You'll need a mean value for 'number of uses identified for the object(s)'. You'll also need a measure of dispersion for the data. In this case, an appropriate measure of dispersion is a standard

---

[4] Doesn't have to be 1 minute. It could be any length of time. Another possibility for changing the procedure to suit your needs.

deviation. Tabulate your results for your own reference. You'll hopefully end up with something that looks a bit like this:

Group	Mean	Standard Deviation
A (one person)	4.3	1.65
B (two people)	5.0	1.40
C (three people)	8.6	1.90

The next thing to do in this situation is to draw a graph. Remember, the type of graph you choose is important. Earlier in the book, where we were busy running after buses, we mentioned the problem that appears to infest many students that seems to remove them of all self-control where graph drawing is concerned. One will do, but make sure it's the correct one. A bar chart will work fine, something like this.

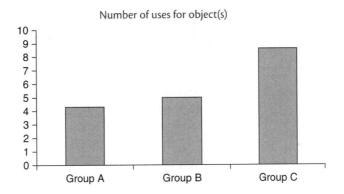

Number of uses for object(s)

That's nice and clear then. The larger the group, the more uses they come up with for the object(s) they were given. That's certainly true for *these* data, but how certain are we that we have really found a reliable relationship between group size and 'creativity' as measured in terms of uses possible with an object or two? How certain are we other people would behave in the same way as this sample?

Statistical thinking

Data analysis will allow you to conclude whether or not the data you have collected are reliable; it will tell you how certain you can be the results you have seen would also be found in the general population. Here your task is to compare the mean scores of three groups. The test usually used for this is one-way Analysis of Variance (ANOVA) with 'group size' (three levels) as your factor. This will give you a p-value telling you how likely it is the group differences seen in your sample were not meaningful. If this p-value is nice and low, the probability is low you will be wrong if you say you have found something happening in your sample.

Discussion

In this practical we have touched on some rather important points in experimental design. All decisions made in the design process are important but some will have an enormous impact on how your project progresses, whereas the impact of other decisions is potentially rather more subtle. The first thing we did here was choose to use an independent-samples design. The problem we were faced with made that decision rather necessary as otherwise practice effects would have distorted our results. However, independent-samples designs come with their own problems. For instance, who is to say that random allocation of participants to the different groups may not have led to the most brilliant participants finding their way into C groups, just by accident? If this really was the case, our result, which appeared to indicate larger groups were better at the task, may not have had anything to do with the size of the group at all: it could have been the result of a confounding variable.

Confounding variables are a worry, because when they appear we cannot be sure that any changes we see in the dependent variable were caused by the independent variable alone. However, random allocation of participants should make this kind of thing rather unlikely. We also chose to use multiple groups (five of each group), which should also limit the influence of individuals on the overall effect, as the more people we test the better our sample should be.

When we did this study we found larger groups performed better than smaller groups. It is, of course, quite possible your research showed that smaller groups performed better than larger groups. If so, you'll have to think why this was the case. One thing to consider is the same between-group differences and individual differences we talked about: it could have been that the most brilliant participants made it into the smaller groups, rather than the larger ones. Again, random allocation and data collection from multiple groups should have helped avoid this. Another explanation if you got different results from ours might come from the task you used.

Alternative versions

There are a number of ways in which this practical might be modified to suit your interests and needs. In our example we have chosen what we have called 'creativity brainstorming' as a method of providing a dependent variable. You might also choose other favourites that often feature at team-building events.

One is 'spaghetti bridge building' where groups are required to build a bridge with a limited supply of dry spaghetti and some glue. The dependent variable is provided by the amount of weight the bridge can take before breaking: a better design will take more weight.

Your manipulations and alterations of the method do not have to be so dramatic. We mentioned earlier in this practical that you could manipulate factors within the procedure we have described, such as the number of objects given to each group or the time you allow each group to come up with uses for them. What is important here is to remember the Keep it Simple rule. If you do decide to introduce 'number of objects' as an independent variable then you should keep group size constant. That way you can be sure any change in the number of uses identified is because of your variable (number of objects) rather than the number of people in each group. It really is important to remember that the only thing you want to influence your dependent variable is one independent variable, so Keep it Simple!

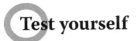

Test yourself

1. What are the major issues involved in choosing an independent samples design and how might you avoid them?
2. Why are standardized instructions a good idea?

chapter 14

practical: head size and intelligence

Topics covered: variables, sampling, experimenter effects, correlation, data assumptions, scatterplots, *p*-values, linearity.
You will need: tape measure, stopwatch.

Background

Back in the nineteenth century, Francis Galton decided it should be possible to know how intelligent somebody was simply by measuring the size of their head. It isn't hard to see his reasoning: the brain is where thinking takes place, so big brains should be better at thinking than small brains. And as the brain is kept inside the head, big heads should hold big brains.

As it happens, subsequent research has shown that Galton might indeed have been on to something. Not only did the US Army once find a relationship between its recruits' IQs and helmet sizes, but the relationships between brain size, head size and intelligence have since been explored with technology unavailable to Galton. Magnetic resonance imaging (MRI) machines, which can accurately measure the volume of people's brains without harming them, have shown that brain size is indeed related to intelligence (Willerman et al., 1991), and also that head size is related to brain size (Tramo et al., 1998). So it seems that we might be able to get an idea of intelligence from head size after all.

Of course, a tremendously important question in all this is how we should define and measure intelligence. Well, we're sorry but we're not going to give you the answer to this one. It would take a whole shelf of books properly to explore the issue, and quite frankly even then you probably wouldn't have a useful answer. Instead, for this practical we are going to use our own special measure of intelligence, the *unipodus* test. In other words, we're going to see how long you can stand on one leg with your eyes closed, which seems as good a measure of intelligence as any other, seeing as our aim here is really to explore research methods rather than intelligence.

Method
Participants

This subject is the sort we discussed back in Section 1, where we ideally want to produce general conclusions that apply to all human beings. Therefore, it would ideally be carried out with a large, completely random – or perhaps stratified – sample of the whole world's population. However, this is almost certainly impractical for you and you will need to get your sample in another way, whilst being aware of the strengths and limitations of the sampling method you use.

If you are doing this practical for a lesson, you will most likely want to test an opportunity sample, such as all the people who are in your class. Although people often view them as second-rate, opportunity samples can work pretty well, especially when the numbers are quite large, and this form of sampling forms the basis for an awful lot of published studies by professional researchers. However, you do have to be careful: we once did this experiment with a class of sports science students who produced quite an unexpected set of data (see *gymnasts.csv* in the online resources). In any study you carry out, you want to be able to generalize from your sample to the population, and if your sample is biased somehow your ability to do this may be compromised. A particular issue for this practical is that the test involves balance, and a student sample is likely to have a relatively low average age. This means your findings are unlikely to generalize well to populations including older people, who may not have quite such good balance.

As with all studies, you also have to decide how many people to test. The best way of doing this is to use power analysis, which is discussed fully in Section 3. However, if you don't want to get involved in that relatively advanced topic for now, just remember that the general rule is: the more the better. For this study, we suggest aiming to test at least 25 people, which will give you enough data for the analysis below. We will say a little more about participant numbers in the Discussion as well.

Data collection

Measure and record the circumference of each participant's head 1 cm above their eyes using a tape-measure (or a piece of string, which you can then measure on a ruler). Then have each participant stand in a clear area of floor, close their eyes and lift one foot from the ground. Use your stopwatch to measure how long they can stay on one leg and record the time next to their head size. If you have a large sample to test, you might want to split into groups to save time and pool your measurements. Of course, if you do this you will need to be aware of possible experimenter effects, as the various people operating stopwatches are unlikely all to have the same reaction times; they are likely also to show differences in where they position the tape measure on people's heads.

If you are not able to collect your own data for this practical, a set is provided on the companion website: www.palgrave.com/psychology/holtwalker in the file called *headsize.csv*.

Results

Looking at your data

Once you have got your data, the first thing to do is to plot them on a graph to get an idea of what the relationship looks like. This is important, as not only will it immediately give you a good idea of whether you have found a relationship between the two measures or not, but it will also allow you to know whether the assumptions that underpin your statistical tests are sound (see discussion below).

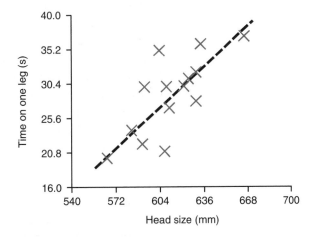

You may well find your data look like those on our plot here, in which there is indeed a tendency for people with bigger heads to be able to stand on one leg for longer than people with little heads. Of course, you may find something very different. A statistical analysis will give you a better idea of whether the data you have plotted in your graph really show a meaningful relationship or not.

Analysis

The simplest way to analyse data like these is to use a form of correlation. Correlation measures the extent to which two variables show a linear relationship. But what does this mean? Perhaps the easiest way to understand what a linear relationship isto say that two variables have a linear relationship when their layout on a scatterplot could be, more or less, summarized by a straight line, like ours above. Sure, the line on our graph isn't a *perfect* summary of the data, but the general layout of the data points is pretty similar to it, with the lowest scores tending to be down at the left-hand side and the highest scores tending to be up at the right-hand side. Yes, the real datapoints are only roughly the same as the line, but, when studying people, rough relationships are the only ones we see.

Behavioural scientists like linear relationships like this because they are simple: they let us reach easily understood conclusions like 'as this thing rises, this other thing also tends to rise'. The data in our graph have a *positive correlation*, which means that as one variable (head size) increases, the other (intelligence) tends also to increase. Other relationships can involve *negative correlations*, which means that as one increases the other tends to decrease. We're all familiar with relationships of this sort – we know, for example, that as our level of tiredness rises, so does the number of mistakes we make when doing difficult tasks (a positive relationship), and that the more alcohol we consume, the less sense we make in conversations (a negative relationship).

Provided you can measure the two variables in question, relationships like these can be precisely determined using correlation statistics, the two most common being Pearson's r and Spearman's rho. r is used for parametric data and rho is used for non-parametric data (you'll be able to see whether your data are parametric or not, from the discussion in Section 1). Both tests provide you with a value – known as a correlation coefficient – between −1 and +1.[1] A correlation of +1 means two variables have a perfect positive correlation: as one goes up by a certain amount, the other goes up by a certain amount. An example of a perfect positive correlation of +1 is the

---

[1] Remember that we want you to understand the concepts of statistics before getting bogged down in the calculations, and we encourage you not to worry how the values are calculated for now but rather to let a computer do the work and give you the statistics. But if you are confident enough to look at how these tests work, or need to do hand-calculations for your lesson, you'll find more information in Section 3.

relationship between distance in centimetres and distance in metres: if we move something by 1 centimetre, we know it has moved exactly 0.01 metres because distance in metres is perfectly related to distance in centimetres. A correlation of -1 means two variables have a perfect negative relationship: as one goes up by a certain amount, the other goes down by a precisely fixed amount.

In the real world, you will probably never see correlations of -1 or 1, and if you do it often means you've done something silly, like in our distance example above, where both variables are just measuring exactly the same thing in two different ways (something it's all too easy to do without realizing). What you will usually see when you do a correlation on real data is an in-between value such as .52 or $-.36$. Values like these indicate that as one variable changes its value, the other value also tends to change, but that this is just a tendency, and the relationship is not perfect. The closer the correlation coefficient is to zero, the weaker the relationship is, and the more it is a tendency rather than a hard-and-fast link. So, for example, research on the relationship between brain size and intelligence has found a correlation of around .50 between the two measures. As this coefficient is not close to zero, we know there is a real relationship. However, as the score is also not close to one, we know the relationship is not perfect, and we would certainly expect to find plenty of people for whom the link between brain size and intelligence does not follow the trend.

Your correlation, like all inferential statistics, will also provide you with a p-value. We discussed the 'official' meaning of p in Section 1, but we also said that there were easier ways to understand it. When doing correlations, we prefer to think of p as *the probability that you would be wrong if you said your two variables are genuinely related*. As you know by now, when p is less than .05 – that is, if there is less than a 5% chance you would be wrong if you said you had found an effect – it is usual to discount that possibility and say that you have indeed found something in your data.

Strong correlations (those with coefficients towards -1 or $+1$) tend to have low p-values. This is because, although it is easy to see small correlations by accident (try correlating two sets of random numbers; the result will almost certainly not be zero), you are unlikely to see a strong correlation when one does not really exist between the two variables in question. So, if you see a low p-value, there is most likely a real relationship between those two variables in the general population.

p will also tend to be smaller the larger your sample is. This is because the more people you test, the less likely it is that any effect you may see is caused by your participants being in some way a funny bunch who are not representative of the wider population.

More advanced techniques suitable for these data include regression analysis, which will not only measure the strength of the relationship in the same way as correlation, but also describe the exact *form* of the relationship between the two variables.

Discussion

In this practical, you have done something that is extremely common in research on people: you have collected two measurements from each person in a sample and measured how strong the relationship is between the two sets of measurements using correlation.

You will come across correlations all over the place when reading other people's research. One thing you must always remember is that correlation relies heavily on the assumption of linearity, and so only works if the relationship between the two variables looks more or less like a straight line when plotted on a graph. This is a critical point, and you have to remember that a correlation coefficient close to zero only lets you conclude that the two variables are not related if you are sure there is no other relationship between them. To illustrate this point, look at the relationship below, which has a shape something like an upside-down U. The data in this plot would have a correlation coefficient fairly close to zero, but this certainly doesn't mean the two variables have no relationship to each other, as they quite clearly do; rather, the low correlation for these data would be because their relationship isn't linear. This is why we recommend always looking at a scatterplot before carrying out a correlation. (It is surprising how many professional researchers fail to do this, and simply leap into carrying out correlations after collecting their data, often concluding that two variables are not related when in fact they are – just not in the linear way their correlation test expected.)

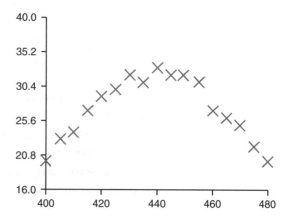

Another thing to be careful of when using correlation is that, just because two variables are correlated, this does not mean that there is a causal relationship between them. If you found a correlation between head size and intelligence in your data, this tells you nothing about whether high intelligence is caused by big heads, or whether big heads are caused by high intelligence, or whether both things are caused by some other factor you haven't tested. The only way you will ever understand causal relationships is by using very different techniques, chiefly the experimental method. This is another mistake people make all too often when using correlation: they see a significant correlation between two variables and conclude that changes in one must lead to changes in the other.

Finally, before you get worried that your small head means you might not do so well on your research methods course, or get ideas above your station because of your large cranium, we should remind you that our *unipodus* test was clearly not a real test of intelligence (although feel free to act as though it were when writing up your findings, as this will give you practice writing in the proper style).

More interestingly, though, even if standing on one leg had been a real measure of intelligence, you would still have to be very careful in interpreting the relationship between this intelligence measure and head size. This is because you are looking at a *correlation of a correlation*: it is actually brain size that correlates with intelligence, and we are using head size as a rough measure of brain size. This means that head size is a totally indirect measure of intelligence.

Alternative versions

This practical could be modified to suit your requirements in various ways. For example, we have chosen standing on one leg as a measure because it is easy to use in a classroom setting, but you might consider using instead a more traditional measure of intelligence such as a part of the Wechsler IQ scale (if you have access to it), or any online IQ test (there are plenty).

Test yourself

1. Is the relationship between stress and illness positive or negative (in the statistical sense!)? What about the relationship between the number of police officers in an area and the number of crimes that are committed?
2. Think of any two positive relationships and any two negative relationships that have not already been mentioned here.

3. A cup of coffee really wakes me up. Two cups make me even more alert! Would you therefore expect to see a correlation between how much coffee I drink and my level of alertness? If not, why not?

References

Tramo, M.J., Loftus, W.C., Stukel, T.A., Green, R.L., Weaver, J.B. and Gazzaniga, M.S. (1998). Brain size, head size, and intelligence quotient in monozygotic twins. *Neurology, 50*(5), 1246–1252.

Willerman, L., Schultz, R., Rutledge, J.N. and Bigler, E.D. (1991). *In vivo* brain size and intelligence. *Intelligence, 15*, 223–228.

3 part

the really
useful
section

In this final part of the book we've included some sections that we think you'll find useful.

There's a 'think critically' section that will give you a chance to flex your research muscles a little more. Also included are two sample write-ups that will show you how, and how not, to approach reporting of your research. We'll finish off with a glossary that should provide a quick reference to many of the terms you'll encounter as you continue your research.

chapter 15

think critically: don't believe everything you read

Take a look at the following descriptions of studies, all of which are faulty in some way. We've made these up, and some may well sound quite ridiculous to you but others may just ring a bell (as we've based them on real mistakes!).

Newspapers are full of claims based on bad science, or on misreadings of good science. When you read over the examples we've included here, use your knowledge of research design to identify the problems with the statements and suggest a better reading of the 'results' we've given you. We've added some of our thoughts to the book's website.

Drinking tea in adolescence causes criminality

Researchers were interested in whether drinking tea during adolescence led to criminal activity in later life. Twenty-four inmates from Crouton County Women's High-Security Prison were asked to recall how much tea they drank each day when they were 14 years old. The participants' ages ranged from 18 to 46 (mean age 38). As shown in the graph, there was a positive correlation between the average amount of tea drunk as a teenager and the number of recorded criminal acts on a person's record. The correlation had a value of $r = .82$,

$p < .0001$. The researchers therefore concluded that drinking tea in adolescence leads people to become criminals in later life and called for tea sales to be severely restricted.

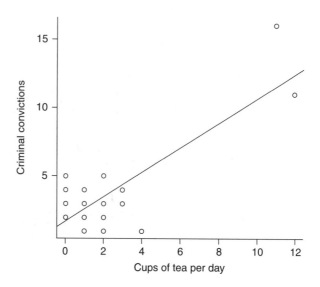

Do parents spend more on computer equipment than non-parents?

The first 40 participants to enter World of Computers on a Monday morning were recruited for this study, giving a sample of 26 men and 14 women. Each person told the researcher how much they spent in the shop during their visit, and also how many children they had. Overall, men were found to spend more than women ($t = 5.71$, $p = .02$). The Pearson correlation between number of children and amount spent was $r = .21$. Therefore, the more children people have the more they spend on computer equipment. Parents are apparently motivated to buy computer equipment for their children and this knowledge will be useful to computer manufacturers, who should clearly make their products more child-friendly.

How can people be encouraged to recycle?

The owners of J & B Recycling wanted to know what prevents people from recycling more of their waste. They paid a researcher to investigate, who carried out a focus group study. The focus group was recruited from people who lived on a residential street and five people took part. The study concluded that people's interest in environmental issues is simply not great enough for them to make any effort to recycle their waste. The researcher recommended that a large-scale publicity campaign is needed to make people more concerned about their environment.

Does eating more tomatoes make you live longer?

Researchers were interested in whether a diet rich in tomatoes increases life expectancy. They took a group of 1,000 people from an island in Greece, where the diet is traditionally rich in tomatoes, and a group of 1,000 people from a religious sect based in the remote highlands of Chile which forbids the eating of tomatoes. The sample was followed for 10 years and at the end of this period 132 people had died from the Greek sample but only 68 had died from the Chilean sample. The researchers concluded that eating tomatoes is associated with a lower life expectancy.

Do false beards make babies smarter?

A rumour spreads in the media that babies who are made to wear a false beard for 30 minutes each day become cleverer as a result. A team of researchers set out to see if there is any truth in this. They find 500 parents who have started making their babies wear stick-on beards and 500 who have not. When tested at 4 years old, the children who had worn the beards during infancy were around 12% better on tests of preschool skills than the children who had not. The researchers concluded that the beards did indeed have a significant impact on the children's development.

Inter-office sports showdown

A large company called Strimpit Holdings has two equally large branches, one on the Eastern side of a city and one on the Western side. The two branches have a long-standing rivalry. They decide to hold a running race in which each branch chooses their best runner to compete in a single 1-kilometre race. The Eastern branch selects their best runner by getting all their employees to run 1 kilometre and selecting the person with the fastest time; the Western branch don't do any running at all but choose their best runner simply by emailing all their employees and asking who is a good runner.

The Western branch's email search produces an employee who regularly runs a kilometre in 5 minutes and has never run this distance in less than 4 minutes 50 seconds; on the day of the Eastern branch's race-off an employee runs a kilometre in 4 minutes 35 seconds. Observers therefore expected the Eastern branch to win the final race, but the employee from the Western branch was faster. Everybody was mystified by the result.

Who needs therapy?

A group of clinical psychologists develop a new form of therapy intended to help people with depression. They take a group of 25 people and measure their levels of depression with an established depression questionnaire. They then administer the new therapy for 8 weeks and at the end of this period measure depression levels again. The average depression level at the start of the study was 56 and at the end, after the therapy, it had gone down to 45. The clinical psychologists conclude that the therapy has been successful at treating depression.

Wearing a hat while driving dramatically increases the likelihood of having an accident

Researchers from the Homburg school of road safety are advising drivers not to wear a hat while driving. A recent survey of 100 delegates at the national league-of-hat-wearers' conference found 27% of them had been involved in a road traffic accident in the previous year. This is 16% higher than the national average. This suggests wearing a hat while driving is significantly more likely to result in an accident than not doing so.

Increase in the price of oil has positive result

Contrary to popular belief, all is not doom and gloom as far as fuel prices are concerned. As the prices of a barrel of oil continue to rise the behaviour of consumers is changing as a result. A sample from the classic Porsche owners' club of Hawaii suggests people are driving less because their fuel is now more expensive. 'The reason for this is obvious,' said Marius von Taxman. 'Our prudent taxation of motoring is forcing drivers to use alternative methods of transport.'

'Education pointless!' says master baker

Lupin DuPain, the famous French baker, has confirmed what we have done already knowed for years: there's no point in going to school. He left school when he was 12 and has now got loads of money. We all know people like this, so school is completely pointless and a waste of time.

Exams are getting easier, says Lord Spottiswood

The minister for education today revealed that exams are getting easier. 'The record results achieved by high-school students can only be because the exams are much easier now than they were when I was a lad', reported his Lordship. Our research has revealed that exams have been getting easier in this way for the last 27 years. Where will it ever end?

You'd have to be insane to drive in New York

Research revealed in a recent meeting of New York's public transport authority has shown that driving is a great deal slower than taking a bus or the subway. Two groups of 20 people travelled from Manhattan's Battery Park to an address on the Upper East Side. One group drove and one group took public transport. The average time taken to drive was 7 minutes longer than the average time taken to travel with public transport: proof that using a car in New York these days is never the best option.

chapter 16
sample write-ups

Talking about how to do research properly is the best bit really. It's enough for a large number of people who do research with people to know what to do and how to do it; they can then take the information they need from their findings and use it in their area of study or work. Often, however, it's not enough to present a graph in a technical report summarizing our findings. Now and again it is necessary to produce a more detailed explanation of why we did what we did, what we did, what we found and what we concluded from our findings. The format of these write-ups depends in part on the discipline in which you work or study, so it's worthwhile reading a few reports in your area to get a feeling for what is required. In fact, that's a very good piece of advice. As with most things, a familiarity with what is needed often really helps your writing, so read around before you start.

In the following section we've included a couple of short reports in note form that give you a good idea of what to do, and more importantly what not to do. Of course, you may want to write in more detail, perhaps focusing on certain aspects of your study depending on the forum in which your report will appear. We've included a good and a not-so-good summary here of the 'It's a matter of taste' practical from earlier in the book. Read both and compare the way that they've addressed the different issues.

GOOD: It's a matter of taste
Introduction

> Opening line gets straight to the point and says what the research question is about.

Since the initial work of Pop and Phizz (1999), there has been a great deal of interest in whether people can tell diet varieties of soft drinks from sugar-based varieties. As McPheelan (2002) pointed

225

out, understanding people's preferences for diet versus sugar-based drinks would be useful for people working in public health promotion, as the ability to shift consumers from high-calorie drinks to lower-calorie alternatives would be useful in combating obesity. However, such a shift will not be easy if people simply do not like the flavour of diet drinks.

Previous work on diet and sugared drinks has shown us that, in general, participants can tell the two categories apart with, on average, an accuracy of 84% (Bobkiss and Tennant, 2004; Kippering and Phlange, 2005; Wartfish and Spadge, 2008). However, all previous studies in this field have focused on people's ability to tell the two types of drink apart, but they have not considered people's *preferences* for one drink over the other. In other words, it is one thing to show that people can tell diet drinks from sugared drinks, but this is not the same as saying that people *prefer* one type of drink, and any preference for one drink over the other would be useful information for people working in, say, health promotion.

A second issue with existing work on diet drink preference is that, to the best of our knowledge, no study in this field to date has controlled the temperature at which the drinks were presented. The temperature of a drink alters its taste quite considerably (Bagshott, 1966), and, in the absence of temperature control in previous studies, it is possible that any effects of drink type on people's responses were really caused by the temperatures at which the drinks were served.

This study, then, will give participants diet and sugared versions of the same drink and look at their preferences. Given Ratchett's (1966) claims that we innately seek sugar in our diets, we predicted that when diet and sugared versions of a drink are served at the same temperature there would be a preference for the sugared version.

Method

Participants

Forty participants (20 male, 20 female) took part in this study. They were recruited as an opportunity sample from amongst the students of Milksop University and did not receive payment for their participation. Ages ranged from 18 to 32 (mean = 20.12, *SD* = 2.45). No participants identified themselves as professional or unusually experienced tasters (catering students, etc.).

Materials

The drinks used in this study were Walkerpop's Cola and Walkerpop's Diet Cola. The drinks were served in white plastic cups of 250 ml

---

Annotation boxes:

Here we justify carrying out the study, in this case by showing it has real-world relevance. Other studies might be justified by their theoretical importance.

We've ended the first paragraph by identifying the key issue.

We introduce what others have found in this field

We then go on to identify the shortcomings of previous work, or the outstanding questions that we plan to address.

Note the reference back to the real-world application we mentioned earlier

Having looked at theoretical issues, we also identify a practical /methodological issue that we can address here.

We've made a statement, so we have to back it up with something. Here we've done this with a citation.

We end the introduction with a statement about what we expect to see.

The key aim of this section is to show people exactly what you did. There should be enough detail that a person could repeat your study exactly as you performed it.

It's good to say whether your participants were paid or not, as it might say something about their motivation.

We felt this was an important issue that might affect the study, so we show here that we addressed the issue.

With materials, it's good to be as specific as possible, citing models, brand names and so on.

capacity (Cup-u-Like model #23). Before the study, the drink bottles were chilled overnight in a single refrigerator and during the study were kept in a single ice bucket to ensure the temperature of the two drinks was as similar as possible. The labels were removed from the bottles and replaced with stickers marked 'A' and 'B'.

Design

If there is some particular debate about whether to use repeated- or independent-measures design, that should usually be in the Introduction rather than here.

One of our aims here is to show that we have done our study in a robust fashion, so we are careful to describe how we control potential problems.

The study was conducted as a repeated-measures design. In order to control for possible order effects, the presentation was counterbalanced such that half the participants tasted the diet drink before the sugared version and half experienced the opposite order. The procedure was carried out single-blind, such that the experimenters knew what drinks A and B were but the participants did not.

Procedure

In many studies, each person experiences essentially the same procedure, so it's often useful to write up a participant's-eye-view of the procedure.

Participants' responses might have been influenced in this study by having other people present, so it's important we explain that participants were tested alone.

Here we show how we tried to achieve consistency across people.

People should be able to leave your procedure in exactly the same state as they entered it. They didn't begin with a sickly cola taste in their mouths, so they should have the option of ending the same way.

Each participant was tested individually in a procedure lasting approximately 5 minutes. For each participant, 25 ml of the first drink (diet or sugared, depending on the counterbalancing condition) was measured into the participant's cup using a measuring cup and the person was asked to drink it all. Immediately, the procedure was repeated with the remaining drink. As soon as this had been consumed, the participant was asked which drink they preferred the flavour of, and their response to this two-alternative forced-choice question was noted by the experimenter. The participant was then thanked for their time, debriefed and offered a drink of water and a mint.

Results

We have presented the data in the text, rather than in a table or graph, because they are so simple that a table or graph would not make them any easier to understand. But if a table or graph makes things clearer, you should definitely use one.

People often don't specify the null hypothesis they tested, but it's good practice.

Generally, it's good to give the exact value of p, but in this case it was so low we decided just to say that it was less than .001 – in other words, there is less than a 1 in 1000 chance of seeing this result in our sample of 40 people if the population really has no preference for one drink over the other.

Note that we always maintain a note of doubt. We can never know anything for certain.

Each of the 40 participants provided a single response, which was a preference for the diet or the sugared drink. These responses were pooled to provide the number of times each drink was chosen, out of the maximum of 40. This showed that the diet version of the drink was chosen 31 times (77.5%) and the sugared version was chosen nine times (12.5%).

A binomial test was used to assess the null hypothesis that there would be no preference for one drink over the other. This showed that for 31 people out of 40 to choose the same drink is significantly different from what we would expect if responses were random ($p < .001$, two-tailed). As such, it appears that responses were affected by the type of drink, such that the diet version of the drink is generally preferred to the sugared version.

Discussion

Previous work showed that people are relatively good at discriminating sugared and diet versions of the same drink, but there was an outstanding question of which variety is preferred when people are asked to choose one. This study assessed this preference by giving people diet and sugared versions of the same drink and asking which they preferred. The results in this study showed a reliable preference for the diet over the sugared version of a drink.

> Discussion begins with a short recap of what the study was for.

> A brief summary of the findings.

The finding that the diet version of the drink was preferred overall to the sugared version was counter to our prediction, and extends our understanding of drink preferences by showing not only that people are able to tell diet and sugared drinks apart with some success (Bobkiss and Tennant, 2004; Kippering and Phlange, 2005; Wartfish and Spadge, 2008), but also that they have a preference for one over the other.

> We refer back to the prediction we made in the introduction.

> Shows how our study contributes to knowledge on this subject.

If, given the choice between sugared and diet versions of the same drink, people tend to prefer the diet version, this suggests that there may be less of a health promotion issue with sugared drinks than McPheelan (2002) suggested.

> We show what our findings say about the real-world issue that we set out to address.

However, we should show some caution before making any public policy decisions based on these data. Although our sample showed a preference which was comfortably different from the 50:50 split we would expect if people did not really prefer one type of drink over the other, our sample was relatively small and came from a fairly constrained population – specifically university students of fairly young age. On a matter such as this, it is quite possible that their preferences would not reflect the preferences of a wider population, such as all adults in the country. This is in fact probable, given that soft drinks are marketed in particular ways to this particular group. As such, it would be valuable now to replicate this study with a sample of a wider population, and with other types of drink, to see whether the preference for diet drinks is still seen.

> This name-and-date approach to citations is known as the Harvard system; some publications use footnotes or endnotes to cite references. Always check which reference system you need to use in your writing.

> We look at possible problems with our study.

> We provide a basis for the issue we have identified.

Conclusion

This study showed that, overall, people appear to prefer a diet version of a drink to a sugared version. This suggests that McPheelan's (2002) concerns about sugared drinks being a problem for health promotion may be less of an issue than she thought: people can tell diet and sugared drinks apart (Bobkiss and Tennant, 2004; Kippering and Phlange, 2005; Wartfish and Spadge, 2008), but these findings suggest that, given the choice, most people would prefer to drink the diet variety.

BAD: It's a matter of taste

Introduction

> No evidence or citation given to back this up.

> Yes it was.

The ability to taste flavours is a product of the tongue. This was not always the case, however: Aristotle's seminal work, *On Taste*, argued that flavours were experienced by the liver, an idea that remained popular right up until the seventeenth century when Descartes commented,

'Gustatory sensation is a product of oral impingement, and the liver is not involved.'

> Actually, no. Participants only tried 2 drinks and may have liked all sorts of other drinks more. Always be as specific as possible with language.

> No justification for the study. No reference to previous work in the area.

This study looked at what type of drink people liked most.

Method

Participants

> Needs much more detail about who they were.

40 people took part in this study.

Materials

> Not enough detail – the materials could affect the study, so people need to know exactly what was used.

The drinks used in this study were some Cola and some Diet Cola of the same brand. The drinks were served in plastic cups. The labels were removed from the bottles and replaced with stickers marked 'A' and 'B'.

Design

> No mention of the counterbalancing. If it's not mentioned, people will assume it wasn't done. The same is true for any other controls or possible confounding variables.

The procedure used a repeated-measures design in which every person tasted both drinks.

Procedure

> Again, simply not enough detail.

Each participant drank one type of cola then the other. They then told the experimenter which they preferred.

Results

> It would be more informative to give the percentages or proportions as well.

> No need to present the same information in more than one way. Here the same numbers are given three times.

> No title. No indication of what the numbers mean. A table should be interpretable on its own.

The diet drink was chosen by 31 people and the sugared drink by nine. This is illustrated in the table and graph below:

Sugared	Diet
9	31

> Again, a graph should be interpretable on its own: title, axis labels, etc. And here, this is the wrong sort of graph: the results show how a group of people breaks down into subgroups, so a pie chart would have been more appropriate – bar charts are really for representing score.

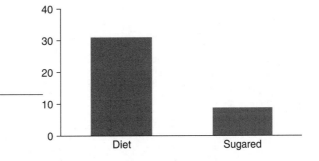

No statistics. And this statement is far too definite: SOME people IN THIS SAMPLE prefer the diet drink. Language needs to be accurate.

Clearly, people prefer the diet drink.

Discussion

No analysis of the data.

This statement is too sweeping.

Can't say 'drinks' as only one was tested.

This study showed that people prefer diet drinks to sugared drinks. As such, manufacturers need to stop producing sugared drinks because they are unhealthy and nobody really likes them anyway.

Conclusion

No evidence given for this statement, and it's nothing to do with this study's results.

This statement is far too strong. Far too much is being inferred from the sample.

This statement does not emerge from the study. The study said nothing about whether one type of drink is 'better' than the other.

Diet drinks are better than sugared drinks.

Glossary

Alpha (α) – the value against which *p*-values (qv) are compared. Every statistical test produces a *p*-value, which is the probability that the null hypothesis (qv) is correct. If this *p*-value is below a certain level, we conclude that the probability of the null hypothesis being correct is so low that it probably isn't correct, and the alternative hypothesis (qv) is probably correct instead. Alpha (α) is traditionally set at .05, although this is just a convention, and it can be set at other levels as well. In strict terms, alpha is the acceptable probability of a Type I error. See also familywise error rate (qv).

Alternative hypothesis – another name for the experimental hypothesis (qv).

Analysis of variance – a statistical technique for looking at the relationship between categorical variables (qv) and a continuous variable (qv). Although, mathematically, it is the same as regression (qv), analysis of variance (often abbreviated to ANOVA) tends to be viewed and used as a separate test. Uses of ANOVA include seeing whether three or more groups of people differ on a particular measure, or whether various groups of people perform differently on a test before and after you do something to them. See also interaction (qv).

Assumptions – all statistical tests have assumptions about the numbers you are testing and where they came from. For example, a Mann-Whitney test assumes there is no way one group of scores could be affected by the other group of scores. However, you could violate this assumption if, for example, you tested two groups of people on an intelligence test and the people in the second group watched the first group being tested, giving them more time to think about their answers. When the assumptions of a test are broken in this way, the results become unreliable. Non-parametric tests make fewer assumptions about the data than parametric tests.

As an illustration of why assumptions are useful to a parametric test, consider this: I have a person sitting next to me who is 35 years of age – are they old? Your answer will almost certainly be 'It depends ...', and you wouldn't be able to give me any sort of definite answer. But what if I told you that you could assume they were a Kindergarten pupil? Being able to make this assumption makes your judgement very easy indeed, and the same principle applies with statistical tests: being able to make assumptions makes judgements easier.

Beta (β) – can mean two different things.

(1) Beta is the probability that a given statistical test is making a Type II error (qv), i.e., the probability that there is an interesting effect in the real world but you are failing to see it in the sample you have tested. See also power (qv).

(2) Beta represents a standardized regression coefficient. In multiple regression (qv), you predict an outcome variable from several predictor variables. Your analysis calculates a *b*-value for each predictor, which can be used to construct the regression equation predicting your outcome variable from your predictor variables. Each of these *b*-values can be converted to a beta value, which allows the various predictors to be compared to one another – the predictor with the highest absolute beta value (i.e., ignoring any minus signs) is the most important predictor for your outcome variable.

Bimodal distribution – a distribution of scores which has two distinct peaks because people tend to get scores around one of two different points. This is often a sign that the sample of people you have studied is really made up of two different groups combined. For example, imagine you measured the heights of 200 people but half were children and half were adults. You would see two peaks in the distribution – one at the average height for each group. In principle, it should also be possible to talk of trinomial distributions as well, in which there are three peaks, but for some reason nobody ever does.

Binomial test – an inferential test for situations where you have two mutually exclusive groups and want to look at how a sample falls within the two categories. For example, you take a sample of 100 children from a school and find there are 65 girls and 35 boys. The binomial test will give you the probability of getting this gender breakdown in your sample if the whole population is really split 50:50 between boys and girls. If the probability of this happening is low, you would conclude the population is probably not split 50:50.

Blind testing – procedures where people are not aware of what is being tested. In a single-blind procedure, the participants do not know which condition they are being tested for. As such, their responses should not be influenced by their knowledge of the procedure. In a double-blind procedure, both the participant and the tester do not know which condition is being tested. This way, not only has the participant no knowledge of their condition, they also cannot pick up subtle clues from the experimenter which might give away this information.

Bonferroni correction – a method for controlling familywise error rate (qv) in which alpha (qv) is divided by the number of tests being carried out. For example: alpha is normally set at .05; if you are doing four analyses to answer a single question, you should divide .05 by 4 (.0125). Each of your four analyses now needs a *p*-value (qv) lower than .0125, rather than .05, to reach statistical significance.

Case study – A form of study design in which a single person (or possibly a single group of people) is studied in depth.

Categorical variable – a variable which consists of categories. Examples of categorical variables include gender (people are either male or female), nationality (people are British, American, Australian, etc.). Categorical variables are in contrast to continuous variables, where people can fall at any point on a scale.

Causal relationship – a causal relationship exists when one of the things you are studying directly causes changes in another of the things you are studying. For example, there is a causal relationship between how long somebody spends practising a musical instrument and how good they are at playing it – it is a causal relationship because the practice was directly responsible for the improved playing ability. It is tremendously important to be sure whether relationships really are causal, and the fact that two measures are correlated is never enough to tell you there is a causal relationship – the experimental method (qv) is the main way to establish whether a relationship is really causal.

Ceiling effect – a problem that arises when a measure you have used leads to all the participants getting very high scores at the top of the scale. This often happens when a test is too easy for the participants. For example, if I give a test designed for 5-year-olds to a group of 10-year-olds I would expect everybody to get the highest possible score, meaning there is no variation between people's scores, which makes them useless for analysis. See also floor effect (qv).

Central tendency – a measure of the midpoint in a set of scores. Known informally as the average. More technically, there are various measures of central tendency, including the mean (qv), median (qv) and mode (qv).

Chi-squared test – a test that measures independent frequency counts or scores taken from a sample.

Cohort – A group of people studied together over time. Usually, if the term cohort is being used, this implies there is more than one group of people being studied with each group going through a process at different times. A classic example would be a study looking at how children perform in their first year of school. If the study lasted five years, the children starting school this year would be the first cohort, the children starting next year would be the second cohort, and so on.

Condition – a 'level' of an independent variable. For instance, if you are measuring memory ability following chocolate eating in an investigation of the idea that the more chocolate you eat the better your memory will be, you might *operationalize* the amount of chocolate as one, two or three chunks. These are 'levels' of the independent variable 'amount of chocolate' and each can be referred to as a 'condition' of the independent variable.

Confidence interval – a range of scores within which a population mean is likely to lie. When we test a sample of people, we hope they are representative of the wider population from which they are drawn. As such, if the mean score for my sample of people is 25, my best guess is that the mean of the whole population, if I could test them all, would also be 25. However, it is quite possible that my sample mean is a little larger or smaller than the real population mean, through sampling error. A confidence interval communicates this possibility, giving a range of scores within which the real population mean almost certainly falls. So if I say my sample has a mean score of 25 with a 95% confidence interval of 22.1 – 27.5, this means that my best guess at the population mean is 25, and that I'm 95% certain that the real population mean, if I were able to test everybody, would lie somewhere between 22.1 and 27.5.

Confounding variable – a variable which makes the interpretation of a relationship problematic. For example, I test a group of children and find the ones who have more contact time with their teacher are better at reading than others. However, I forgot to make sure the children were all the same age before I carried out the study, and some of them are much older than others. Because older children read better than younger children anyway, my failure to control age means age is a confounding variable, and is probably disrupting my ability to look at the relationship between teacher contact time and reading. Confounding variables can often be removed with partial correlation and analysis of covariance.

Continuous variable – a measure on which people can fall at any point. If you measure categorical variables (qv), such as gender and nationality, there is only a limited range of answers people can give; if you measure continuous variables such as height or weight, there is a vast range of answers they can give and people can vary by all sorts of different amounts.

Convenience sample – see opportunity sample.

Correlation – as the name (co-relation) suggests, this is a measure of how closely two variables (qv) are related to each other. By related, we mean that as one variable changes, the other also tends to change in a predictable way. The extent to which changes in one variable are associated with changes in the other can be precisely measured using a correlation coefficient. Correlations can be positive, so that as one variable increases the other tends also to increase, or they can be negative, such that as one variable tends to increase the other tends to decrease. An example of a positive correlation is the relationship between air temperature and how many ice creams people buy: the hotter it is, the more ice creams they buy. An example of a negative relationship is that between air temperature and how many clothes people wear – as temperature goes up, the number of clothes tends to go down.

Correlation coefficient – a numerical measure of how closely two variables are related. Correlation coefficients (usually represented by the letter r) can range from –1 to 1. A coefficient of 1 or –1 means there is a perfect correlation, such that a given change in one variable is associated with a precise amount of change in the other variable; as the value gets closer to 0, this tells us that a change in one variable is less tightly linked to changes in the other. When the correlation is close to 0, changes in one variable are unrelated to changes in the other.

Counterbalancing – in repeated-measures designs, a method for ensuring there is no systematic bias in the order in which people experience conditions; a way of overcoming order effects. If all your participants took test A then test B, your results would probably be biased as everybody taking test B would be (a) more fatigued and (b) more practised than when they took test A. As such, any differences in performance between test A and test B cannot be interpreted reliably as they could be caused by the order of presentation rather than actual differences between the tests. This issue is solved through counterbalancing, where you ensure that half the participants take test A first and half take test B first, so any order effects balance out.

Criterion variable – in regression, this is the variable you are predicting from another variable (or variables). In an experiment it would be called the dependent variable, but in regression we use the term criterion variable instead, as the term 'dependent variable' is saved only for experimental designs. Regression cannot tell you whether two variables have a causal relationship or not, so we use the terms criterion variable and predictor variable instead of dependent variable and independent variable to reflect this.

Curvilinear – a relationship which does not approximate to a straight line on a scatterplot (see linear, qv), but which rather approximates to some sort of curved line.

Data – two or more pieces of information, such as measurements taken from people. The singular is 'datum'; the plural is 'data'. I am 180 cm tall, so 180 cm is a datum. If I measure another person's height and write it next to mine THEN I have some data. The word 'data' is plural. It really is. Phrases such as 'The data was analysed…', 'This data is skewed…' are all wrong, wrong, wrongity-wrong. The data WERE analysed and THESE data ARE skewed. There, I've said it.

Debrief – the process of explaining your study to participants after they have taken part. The main purpose of a debrief is to get each participant back into the state they would have been in had they not taken part in your study, so that taking part in your study has no lasting effect on them. As such, any deceits should be explained, any anxiety induced by your study reduced to what it was at the start, etc.

Dependent variable (DV) – see experimental method (qv).

Descriptive statistics – measures which describe a set of data. For example, measure of central tendency (averages), dispersion (qv), etc.

Dichotomous variable – a variable that can only take one of two levels, such as gender (either male or female) or life status (people are either alive or dead).

Discrete variable – another name for a categorical variable (qv).

Dispersion – the way in which scores are distributed around their central point (usually the mean). For example, the scores 9, 10, 11 have a mean of 10, as do the scores 5, 10, 15. However the first set has much less dispersion, as the scores are all closer to the mean. Dispersion is assessed with measures such as the standard deviation (qv), variance (qv) and range (qv).

Distribution – how a set of scores is arranged across a group of people; a measure of how often each particular score is seen in a dataset. See also normal distribution, bimodal distribution, skew.

Double-blind testing – see blind testing (qv).

Effect size – if you find something interesting in your data, such as a correlation between two measures or a difference between two groups' scores, the effect size is a measure of how large your finding really is.

Measuring effect size is an important addition to null hypothesis testing (qv). This is because even a trivial difference between two groups will become statistically significant if you test enough people. Effect size measures ignore the size of the sample – instead they measure how big your finding is. There are many measures of effect size, but the most common are r, the correlation coefficient, and Cohen's d (which is used for t-tests and similar procedures). Both of these tell us exactly how strong the effect we have seen is: high values mean a big effect.

Empiricism – A school of thought that argues that we learn through observation, through experience.

Errors – in null hypothesis testing, you can make two errors. You can either incorrectly reject the null hypothesis (i.e., claim to have found an effect when really there isn't one in the population) or incorrectly accept the null hypothesis (i.e., conclude there is no effect when really there is one in the population). The first type of error, where you incorrectly reject the null hypothesis, is called a Type I error and the second type of error, where you incorrectly accept the null hypothesis, is called a Type II error. This is incredibly difficult to remember, so a useful aide memoire from *The Psychologist* is: 'Error Type I – the results are a con. Error Type II – the results slipped through.'

Putting it in loose terms, a Type I error is where you see an effect in your sample but this is just a chance effect caused by your sample being odd in some way. A Type II error is where there is an interesting effect in the real world but you miss it, because the people in your sample happened not to show it sufficiently. See also p, alpha, beta.

Eta-squared – a measure of effect size (qv). Used primarily with analysis of variance (qv), although it does have other uses, such as checking data for linearity (qv), eta-squared is a main effect or interaction's sum of squares divided by the total sum of squares – i.e., the proportion of the total variance in the data attributable to that main effect or interaction. An alternative form, partial eta-squared, divides the main effect or interaction's sum of squares by itself plus the error sum of squares. Partial eta-squared thus shows how much of the variance (qv) that could be explained by an analysis of variance term IS explained by that term.

Ethics – principles of what is and what is not acceptable behaviour. Carrying out research is subject to various ethical principles. In particular research should not be carried out when unnecessary, or when the methodology is flawed, and should aim not to cause any unnecessary distress to the participants. A debrief (qv) is often a key component of avoiding distress. Moreover, research participants should give informed consent (qv), which means they know what they are letting themselves in for before the study begins.

Ethnography – a form of data-gathering in which the experimenter embeds themselves in an environment to act as an observer. Uses of ethnography range from studies of other cultures to studies of workplaces and human-computer interaction.

Experimental hypothesis – the opposite to the null hypothesis (qv). The experimental (or alternative) hypothesis states the idea you actually wish to test, and is the idea you will accept if your analysis suggests the null hypothesis is unlikely to be true. So if your null hypothesis stated that poverty and crime are not related, your experimental hypothesis would be that they *are* related. If your analysis said that the null hypothesis was probably not true, the conclusion to your analysis would be the experimental hypothesis. For an explanation of the logic of all this, see Part 1 of this book.

Experimental method – a way of gaining knowledge in which you deliberately make adjustments to some aspect of the world, aiming to keep all other aspects of the world the same, and observe the effects of your adjustments. The thing you adjust is known as the independent variable and the thing you observe is known as the dependent variable. The experimental method helps you establish whether there is a causal relationship between the two.

For example, if you wanted to know whether eating broccoli makes people sick, you would manipulate the independent variable of diet – perhaps giving people broccoli on some occasions and different foods on other occasions. Your dependent variable – the thing you are observing – would be whether they got sick or not. If you found that it was only when you switched the diet to broccoli that the level of sickness went up, then, provided you had managed to keep everything else constant, this would definitely suggest it was the broccoli that was making the people sick.

Experimenter effects – when you test a group of people, their scores all tend to be different to some extent. These differences come from various sources. Experimenter effects are systematic variations in data caused by the particular people who collected them. For example, if you are a rude and abrupt person, you will probably get different scores when you test people than a friendlier experimenter would. Experimenter effects will be less pronounced when measuring very objective variables like height and weight, as these can't change depending on a person's mood. However, many other measures can change depending on a participant's mood, including measures of any psychological variables, how long it takes them to complete a task, etc. In an ideal world, it is best to have just one person collect all the data for a study as this way, whatever experimenter effects are present, they will at least be similar for all the participants. See also random effects (qv).

Extraneous variable – A variable that may interfere with the relationship between the dependent and independent variables, so you need to control for it, and consider it in your research design.

Face validity – The measure you are using appears, on the face of it, to be measuring what you want it to.

Familywise error rate – The probability that a set of related analyses will make a Type I error. Each inferential statistical test carries a probability of making a Type I error. In advance, this probability is alpha, usually set at .05. If more than one inferential test is carried out to answer a question, the overall probability of making a Type I error will be higher than .05, as the probabilities from each test add up. This new probability is the familywise error rate, and the issue can be dealt with by using lower alpha values. See Bonferroni correction; omnibus tests.

Floor effect – a problem that arises when a measure you have used leads to all the participants getting very low scores at the bottom of the scale. This often happens when a test is too difficult for the participants. For example, if I give a test designed for 10-year-olds to a group of 5-year-olds I would expect everybody to get a very low score, meaning there is no variation between people's scores, which makes them useless for analysis. See also ceiling effect.

Hypothesis (plural hypothe*ses*) – specific predictions that we make during research. See null hypothesis, experimental hypothesis, and alternative hypothesis (qv).

Independent variable (IV) – see experimental method (qv).

Inferential research – research which aims to study a group of people with the aim of discovering a general principle which can be applied to further people. Inferential research is in contrast to summative research (qv) and nearly always involves the use of inferential statistics (qv).

Inferential statistics – procedures used to test hypotheses. Usually the point of inferential statistical tests is to estimate how likely it is that what you have seen in a sample of people would also be seen if you could test the wider population from which the sample comes. Any procedure that produces a p-value (e.g., a t-test) is an inferential test and any procedure that does not produce a p-value (e.g., calculating a mean) is a descriptive test.

Informed consent – consent is permission from a participant for an experimenter to test them. Informed consent means the participant is told the real purpose of the study before taking part and is not deceived in any way about what the experimenter is planning to do. Research which does not involve informed consent is ethically problematic and should not take place without a very good justification, and permission from a suitable body such as an ethics committee.

Interaction – in analysis of variance, a finding in which the influence of one factor depends upon the level of another. For example, if men and women are given both low and high doses of a drug, the influence of the dose might be different for men and women, e.g., men might show no side-effects at both dose levels, but women might show side-effects at a high dose but not a low dose. If this is the case, there is said to be an interaction between dose and gender. You need to know which gender you are talking about before you can understand the effects of drug dose; similarly you need to know which drug dose you are talking about before you can understand the effects of gender.

Inter-rater reliability – a measure of how consistently two raters are scoring something. If two people are rating the same thing, they should generally agree on what they are seeing. As such, their ratings should correlate, and typically a correlation between two raters' scores of .80 or more is considered necessary if we are to say their ratings are reliable – i.e., they're both assessing the same thing.

Interval data – numbers which can be arranged in order and in which the intervals between numbers are meaningful. For example, temperatures in degrees Celsius are an interval measure: the distance between 5 degrees and 10 degrees is the same amount of change as the distance between 20 degrees and 25 degrees. Interval data differs from ratio data by not having a proper zero point, at which 0 means a complete absence. For example, calendar year is an interval measure as 0 does not mean the beginning of all time. Similarly temperature in Celsius or Fahrenheit is an interval measure as 0 does not mean a complete absence of temperature. See also nominal, ordinal, ratio.

Interviewer bias – An error that may occur because of a conscious or subconscious propensity of an interviewer to record data of a certain kind. For instance, the interviewer may not be aware that they are attracted to their participant and this may influence their subjectivity in the interview.

IQ – a measure of intelligence. Originally intended as an objective measure, these days the difficulty of defining exactly what intelligence is means that IQ is now primarily a statistical phenomenon: a set of tests designed so that a large group of people will produce a normal distribution of scores.

Level – in analysis of variance, the number of difference points at which each independent variable is measured. For example, if you have a factor of gender, comparing men and women, this factor has two levels: male and female. If you test a group of people on a task under three different levels of background noise you have a factor called noise with three levels.

Levels of measurement – a number such as '8' or '26' can hold varying amounts of information depending on how it is used. Nominal data (qv) have the least amount of information and ratio data (qv) have the most. In between these extremes are ordinal data (qv) and interval data (qv). It is only interval and ratio data, which hold the most information, which are suitable for parametric analysis (qv).

Likert scale – A scale in which participants indicate their level of agreement to a number of statements that are chosen carefully to express a favourable or unfavourable view of a concept under investigation.

Linear relationship – A relationship between two continuous variables which approximates to a straight line when plotted on a scatterplot.

Matched pairs – A type of independent-samples design where two groups of people are each tested with different levels of an independent variable. Each member of each group is matched as closely as possible to a member in the other group in an attempt to limit any between-group variability that may introduce a confound and influence the results.

Mean – the most common measure of central tendency. The mean is what most people think of as the 'average', i.e., the sum of all the scores divided by the number of scores. For example, if we measure 20 people's height, the mean for that group is the sum of all their heights divided by 20. The mean score of '20, 30, 40' is 30.

Median – the middle score in a set of data when all the data are arranged from lowest to highest. When there is an odd number of scores in a dataset, the median will be the middle value; when there is an even number of scores the median will be half-way between the two middle values. The median can be a better measure of central tendency (average) than the mean when a set of measurements is skewed, i.e., has more high values than low values or vice versa. When data are skewed the mean is a poor average but the median is still pretty accurate. The mean and median will be similar in a set of data that are not skewed and this can be a useful way to check your data.

Meta-analysis – a technique for combining the inferential results from a number of studies. For example, if 10 studies have looked at the same issue, and each has 100 participants, conducting a meta-analysis combines all the results into one study and is the equivalent of carrying out a single study with 1,000 participants. Meta-analysis is based around the calculation of effect sizes (qv).

Mode – the most common score in a set of data. A type of 'average' for dealing with categorical data. For example, if a museum curator wanted to know what their 'average' visitor was like, they would look at the mean age but the modal nationality (i.e., the most common nationality) and the modal gender, as these are categories and modes and medians are no good (e.g., it doesn't make sense to say the average visitor is half-female).

Monotonic – a positive monotonic relationship is one in which each point is either the same as or higher than the previous point; a negative monotonic relationship is one in which each point is either the same as or lower than the previous point.

Mundane realism – the extent to which the results of your research can be applied to a real-world situation to which the results will be applied.

Naturalistic – a 'real' or 'natural' representation of behaviour.

Negative relationship – a linear relationship (qv) in which as one variable increases, the other tends to decrease.

Nominal data – data in which the numbers are simply acting as names, such that putting them into order is meaningless. Examples of nominal data include bus routes and numbers on sports shirts. Bus route number 25 is not necessarily longer, faster or better than route 24, so the differences between numbers tell us nothing. In nominal data the numbers have very little information and are unsuitable for most statistics.

Non-parametric – see parametric.

Normal distribution – with many measures, most people score close to the average, with fewer people achieving a given score the further it is from the average. A normal distribution is a very specific, bell-shaped curve describing a common situation like this. The normal distribution is useful as its properties are well known. For example, 67% of all people fall within one standard deviation of the mean score. Also known as a Gaussian distribution.

Null hypothesis – the prediction that there is no effect in the data you are analysing; the opposite to the alternative hypothesis (qv). Inferential statistics are largely based around assessing the probability that the null hypothesis is true; when this probability is low (i.e., less than alpha, qv), we reject the null hypothesis and instead accept the alternative.

Null hypothesis testing – an approach to research in which you test the idea that the thing you are interested in has no effect, or that there is no association between some measures. Null hypothesis testing involves calculating the probability of your null hypothesis being true. When this probability is low, less than alpha (qv), you reject the null hypothesis and assume the experimental hypothesis (qv) is true instead.

Omnibus test – a statistical test such as analysis of variance which is effectively doing more than one test, but which makes allowance for the familywise error (qv) this would otherwise cause.

One-tailed hypothesis – an experimental or alternative hypothesis which not only predicts an effect, but also predicts the direction of the effect. For example, predicting that men and women will perform differently is a two-tailed hypothesis; predicting that women will have a higher score than men (a difference, and the direction of that difference) is a one-tailed hypothesis. So named because we are only interested in one of the tails of a probability distribution.

Opportunity sample – A sample of a population chosen by convenience, so also known as a convenience sample. For example, if you study human memory by testing everybody in your class this is an opportunity sample. Opportunity sampling is usually fine for testing basic cognitive and perceptual skills – which are much the same for everyone – but not ideal for testing learnt abilities or opinions, as the samples can easily be unrepresentative of the wider population. Opportunity samples are often used for pilot testing (qv).

Order effect – a potential bias in data caused by the order in which people were tested. This issue arises where people are tested on more than one task. If task A is always completed before task B, the experience of having done task A is likely to alter the task B scores, either through practice or through tiredness/boredom. Order effects can be dealt with through counterbalancing (qv).

Ordinal data – numerical data which can be put into order but where the intervals between numbers are meaningless. A good example is hotel star ratings: a four-star hotel is better than a three-star rating, so the order of the numbers tells us something (4 is higher than 3), but the difference between ratings isn't fixed, so the difference between a four- and a three-star hotel is not exactly the same as the difference between a three- and a two-star hotel.

Outcome variable – in regression, an alternative term for 'criterion variable'.

_p_-value, _p_ – in inferential statistics tests, the probability that the null hypothesis is correct, or the probability that you would make a Type I error if you rejected the null hypothesis.

An informal but helpful way to think of _p_ is as the probability you will be wrong if you conclude you've found something interesting in your data.

Parametric – inferential statistical tests can either be parametric or non-parametric. In general, there is a non-parametric version of each parametric test: independent-samples _t_-test (parametric) vs Mann-Whitney (non-parametric); repeated-measures _t_-test (parametric) vs Wilcoxon test (non-parametric); analysis of variance (parametric) vs Kruskall-Wallis test (non-parametric). Parametric tests make more assumptions about the data and cannot be used if these assumptions are not met. The advantage of using parametric tests is that they have more statistical power – i.e., they are less likely to make a Type II error (they are more likely to see an effect if it exists).

In practice, the mathematics of parametric and non-parametric tests tend to be the same; the difference is that parametric tests do their calculations on the actual scores that people produced and non-parametric tests put the scores into order, assign each a rank (lowest score = 1, next lowest = 2, etc.) and do their calculations on these ranks instead of the original scores. This works because ranks always meet the assumptions for a parametric test.

The greater power of parametric tests arises because, as they work on the original scores rather than the ranks, they have more information to work with in their calculations.

Partial correlation – the degree of association between two variables with the influence of another variable mathematically removed.

Pearson's r – the most common parametric correlation coefficient.

Percentile – the position of a data point, such as a person's salary or test score, expressed as a percentage of people who are at the same level or below them on the salary or test-score scale. So if you are at the 99th percentile, 99 percent of people are at your level or below you.

Pie-chart – a graphical representation which shows a disc divided into segments. Pie-charts are useful for showing how some quantity divides into parts, but are never used for showing means or other such data.

Pilot study – a study carried out quickly, cheaply and with less rigour than a full study, with the intention of testing materials or a methodology before committing to carrying out a full study.

Placebo – a manipulation which produces a change in a variable through a participant's knowledge of the manipulation rather than through any causal relationship (qv) between the placebo and the outcome measure. The classic example is a dummy medicine which produces effects simply because the recipient thinks it should, rather than because it has any medicinal benefit. When testing medicines, it used to be normal to compare the effect of the treatment with no medicine. But because people can recover simply because they know they have taken *something* it is now common to compare the medicine with a placebo, rather than with no medicine.

Population – The overall group of people you want to know about in a study. Sometimes the population is quite small – for example, if you want to know how many people in your street ride a bicycle, the population is all the people in your street, and you would want to survey them all. A lot of the time, however, when studying people we want to learn things that apply to everybody. For example, if I want to know whether taking drug X cures a certain illness, I want to know whether this is generally true for everybody – not just the people on my street. However, studying the whole population of the world is impossible, so generally a representative sample is studied instead and inferential statistics used to calculate how likely it is that what is seen in the sample would also be seen in the whole population.

Positive relationship – In correlation, when one variable increases so too does another. Shoe size, for instance, may be regarded as positively related to height. Generally speaking, the taller you are, the larger your feet.

Power – the ability of a statistical test to reveal an effect if one really exists. If the people you have studied really have something going on (e.g., a relationship between two measures, or a difference between two groups), a powerful test is more likely to show you this. In formal terms, a powerful test is less likely to make a Type II error. Power is defined as 1 – beta, where beta is the probability of making a Type II error.

Power analysis – a technique for estimating either how many people you need to study to find a significant effect (a priori power analysis) or how large the effect is that you have found with the people you have tested (post hoc power analysis). Power analysis is tied to the measurement of effect sizes, and also considers Type I and Type II errors. Researchers most commonly use a priori power analysis when planning studies, asking questions like 'If I'm expecting a medium effect size, and want the probability of both Type I and Type II errors to be below .05 (5%), how many people do I need to test to get a statistically significant result?'

Predictive validity – the ability to predict the thing you are attempting to predict. Something has predictive validity if it predicts the thing in which you are interested. For instance, we would *hope* that high-school examination results *predict* whether a student is good enough to come to university or not. Unfortunately this may not be the case at all.

Predictor variable – in regression, this is a variable you are using to predict another variable. In an experiment it would be called the independent variable, but in regression we use the term predictor variable instead, as the term 'independent variable' is saved only for situations where there is a causal relationship between the two measures. Regression cannot tell you whether two variables have a causal relationship or not, so we use the terms criterion variable and predictor variable instead of dependent variable and independent variable to reflect this.

Probability – a measure of how likely something is to happen, or to be correct. Mathematically we measure probability as with a value ranging from 0 to 1. A probability of 0 means something will never happen; a probability of 1 means it will always happen. A probability of .7 means it will happen on 70% of occasions.

Quota sampling – A type of sampling where quotas are set for certain subsections of the population. For instance, a supermarket chain may be interested in the type of foods it needs to stock in certain stores. If most people that shop there are from high-income families then a higher quota of this type of people will be required for the research carried out by the market research company. Similarly, if very few families with low incomes shop there then fewer of these families will be included in the quota sample.

Random effects – when you test a group of people, their scores all tend to be different to some extent. These differences come from various sources. Random effects are differences between people's scores that are not systematic but rather caused by individual or chance factors. For example, if you take a group of people and measure how long each sleeps in your laboratory, some of the variation between the people will be caused by factors you might be interested in (e.g., how much coffee they have drunk) but a lot of the variation will usually be caused by random effects – things you have no control over, such as how much sleep your participants had the night before, the fact some people naturally sleep more than others, the room being noisier for some people than others, etc.

Random sample – A sample of a population chosen by selecting people at random. Strictly speaking, everybody in the entire population should have an equal chance of being included. The only real way to achieve this is to draw names at random, or something similar.

Randomization – using random numbers or processes in experimental design. Randomization is used primarily (a) to select random samples (qv), and (b) to combat order effects, by giving each participant a series of tests in a random order.

Randomized control trial – this is where the participants are randomly allocated to the various conditions in a study. Let's say we are testing a new drug and need to give some of the participants the drug and some a placebo. A way of doing this without bias would be to use a random process for each person – for example, you could toss a coin for each person to decide whether they got the drug or the placebo. Note that what we have described here, with the coin-tossing, is a *true* RCT, and it is possible the two groups would end up with different numbers of people in them. It is common to see pseudo-RCTs, where the researchers ensure the two groups are the same size.

Range – a measure of dispersion (qv), which simply cites the lowest and highest scores in a dataset.

Ratio data – Data that have the properties of interval data, but which also have a genuine zero point, i.e., 0 means a complete lack of something. This is in contrast to interval data which do not have a proper zero point. Most everyday measures are ratio, e.g., money, where 0 means no money at all, or length, where 0 means no length at all. This is in contrast to temperature systems like degrees Celsius, where zero does not mean there is no temperature at all. Similarly, calendar year is not a ratio measure as the year 0 does not mean the beginning of all time.

The interesting thing about having the zero point, and the reason for the name ratio data, is that when a genuine zero point exists we are able to use ratio phrases like 'twice as much...' and "half as much...". For example, if you have 30 pencils and I have 15, I can say you have 'twice as many pencils' because the number of pencils is a ratio measure. If you are in a room at 30 degrees Celsius and I am in a room at 15 degrees Celsius, I cannot say you are twice as hot as me, because temperature in Celsius is not a ratio measure.

Regression – a technique for examining the relationship between two or more variables. In regression, changes in one variable (the criterion variable) are predicted from one or more predictor variables. The technique allows us to know exactly how the criterion variable changes as the predictor variable(s) change, and also how closely the variables are related to one another. See also regression to the mean (qv), regression fallacy (qv), for alternative uses of the word 'regression'.

Regression fallacy – along with the placebo effect (qv), the phenomenon underpinning most quackery and New Age pseudo-medical nonsense. Chronic conditions, such as arthritis, long-term pain etc., tend to vary between good and bad periods. After a bad period, a better period will follow because the pain level naturally goes back, or regresses, towards its average level (see regression to the mean, qv). People living in pain tend only to seek help when their conditions are particularly bad. But because these bad periods will nearly always be followed by a better period anyway, absolutely anything you do to somebody during a bad period will appear to make them better, at least for a while, hence the continued existence of ear candles, angel therapists, crystals and all other such guff.

Regression to the mean – the tendency for extreme scores to become less extreme; the tendency for everything to become more average over time. For example, if a group of people is given a task and the highest-scorers selected for further testing, the tendency will be for this group to perform closer to the population mean – i.e., worse – when you retest them. Regression to the mean was first noticed in children by Francis Galton, and can often be seen in this context: two very tall parents will tend to have a child who is shorter than they are – the child's height has gone back, or regressed, towards the population's mean. In short, extreme cases tend not to beget even more extreme cases. For an application of this, see the regression fallacy (qv).

Reliability – the consistency with which something is measured.

Repeated-measures – a form of experimental design (qv) in which each participant is tested more than once.

Replication – usually means repeating an experiment to see whether the findings remain the same. Replication is a key component of good science: one person makes a discovery and other people attempt to replicate their findings, to be extra-sure they are real.

Particularly in biology, the term replication can be used also to mean testing more than one person in a study ('We replicated the measurement on 30 people').

Research question – the question you are hoping to answer with a piece of research. This usually takes the form of a straightforward everyday question such as 'Does eating cheese make people more intelligent?'

Sample – see sampling (qv).

Sampling – selecting the participants for a study. The aim of sampling is usually to get a group of people – a sample – which is representative of the general population from which the sample comes.

In other words, you want to test a small number of people who will behave just like the wider population. Your sample is a microcosm of the population.

For example, if you want to know something about all the people in your country, because it is impractical to test them all you would want to study a subgroup which has the same sort of balance of sex, ethnicity, socio-economic status etc. as your whole country. Because this is such an important yet difficult issue, various methods of sampling have been developed: see random sample (qv), stratified sample (qv), opportunity sample (qv), snowball sample (qv).

Sampling error – any bias in your sample which means it is not perfectly representative of the population from which it is drawn. Inferential statistics can be seen as being all about assessing the amount of sampling error you are likely to have in your sample.

Sensitivity – If a test identifies an issue very accurately then it can be said to be very sensitive.

Significance – in statistics, significance has a very specific meaning. In strict terms, it means that the probability of a Type I error is below the alpha criterion. More loosely, it means the probability that you have found nothing of interest is low enough that you reject that possibility and instead conclude that you have found something of interest.

Single-blind testing – see blind testing (qv).

Skew – a property of a distribution (qv) when it is not symmetrical. Ideally, most distributions of scores are symmetrical with a roughly equal number of scores above and below the mean. If there are more people scoring above the mean, such that there is a long tail on the right-hand side of the distribution, the distribution is described as positively skewed; when the long tail is to the left the distribution is known as negatively skewed. Potentially a problem for parametric (qv) analyses, skew can often be corrected, e.g., by taking the square root of all the scores and doing your analyses on these.

Snowball sample – a method for sampling hard-to-find or naturally secretive groups like criminals, people with mental illnesses, etc. There is no way you could carry out, say, a random sample (qv) of criminals as you have no way of knowing who they all are (if you do, your government would be keen to speak to you). With a snowball sample all you need is one participant. You study this person and then ask them to tell at least one other person about your study. You then ask each person who comes forward also to tell other people about your study, and so on until you have enough people. Snowball sampling is not ideal, as everybody in your sample knows one another, which could introduce biases. If nothing else, your sample is likely to come from a small geographical area. However, when you want to deal with groups you cannot find any other way to sample, snowball sampling may be the only way to work.

Spearman's rho – the most common non-parametric correlation coefficient.

Standard deviation – measures how spread out your data are. It is a measure of dispersion. See also standard error.

Standard error – the standard deviation (qv) associated with a mean score (qv), divided by the square root of the number of participants who produced that mean. Standard errors are closely related to confidence intervals (qv), and give us an idea of how likely our sample mean is to be an accurate estimate of the population mean. Standard error goes down as dispersion (qv) goes down, and also goes down as the number of people tested rises – this latter point should make sense, as the more people tested, the closer your sample must be to the whole population.

Standardized instructions – a set of instructions explaining what the participants need to do in a study. By writing the instructions down and reading them to the participants – or allowing the participants to read them to themselves – you can ensure that any differences in how people perform cannot be explained by them having heard subtly different instructions.

Statistical significance – see significance.

Stratified sample – a sample of a population chosen so that the demographic mixture of your participants matches the demographic mixture of people in the general population. For example, if the whole population has 50% men and 50% women, you would choose people for your sample to ensure the same mix. If the whole population also had 10% of people aged over 75%, you would make sure your sample was the same. Stratified samples are nearly always large (e.g., over 1,000 people) and are frequently used in surveys and opinion polls.

Study – an umbrella term referring to any type of research; the term is useful as it includes all methodologies such as experiments, case studies, etc.

Summative research – research aimed simply at describing, or summing up, a group of people. This is in contrast to inferential research (qv), which studies a group of people with the aim of finding general lessons.

Systematic observation – an observation that follows a carefully constructed plan. The behaviours to watch out for in the observation are carefully decided upon and systematic recordings made during the observation period.

t-**test** – a parametric (qv) test for comparing two means. A significant result suggests that the two means come from two fundamentally different sets of scores.

Test-retest reliability – if a test provides you with a particular score one day, it should also provide you with a similar score on another day. If it does, then you can say that you have achieved test-retest reliability.

Transferable skill – a skill or ability which can be used in many different fields. For example, being able to write clearly is a transferable skill: it is something that will serve you well whether you become a novelist or a financier. Learning research teaches you many transferable skills: clear writing, problem-solving, handling numerical information, critical ability and so on.

Two-tailed hypothesis – see one-tailed hypothesis (qv).

Type I error – see Errors (qv).

Type II error – see Errors (qv).

Variable – anything you have measured or manipulated in a study. Variables can take different forms – they can be groups (e.g., gender could be a variable in a study), in which case they are called categorical variables, or they can be normal measurements such as length or temperature, in which case they are called continuous variables.

Variance – when you collect a set of measurements from people, such as all the heights of the people in a room, it is extremely unusual for all the measurements to be identical. Variance is the term for this natural variation between measurements, as in analysis of variance (qv). More specifically, variance can be quantified as the square of the standard deviation.

x-bar – a common mathematical symbol used to represent the mean (qv) score for a group – the letter x with a bar over the top $\bar{x}$. Often we used M instead, but either form is fine.

Z-**score** – a common form of standardized score in which scores are transformed into standard deviations from the mean (so 0 is the mean score, +1 is one standard deviation above the mean). If we test a group of people on various different tests, each with its own scoring system, converting these scores to Z-scores allows us easily to compare performance on various tasks. For example, if I have a Z-score of 1.20 on one task, and a Z-score of 1.21 on another, it is easy to see that I am performing at a very similar level at the two tasks, at least in relation to the group of people tested.

Index